Earning a Doctorate Degree in the 21st Century

Challenges and Joys

Be a Protector of Wisdom!

Bahaudin G. Mujtaba
Michael M. Scharff

☆ International ☆
LEAD ACADEMY
Leadership Education and Associate Development Academy

Foreword by Dr. Paul Hersey

Bahaudin G. Mujtaba, & Michael M. Scharff, 2007. Earning a Doctorate Degree in the 21st Century: Challenges and Joys

Produced by:
        Dr. Bahaudin G. Mujtaba
        Nova Southeastern University
        3301 College Avenue
        Fort Lauderdale FL 33315-3025
        Phone: (954) 262-5000 Or (800) 672-7223
        Email: mujtaba@sbe.nova.edu

Cover Design By: Cagri Tanyar

Amaguk Sculptor & Artist: Marie Barbera,

Amaguk's Sponsors: Dr. Paul Hersey, Mrs. Suzanne Hersey, Dr. Ronald Campbell, and Mrs. Dorothy Campbell at the Center for Leadership Studies in Escondido, California.

ISBN 10: 0-9774211-3-9
ISBN 13: 978-0-9774211-3-8

    1. Business & Economics-Education.
    2. Education-General.
    3. Education-Adult & Continuing Education.

ILEAD Academy, LLC
Davie, Florida. United States
www.ileadacademy.com

Review Comments

After completing my master's degree, I was certain it was just a matter of time before I would begin a doctoral program. The most frightening part in making that step was the idea of the dissertation. In my very first class, a Research course, on the first day, the professor asked us each to write on a blank piece of paper a statement of what the purpose of our research was going to be. That's when I realized not only the importance of choosing a topic early in the program, but also choosing one that is truly interesting to me. *"Earning a Doctorate Degree in the 21ˢᵗ Century: Challenges and Joys"* discusses in great detail the difficulty involved in selecting a research topic. It also examines the different options for students that do not have an exact direction yet for their dissertation. With marketing as my specialization, and music as my passion, my statement for the Research course became extremely obvious to me – 'The purpose of this research is to determine how the music industry is developing marketing strategies that can be used to overcome online music piracy.' Now instead of being terrified of the dissertation, I'm overwhelmed with excitement to begin the journey. *"Earning a Doctorate Degree"* book encourages doctoral students to discover, express, and maintain this type of excitement in regard to their research.

– Laura Enneian, Doctoral Candidate

In this text you'll benefit from the counsel of the authors who have coached numerous others before you through this process.

– Dr. Paul Hersey, Chairman, Center for Leadership Studies

This book is your *ace in the hole* to completing a doctoral program. If you have the thirst for knowledge, but are unsure if you have the wherewithal to complete a doctoral program, this book is for you. You will find helpful tips for succeeding, learn from the experiences of others who have struggled to achieve and succeeded in the process, and probably change your way of thinking about yourself. You will find yourself thinking about where you have been, where you are going, and the motivations, attitude, and strategy you need to complete a doctoral program.

– Dr. Tamara S. Terry, Assistant Dean and Chief Financial Officer of the H. Wayne Huizenga School of Business and Entrepreneurship

This book is long overdue. Being a doctoral student is in many ways a very lonely, frustrating experience. I remember ever so clearly my feelings of anxiety from not knowing what to expect as I proceeded through my doctoral program. If a book like *"Earning a Doctorate Degree in the 21ˢᵗ Century: Challenges and Joys"* had existed, my life as a doctoral student would have been so much easier and satisfying. Just knowing that other doctoral students shared my feelings would have been a major source of comfort. Also, the many helpful tips provided throughout the book would have helped me to save valuable time. Every potential doctoral student should make this book a well-used part of their library.

– Dr. Terrell G. Manyak, Professor of Management

"Earning a Doctorate Degree in the 21ˢᵗ Century: Challenges and Joys" is a step by step guide to the successful completion of a doctoral program. It is easy to follow and provides invaluable information on beginning a doctoral program, passing the comprehensive exam, selecting a research topic /committee, and completing the dissertation project. It features a range of practical, personal examples and guidance on how to avoid the pitfalls in pursuing a doctoral degree. I find it to be a comprehensive collection of hard to find information, resources, and advice. It is indispensable for any one pursuing/intending to pursue a doctoral program.

– Dr. Belay Seyoum, Professor of International Business

Drs. Mujtaba and Scharff, in their very readable and comprehensive book, *Earning a Doctorate Degree in the 21st Century: Challenges and Joys*, have made a very significant contribution to the academic and practical literature concerning attaining a doctoral degree. Of particular worth are the chapters dealing with the most challenging aspect of the doctoral process-the dissertation. This book obviously will be very important to the student contemplating doctoral studies, but also quite valuable to school administrators and faculty members who continually grapple with the "ABD" dilemma. Also of great interest and appeal in the book are the inspirational stories, replete with practical wisdom, as to how the authors, as well as several contributors, mastered the doctoral process to achieve academic, professional, and business success. The book, therefore, is a "must" read, particularly so for the aspiring doctoral student.
– Dr. Frank Cavico, Professor of Business Law and Ethics

"Earning a Doctorate Degree" is an excellent compilation of facts and testimonies that anyone who is considering a doctorate degree should read. This book also gives insights for international doctoral candidates. Furthermore, this book is a recommended reading for all new doctoral students and can be incorporated in graduate programs. As a new doctoral student, you will get a solid head-start with the information provided in this book.
– Dr. Albert Williams, Professor of Finance and Economics

Dr. Mujtaba and Dr. Scharff have developed a well thought out overview of the joys and challenges in earning a doctorate degree. The chapters are organized well and the book will be helpful to students currently working on their terminal degree or professionals who are considering starting the process. Personal trials and tribulations are communicated through the stories of several colleagues who have made the journey. This is a great read with practical advice and helpful information to encourage those considering joining the ranks of the educational elite. The journey is not easy nor without great cost, but the rewards can be enormous both personally and professionally.
– Dr. Daniel Sullivan, Director of Student Development

Earning a Doctorate Degree, by Bahaudin G. Mujtaba and Michael M. Scharff, is an excellent source of inspiration for those who have the motivation to culminate their professional dreams and aspirations. The book further offers guidelines and specific suggestions on how to achieve one's higher education academic goals. Congratulations to Bahaudin and Michael.
– Dr. Pedro F. Pellet, Professor of Economics

This is one of the best works that give us general ideas for a doctoral program. You can get detailed information about the general steps from how to choose your program to the career developments after the completion. Specially taking the beginners' perspective, the book is beneficial to the readers who are not totally familiar with the graduate program.
– Dr. Joung W. Kim, Associate Professor of Accounting.

"Earning a Doctorate Degree" lays out the realities of why so many students fail to make it to the finish line. The authors build a solid case for why doctoral programs build unnecessary barriers leading to discouragement and high failure rates. Written in a clearly understood and anecdotal fashion, Mujtaba and Scharff argue a case of student/faculty disconnect and false expectations. At the heart of their argument for boosting doctoral completion is an intrinsic appreciation for the value of learning that has been lost in the luster of "doc-in-the-box" approaches to boosting a candidate's job credentials. The book is based on practitioner perspectives adding to its credibility and readership. Both school administrators and doctoral student prospects will benefit from these long overdue ideas for boosting retention.
– Dr. James Barry, Professor of Marketing

While the path to completing a doctoral degree contains numerous obstacles, in *"Earning a Doctorate Degree"* Drs. Mujtaba and Scharff provide a useful roadmap to avoid them. Each section contains personal insights of the authors and others who have successfully completed the journey. From the beginning of why one would want to undertake the goal of a doctorate to completing the dissertation, the reader is provided with key issues related to challenges and how to overcome the barriers. The book should be read when a potential student is considering a doctorate to help in the decision-making process, and once a student enrolls, it should be re-read as the student progresses through a program to keep him/her on course for completion.

– Dr. Les Carter, Entrepreneurship Chair, St. Edward's University

The road toward a doctorate degree can feel as challenging as a walk through a mind field and without proper planning and guidance you will never make it. Mujtaba and Scharff have created a great resource for any student thinking about a doctorate degree and a must have book for those that decide to enter a doctoral program. This book addresses key issues that go beyond the classroom that most students don't think about when they get started in a doctoral program, being able to identify and survive the pitfalls is essential. The strategies on managing time and stress along with the great advice on selecting your research topic and of course selecting your committee are extremely helpful. I highly recommend this book for anybody that is entering a doctoral program because the best way to travel down the road toward a doctorate degree is with the directions right next to you.

– Dr. Jeffrey Fountain, Assistant Professor of Sports and Recreation Management

This book is an invaluable guide for every doctoral student and those contemplating entering a doctoral program. It is a mentor and guide available 24-7. The authors' personal experiences in successfully completing the doctorate model the path to obtaining a terminal degree.

– Dr. Barbara Dastoor, Professor of Human Resources and Qualitative Research

The *"Earning a Doctorate Degree"* book is useful for those who are contemplating a decision about continuing their higher education specialization and earning a terminal degree. The book explores the motivational requirements for such a prestigious degree, the choices for enrolling into a higher education institution, balancing the course and research work with one's current job responsibilities, and strategically completing each required step in the allotted time. It is a recommended reading for current master's program students and graduates.

– Farzana Rahman, Teacher and a Doctoral Prospect

This book is dedicated to those who bring about positive changes in themselves and for others in society through higher education and continuous learning.

TABLE OF CONTENTS

Foreword

Right in the first few paragraphs and pages of chapter one you discover why the authors wrote this book...

- People love to learn...
- Personal fulfillment...
- Seeking knowledge never ends...
- In the seeking you find joy!

With this book, and therefore the authors' help, as a doctoral candidate you too will better navigate the enormous challenge before you. In this text you'll benefit from the counsel of the authors who have coached numerous others before you through this process.

I wish you could sit in the office in conversation one on one with the authors. You then could add the warmth and excitement to the information contained in the book.

I wish you all the rewards of your dreams in "*Earning a Doctorate Degree.*"

Warm regards,

Dr. Paul Hersey, Chairman
Center for Leadership Studies

Acknowledgements

There are many individuals that have formally or informally contributed to this book. *First,* we would like to thank the following colleagues for their contributions and guidance in preparing the content of this book:

- Albert Williams
- Anisa Qadir
- Art Weinstein
- Audrey Ellison
- Barbara Dastoor
- Belay Seyoum
- Cagri Tanyar
- Charlie Blackwell
- Charmaine Walters Balfour
- Dan Meyerson
- Dan Sullivan
- Eleanor Marschke
- Farzana Rahman
- Frank Darguzaz
- Freda Turner
- Frank Cavico
- Ike I. Udechukwu
- James Barry
- Jane Gibson
- Joann Adeogun
- Joel Rossmaier
- Joel Schlesinger
- Joung W. Kim
- Kristie Tetrault

- Laura Enneian
- Len Samborowski
- Mike Bendixen
- Mustafa G. Mujtaba
- Natcha Limthanakom
- Nilofar Jamasi
- Paul Hersey
- Pedro F. Pellet
- Peter DiPaolo
- Preston Jones
- Raimi Abiodun
- Randolph Pohlman
- Robert M. Wolk
- Ronald Campbell
- Roy Nafarrete
- Robert Preziosi
- Robert Sellani
- Robert J. Mullaney
- Russell Abratt
- Tamara S. Terry
- Terrell Manyak
- Thomas Box
- Timothy McCartney
- Stefanie D. Wilson

Second, we would like to thank all those who have helped us both personally and professionally get to this point.

Third, we thank you for reading this material. For suggestions and questions, you can contact either of us (mujtaba@sbe.nova.edu or mscharff@limestone.edu) at any time.

Bahaudin G. Mujtaba and Michael Scharff

Amaguk, Protector of Wisdom

The bronze Native American statue, on the cover of this book, named Amaguk (which means "Protector of Wisdom") was unveiled at the H. Wayne Huizenga School of Business & Entrepreneurship at Nova Southeastern University on Monday, October 30, 2006. The statue's artist is Marie Barbera, one of the world's foremost sculptors of Native American Indians. Much of her work is featured in Dr. Paul Hersey's Center for Leadership Studies in Escondido, California. You can learn more about Barbera's work at her website: www.mbarbera.com.

The bronze statue, Amaguk, was donated through the generosity of Dr. Paul Hersey, Mrs. Suzanne Hersey, Dr. Ronald Campbell, and Mrs. Dorothy Campbell. Dr. Hersey continues to share his knowledge and wisdom with students throughout the world and has built life-long relationships with leading faculty members at various prestigious institutions. He was key to the development of the Huizenga School's master's degree program in Leadership. Dr. Hersey humbly stated that outstanding institutions are fitting places for Amaguk, Keeper and Protector of Wisdom, a symbol of knowledge and imparting of understanding.

Accordingly, special thanks go to Dr. Paul Hersey, Mrs. Suzanne Hersey, Dr. Ronald Campbell, and Mrs. Dorothy Campbell for their contributions to the field of education and research.

1 – Why Earn a Graduate Degree

Advanced degrees are now becoming the norm in various professions, to be able to teach college courses, and to conduct research in one's field or industry. There may be a number of great reasons for each individual to pursue a graduate degree and specialize in a specific field of his or her interest. One of the most popular reasons is that when job hunting, finding other applicants with undergraduate degrees is now very common in the United States and most other developed countries. In order to distinguish oneself, possessing a master's degree or doctorate degree surely will be a determining factor on whether to hire someone or not. According to experts, a doctorate degree can open doors that are not otherwise accessible to a person in today's competitive work environment. These opportunities can include research positions at corporations and government laboratories, as well as teaching and development opportunities in higher education. Furthermore, continually learning through a graduate degree further allows one to expand his/her knowledge and capacity to do more. Most management and upper level leadership positions prefer a high level of education. Even in the government, whether it is in the United States or other countries, the higher the degree, the higher the grade level will likely be for applicants who seek employment through public service. With a graduate degree in business or management, companies know that you have been developed to manage people and to understand business practices at a higher level. Hence, one is afforded more responsibility and career challenges leading to greater management opportunities.

Some people love to learn and take classes throughout their lifetime. For those individuals, a master's and doctorate degree may be part of the natural cycle of learning. Personal fulfillment may be found in educational pursuits. The wonderful thing about seeking knowledge is that it never ends. You may spend a lifetime seeking knowledge and in the end discover that it was in the seeking that you found joy. In general, people are likely to pursue a doctorate degree in order to obtain certain intrinsic and extrinsic benefits and advantages associated with completing and obtaining it. Intrinsic benefits are the tangible, concrete, and readily apparent results of obtaining and having a graduate degree. One can earn a doctorate degree for hundreds of different reasons and each reason might be unique. While there might be patterns and general categories, most people enroll in a doctorate program because of an intrinsic motivation that is unique to them. These motivations may include family pressures, career change possibilities, organizational or governmental requirements, or the appeal of being called *doctor*.

According to James Faust (2003), a great leader said, "My dear young friends, there is another great truth that you young men must learn. It is that everything has a price. There is a price to pay for success, fulfillment, accomplishment, and joy. There are no freebies. If you don't pay the price that is needed for success, you will pay the price of failure. Preparation, work, study, and service are required to achieve and find happiness. Disobedience and lack of preparation carry a terrible price tag." Earning a doctorate is an accomplishment that is worth the time and effort needed to bring success in both one's career and personal dreams; however, as noted in Faust's quote, it does come at a price. Besides taking several years of hard work and focus, most doctoral programs are expensive and only about 40-60% of those entering terminal programs complete their degree (Smallwood, 2004). It is the overriding objective of this book to offer tools and techniques that can help candidates successfully overcome these statistics and earn a doctorate degree.

Reasons for Earning a Doctorate Degree

A colleague once said that "I joined the doctoral program because I needed two things for my continued happiness: first, intellectual stimulation; and, then physical stimulation. Years ago when I first got married, I received both forms of stimulation from my husband; shortly after, I needed new sources of excitement and invigoration which the doctoral program fulfilled." Another colleague named Kelvin A. Massey (Personal Communication, January 25, 2007) mentioned that he was pursuing graduate studies, not necessarily for improving job potential, but to learn the vocabulary and language of business and high education research. In his real estate law practice, he was frequently called upon to resolve disputes and negotiate contracts between parties as well as implement the terms and conditions of previously negotiated agreements and contracts. During the course of his solo practice, he learned the concepts of managing a business such as marketing, organizational structure, financing, accounting, and strategic planning. Although he operated a highly successful practice, the limited business education relegated him to decision-making based on "what made sense" and other intuitive factors. After the sale of the business, he decided to satisfy a long deferred personal goal as well as satisfy his craving to learn "the language" of business and higher education regarding research and enrolled in the graduate business program.

While everyone can use intellectual stimulation, there are many ways to get it, and a doctoral program is just one possible source. However, intellectual stimulation is not the only reason people pursue a doctoral degree. As previously mentioned, there are many reasons for pursuing a doctoral degree. One of the biggest may be the shortage in qualified terminally-degreed faculty members on college campuses. Regardless of the reason, studying for a doctoral degree is entirely different from the previous education. Hawley (1993) believed that doctoral study differs from earlier educational pursuits in two ways: intellectual and psychological. In terms of intellectual, doctorate study must produce scholars; as such, it involves doing a number of intensive researches and completing area-focused studies. In addition, there are a number of psychological aspects unique to doctoral studies. In some cases, doctoral students also have to deal with difficult feelings such as boredom, frustration, and loneliness. Planning to get a doctoral degree, students should evaluate and ask themselves why they need a doctoral degree. Not being able to adequately identify one's personal motivation for pursuing the degree may lead to additional stress and frustration and ultimately to dropping out of the program during some of the more difficult moments...yes, there can be challenging moments that make one think and stretch beyond his or her original abilities and boundaries. Of course, it is often the desire and objective of wanting to know more about a specific topic that people start their journey of education and higher levels of learning as demonstrated by Professor Mustafa G. Mujtaba's statement:

> The reasons for why I chose to obtain a higher education, as in obtaining a doctorate degree, are many. Growing up I was always under the impression that in order for me to understand the world around me, I must attend school and continue learning. I assumed, maybe subconsciously, that by the time I finish high school, I would know everything there is to know about the world. However, I was negatively surprised! Once I graduated from Columbia High School in Lake City, Florida, and stepped into the "real world," I felt as if I was going back to kindergarten. I felt that I did not know anything, or the things that I should have known by then. Of course, I knew how to solve calculus problems, do basic and advanced chemistry problems, and even write short stories. But, I was still missing something. And that was the yearning for more knowledge. That is when I knew I had to start kindergarten again, and thus I began my college years. Again, I thought, by the time I have my bachelor's degree, I will be set. However, I was wrong! I learned much, yet I still did not know what I wanted to have known. From the beginning of mankind, infectious diseases have existed, and we have always been haunted by them. How could a bacterium that is not even visible to the naked eye cause so much harm! The more I learned, the more questions I had. Just like new computers are being introduced each year with bigger hard drives, similarly my brain capacity was being upgraded with every year I spent at the university level doing graduate research. Thus, I continued my research and doctoral studies in Microbiology at the University of Florida. Those years were time well spent. Truly, I did gain much understanding of the microscopic world, yet I still did not know. I was left with many questions. But, it took a doctoral degree for me to realize that I will never understand any topic fully no matter how long I research it. For me, it is the satisfaction of gaining that extra knowledge and "know how" that drove me to get a higher education and learn to research (Personal Communication, February 20, 2007).

A doctorate program can certainly fulfill one's desire for knowledge as well as provide the researcher with the understanding that there is so much more that can be studied in the coming years and generations as demonstrated by Mustafa's educational journey and experience. Mustafa finished his doctorate degree and then completed three years of fellowship at Harvard University before taking a research faculty position at the University of Florida. Today, he is teaching at the Florida Gulf Coast University in Fort Myers, Florida. Of course, while Mustafa's reasons for higher education stemmed from a desire to gain more knowledge in hopes of researching and understanding what causes certain diseases and how to prevent them from hurting human beings, everyone else can have his or her own reasons for pursuing a doctorate or an advanced degree in his or her profession. For example, according to Dr. Nilofar Jamasi, dentist in Central Florida:

> A dentist may pursue a postdoctoral dental degree because he or she enjoys performing specific procedures in dentistry and feels fulfilled while performing those procedures. While practicing comprehensive dentistry, a dentist may develop a rising interest toward a specific field of dentistry encouraging him/her to seek more education. This newly-gained knowledge will be invaluable to the patients, as more services can be provided to them. Another reason a dentist may pursue further education is to teach and research in the dentistry field at the university level. This high level of expertise will allow one to contribute effectively to the future generations of learners, and such experts will be able to participate in the creation and progress of innovative research projects. In addition, in the developed economies, now we have access to such great learning opportunities that it often makes people feel fortunate and compelled to study and get more advanced levels of expertise. For example, a general dentist may seek a postdoctoral degree mainly because he or she is personally motivated to do so for his or her intrinsic reasons, concerned for the wellbeing of others, and have the desire to explore his/her interest further in one specific area (Personal Communication, February 20, 2007).

Medical experts who are practicing dentistry, microbiology, or medicine, for example, often earn advanced educational degrees to provide more services to patients and/or to conduct clinical and academic research in hopes of discovering new knowledge and advancing their professions. Of course, most business, leadership and management professionals also seek higher levels of knowledge in hopes of gaining new knowledge and advancing their professions. At the mean time, they too wish to better serve their customers, employees, third party beneficiaries, and others in the community. Perhaps there are no wrong reasons for gaining more knowledge and pursuing a doctorate degree when such learning benefits society through the advancement of knowledge or prevention of catastrophes.

Bahaudin's reasons for earning a doctorate degree in business and management can be summed up as follows: personal and intellectual development, recognition of contribution, entrance into academia (research, professorship, lecturing), better employment opportunities, and social mobilization or networking with professional colleagues. Of course, regardless of the reasons, earning such an achievement also depends on many other situational variables such as time, money, parental status, martial status, and overall family support.

For Michael, his reasons for earning a terminal degree focused around a better work-life balance. He started his doctoral studies when his son was very young so that when his son started school he would be completing his doctoral program and be able to look for opportunities at a college or university so that his schedule would better match his son's as he went through elementary, middle, and high school. As it turned out, he was able to complete his doctorate studies and obtain a teaching position at Limestone College in Gaffney, SC by the time his son was in 1ˢᵗ grade. While Michael and Bahaudin's reasons were strong enough to successfully get them through the challenging moments of higher education, especially the dissertation project, there might be many other great reasons for pursuing a doctoral degree. Several of the commonly mentioned reasons[1] for pursuing a doctoral degree are briefly highlighted below.

Personal Development

Pursuing a doctoral degree is a unique and valuable experience as it is a research degree. Because a doctoral degree is a research degree, for many students it will be the first time they work within the community of scholars and the distinct characteristics involved with creating new research. For example, students may have to learn to narrow their focus, control personal opinions, focus their studies, and think logically. Also, they need to learn how to work in a team and communicate with their supervisors, mentors, and committee members. Teamwork and communications skills will be important to making it through the coursework and paramount to successfully completing the dissertation. Thus, pursuing a doctoral degree fosters the abilities to think systematically and analytically. In addition, doctoral students experience not only how to manage themselves, but also how to communicate with others.

Contributing to Knowledge

Doing research is the main responsibility for doctoral students; thus, they have opportunities to make a significant contribution to their field of study. Hawley (1993) believed that doctoral students need to change themselves from being just a consumer of research to a producer of research. Also, works produced by students represent a very significant element in national knowledge production (Leonard, 2001).

Benefiting Society

Some non-Western students and political activists, such as feminists, can help their society by getting a doctorate degree, then going back to work for their communities. For example, many doctorates become professors in their own countries even though they may earn less income and, at times, live with fewer luxuries than are available in developed economies. Yet, they continue doing their research, generating ideas to develop their professions, schools, and/or countries. For example, some doctoral students plan to further their specific area of research to improve their countries' situation, while others attempt to produce and publish competitive research articles to enhance the credibility of their schools.

---

[1] Coauthored with Natcha Limthanakom, Nova Southeastern University.

Financial Freedom

An important motivational factor in going to graduate school is the income ratio between bachelor level and graduate level employees. People who continue their education are the ones who typically end up with higher positions and larger salaries in their organizations. According to some reports in the United States, graduate degrees can pay off in terms of income as the median annual household income in the year 2000 was around $65,922.00 for people with bachelor degrees and $77,935.00 for those with master's degrees. Yet, others have claimed that the lifetime income of those holding masters degrees surpasses people who received only a bachelor's by $333,265.00, while professional and doctoral graduates earn $889,154.00 more than the bachelor's holders.

Earning a doctorate degree is not necessarily going to make a person rich or a millionaire, but it can provide one with more opportunities in regard to research, consulting, and teaching. While somewhat outdated, according to statistics reported by the U.S. Department of the Census during 1995, mean annual income of persons who are 18 years of age and older can expected to be $82,749 for those with professional degrees, $67,785 for those with doctorate degrees, $46,332 for people who have earned a masters degree, and about $37,724 for those with bachelor's degrees.

The Chronicle of Higher Education, in their August 25, 2006 issue, reported that the average faculty salaries for a 4-year institution in the 2005-2006 academic year in the United States was $102,702 for a professor rank, $84,095 for an associate professor rank, $78,151 for an assistant professor rank, and $49,271 for an instructor in business, management, and marketing related courses. In these 4-year institutions, the faculty members teaching in engineering and in legal studies were paid slightly higher than business faculty. Those with doctorate degrees are expected to be paid at the highest level of each rank, as many 4-year institutions do have ranked faculty members who do not have terminal degrees.

As a doctoral student, or a potential doctoral student, one should realize that having an advanced degree is not an end in itself and should not be seen as a panacea for world peace, financial stability, or wisdom. Having an advanced degree simply means one is passionate about a specific subject area and has developed a mastery of a few topics in the designated area. Nonetheless, it is an achievement that should be respected and admired in society. However, it is not the degree that makes one an expert or a better philosopher; but rather, it is one's level of effort and how one uses the gained knowledge to create an identity for oneself. Overall, it is worthwhile to repeat that earning a doctorate is an accomplishment that is well worth the time and effort needed to bring success in both one's career and personal dreams.

A Three-Dimensional Analysis of Motivation for a Doctoral Degree[2]

The majority of students who acquire a Masters Degree do not move on to pursue a terminal degree. These persons have perhaps reached intellectual self-actualization or maybe just do not see the need for such a pursuit. Why then do others move on to pursue terminal degrees? What motivates one to achieve a doctoral degree? The first systematic approach to develop the concept of achievement

---

[2] Contributed by Charmaine Walters Balfour, Nova Southeastern University.

motivation was conducted by David McClelland and his associates in 1947. McClelland and others defined achievement motivation as a learned motive, unconscious in nature, resulting from reward or punishment for specific behavior (Castenell, 1984). Today, researchers are still trying to find out the true motivation of doctoral candidates and graduates.

A three dimensional approach in discussing the motivation behind the pursuit of a terminal degree involves the pre-motivational factors which can include: (1) Better employment opportunities, (2) To enter into academia, (3) Personal/Intellectual development, (4) Affordability, (5) Status, (6) Social mobilization, (7) Recognition, (8) Like to study, and others. The second dimension includes the present motivational factors that influence the completion of a terminal degree, and the third dimension includes the post motivational factors that ensure the degree is used for its intended purpose and not become 'dead stock.' During 2006 and early 2007 academic years, an informal questionnaire was sent to 45 current and post doctoral colleagues as well as terminally-degreed individuals to determine their top five reasons for pursuing such an advanced and specialized degree. These questionnaires were sent via email and responses received in like manner. The results were tabulated to show the percentage of respondents who chose a specific variable as their first five choices.

Pre-motivation. Seventy one percent (71% or the highest percentage choices) of the respondents chose better employment opportunities as either their top or second highest reason in pursuing a terminal degree. Sixty five percent (65%) chose personal and intellectual development as their first or second choice. Ninety eight percent (98%) did not see affordability as a factor in pursuing a terminal degree. Based on the responses, it is believed that being more qualified will result in better employment opportunities in terms of positions and consequently higher salaries. Although many theorists do not believe that money is the key motivational factor, this small survey of doctoral students and post-doctoral colleagues suggests otherwise. While one might argue that better employment opportunities do not necessarily mean more money, money is actually what it "boils down to" for many individuals. Therefore, if the student thinks that pursuing a terminal degree will place him/her in a better position, job wise, then he/she will be more likely to pursue it.

As a student moves on to pursue a terminal degree, a certain amount of personal and intellectual growth is expected. There is a certain intellectual curiosity and willingness to explore in new areas that would characterize the doctoral student (Roth, 1955). In applying the results to Maslow's Hierarchy of Needs Theory, we see that recognition and social mobility would tie in with the esteem need, which is the fourth stage in the hierarchy, and personal and intellectual development along with employment opportunities would tie in with self actualization.

The results of the respondents to this informal survey can also be related to the Hawthorne Studies, which found that employees became more motivated as soon as they recognized that they received more attention. Knowing that he/she will be moving up in the echelons of society is what motivates some students to pursue doctoral studies – the recognition, the attention. Equity Theory is often described as a relationship between employees' motivation and their perception of being treated fairly by their bosses in the organization. The doctoral student sees good pay as an equitable output for a doctoral degree input.

Present motivation. There is usually a high level of motivation to start a terminal degree but too often students give up their dream in the process. It takes determination and drive to complete the degree. Good attitude, discipline, finances, effort, strategies, focus, performance, and goal setting all play a role in ensuring the degree is completed. A good or positive attitude creates optimism for the future and facilitates the handling of both unexpected and expected obstacles. Failure is usually the result of a poor attitude towards whatever one is doing (King, 2006).

Discipline is the ability to stick to one's plans when tempted to do otherwise. Whenever there is a deviation from plans every other plan is affected and then things tend to go awry. Highly self-disciplined students usually outperform their more impulsive peers on every academic-performance variable (Duckworth & Seligman, 2005).

Finances have to be in place in order to ensure the completion of the degree. This can come in the forms of scholarships, loans, aids, or from savings. However, proper financial planning is essential in ensuring the completion in a timely manner.

The doctoral student should earnestly endeavor to do whatever it takes to complete the degree. Strategies should be developed and carried out. Many doctoral students lose focus and end up either taking many years to complete the degree or not completing it at all. The student must never "take his or her eyes off the prize." The doctoral student should set clearly defined goals and constantly perform assessments to determine if efforts to meet these goals are being made. Keep in mind that achieving these goals will satisfy the pre-motivation needs that drove the pursuit of the degree in the first place.

Post-motivation. Many graduates pursue terminal degrees with no intention of doing anything with it. That might be the case for those who want it only for personal development. Some may question, why spend so much time, effort and money just to say you have a terminal degree. We recommend that each individual should put the degree to the best use possible in order to maximize on its returns. Seek out opportunities in which it can be used, such as consultations, lecturing, research, or a desired and lucrative position in a company.

As previously mentioned, there are various reasons for pursuing a terminal degree. Self actualization, personal development, entering into academia, family influences, status, and recognition are some of the reasons students pursue a terminal degree. Based on personal discussions and surveys, many individuals seem to pursue a doctoral degree to gain better employment opportunities. Another main reason is for personal and intellectual development. For others, the key reason is for social mobilization and recognition. There is no one motivational factor that will drive a doctoral student to succeed. The student has to want to succeed and be determined to take the necessary steps to achieve. There has to be a constant drive and desire to achieve while staying focused. Develop realistic goals and be disciplined enough to take the necessary actions to achieve these goals. Many students have pursued terminal degrees and many are doing it. It undoubtedly is not an easy road, but through hard work and perseverance it can indeed be done.

Educator's Rationale for Pursuing a Doctorate[3]

Attaining a doctoral degree is an expensive and time-consuming task for everyone, but perhaps a necessity for educators. The pursuit of a terminal degree generally demands a great deal of effort and sacrifice; it should not be undertaken lightly. Failure to earn the degree after having begun a program of study can have a significant and detrimental psychological impact on the unsuccessful candidate. Such a failure also may result in a severe financial reversal for the student, either due to loans which will be difficult to repay or the liquidation of personal financial resources that cannot be recovered. The effort and sacrifice, then, have to be weighed against the perceived benefits or advantages of having a terminal degree over not having one. Once the decision has been made to pursue graduate studies, it is critical to approach such a pursuit in a manner that increases the likelihood of success. The motivation for obtaining a doctorate comes from many sources. As previously mentioned, not all individuals who seek a doctorate do so for the same reasons nor are the rationale felt to the same extent or degree by all candidates. From an academic perspective, some of the most prevalent reasons why individuals might pursue a doctorate degree could be as follows.

Demand for the terminal degree. Demand for college accounting instructors, as one example, with a terminal degree is already greater than the supply; and the situation is only expected to become more critical in the future. One study indicated that over the academic years 2005 – 2008 the shortfall is expected to be almost 500 unfilled positions (Plumlee, Kachelmeier, Madeo, Pratt, and Krull, 2006). Some of these positions may be filled by instructors without terminal degrees. Moreover, Plumlee et al. (2006) cautioned that the projected shortfall may be even greater than expected since their study assumed a 100% completion rate for all doctoral candidates studied; realistically, some attrition in these programs will occur and not all candidates will complete their programs. The expected shortfall is reflected in salaries being offered for instructors with full terminal degrees. Instructors with doctorates whose duties are primarily teaching may expect annual salaries averaging 8% - 10% higher than salaries for instructors without doctorates (Plumlee et al., 2006). Thus, candidates completing doctoral programs in accounting may expect to find not only a wide selection of positions available in the next few years but may also expect to be better compensated for attaining the terminal degree.

Personal growth/dissatisfaction with career. A second important motivation, especially affecting individuals who already have established careers in the business world, is the desire for personal intellectual growth and new challenges. Similar to the authors of this book, many current doctoral candidates left behind lucrative, or at least comfortable, lifestyles in the business world to go back to school. A feeling of stunted growth, both professionally and intellectually, was an important rationale for many of these candidates (Mangan, 2006). Also, important was the opportunity to mentor new professionals and be on the cutting edge of research in their field. Another rationale for doctoral candidates who leave the business world to return to school is job security. As was pointed out by one researcher (Mangan, 2006) universities do not merge, send jobs offshore, relocate headquarters, or (generally) go out of business. Thus, a tenured professor at a university with a relatively well-paying job has a certain degree of security that is not available in the traditional business career. Nor

---

[3] Contributed by Joel Rossmaier, University of the Ozarks.

does this situation seem likely to change in the near future. As indicated above, the demand for accounting doctorates is expected to exceed supply in the near term. Mangan (2006) reports on a study by the Association to Advance Collegiate Schools of Business (AACSB) that projects shortages across all business disciplines amounting to 1,100 by 2007 and 2,400 by 2013. Current trends in doctoral programs support this projection; although the total number of doctorates awarded increased in the United States in both 2003 and again in 2005, the number of new doctorates in business actually declined in those years (Gravois, 2005; Smallwood, 2006).

Respect of students. For those individuals who have already made a commitment to a career in education at the college level, gaining the prestige and respect of students may provide another motivation or rationale for obtaining a doctorate. Research indicates that undergraduate accounting students place a relatively high value on the attainment of a doctorate; such an achievement, especially combined with significant practical experience, is an important determinant of students' choice of instructor (Mounce, Mauldin, & Braun, 2004).

Respect of peers. It is generally conceded that the doctorate is perceived by other doctorate-holding professors, and other instructors, as indicating a penultimate level of teaching quality at the university level. This is so even as educators decry the perception that a doctorate prepares one only for a career in academia (Heathcott, 2005). Thus, another motivation for pursuing a doctorate would be to gain the respect of one's teaching colleagues who have already achieved the terminal degree and may tend, however inadvertently, to judge others by the same standard, particularly on matters of promotion and tenure.

Rarely will all the above rationales be indicated by a specific individual pursuing a doctorate in a specific program. Some will be more important than others, some will not be mentioned at all, and some individuals may use rationales that are not generally recognized as important to pursuing the terminal degree. For example, one individual pursuing a doctorate may conclude that the demand for the degree (and commensurate financial reward), desire for student respect, and desire for intellectual stimulation and growth are, in that order, sufficient rationale for accepting the sacrifice and challenges of the program of study. The individual may also justify the doctorate as a way of observing and emulating professors whose teaching styles he or she most appreciates or sees as most desirable; such a rationale would be most likely indicated by someone who had already made the commitment to a new career as an educator. Similarly, an individual who has made a commitment to education at a particular institution or in a particular area may justify the doctorate as a job security issue—seeking and holding the doctorate reduces the risk that the institution will hire an instructor who has more substantial academic credentials.

New candidates can use a variety of techniques to successfully complete the doctorate degree. Both students and institutions have a vested interest in how the pursuit of a doctorate may be brought to a successful conclusion. But current trends indicate that this vested interest is not being as aggressively protected as it could be or should be. Recent studies indicate that up to 50% of the students who begin a doctoral program fail to attain the degree (Jacobson, 2001; Smallwood, 2006). Recognizing the fact that both institutions and students have an interest in completing the degree, factors affecting the successful completion frequently are under the control of the institution or the student, but rarely under the control of both.

Organizational factors are those factors under the control of the institution. Such factors would include, for example, the student selection and admission process, the program structure, assigning advisors and mentors, and the overall responsiveness or flexibility of the program (Smith, Maroney, Nelson, Abel, and Abel, 2006). As noted, students will rarely exercise even slight control over these factors. Thus, it would seem that students should concentrate on those factors which may be more personal in nature.

Personal factors include relationships with family, financial strains, employment responsibilities, and personal support systems (Smith, et al., 2006). Techniques for managing these factors would include such things as improving time and project management skills, communication with family members to make sure everyone (including significant others) knows what to expect from the candidate during the program, and establishing a financial budget so that the financial strains are at least anticipated and planned for appropriately.

One factor which is consistently cited as important is a sense of community or belonging among students that provides additional support (Jacobson, 2001; Mangan, 2006; Smith, et al., 2006). This is a factor which is at least partly under control of the students. Clearly, it helps to have an environment fostered by the institution which contributes to the sense of community, for example, by setting up student lounges and study areas, sponsoring colloquia, having "brown-bag lunch" days when students can meet and talk informally. However, each student can also actively establish a sense of community by seeking out and establishing relationships with fellow students outside the institution. These relationships would have as their starting point the collegial feeling brought about by shared experiences in the doctoral program but could also build on other common characteristics as well (e.g., hobbies, interests, family, etc.).

Pursuit of a doctorate is a time-consuming, expensive task requiring a great deal of commitment and sacrifice. Understanding the motivations for such an enterprise as well as the techniques which may be employed to facilitate attaining the degree can have a significant impact on the chances for a successful completion of the program. Educators should know that obtaining such a terminal degree can be beneficial to themselves, their students and their respective institutions. Regardless of the temporary financial costs, for many individuals these are sufficient reasons to earn a doctorate degree.

Motivation for a Doctorate in the Healthcare Field[4]

Dynamic, unpredictable, invaluable, evolving- these are all terms that can be used to describe healthcare and the management of healthcare in today's U.S. society. There is very little, if anything, that is more important to people than their health and well-being. With consideration of rising healthcare costs, the under or uninsured population, and rising occurrences of health epidemics such as diabetes and obesity, it is no wonder one must continue on to higher levels of education for basic comprehension. Higher education, for that matter, would only serve to catch-up, not necessarily keep students abreast of current events. Such familiar statistics describing how "children from low-income families were more likely than children from middle-

---

[4] Contributed by Robert J. Mullaney, Nova Southeastern University.

high income families to be uninsured" (Simpson, 2005) can remain unchallenged without inquiry if not for academic programs and research requirements. It is only with pertinent continuous education and direct, on-going experience within the field of healthcare that decisions of substance can be made. Knowledge is the prerequisite to making an informed difference.

With colleges and universities popping up all over the world, especially in the developed economies, a bachelor's degree is becoming as valuable and useful as a high school diploma was many years ago. The level of research associated with doctorate level course work is the key element in its value. Many, but not all, master's programs require a thesis or dissertation paper of some sort. A doctorate degree transforms a typical "college student" into a potential research machine. Armed with the skill, resources, and practice it takes to implement long lasting, substantially relative differences in society not only takes determination and stamina of "...doctoral candidates, but it also requires passion" (Leedy, 2005). As mentioned in many research methodology textbooks, passion is an essential element for successful completion of doctorate level course work. The only way one can realize his or her passion is to acknowledge the actual value of their chosen terminal degree and its alignment with their own personal attributes.

It is supposed that many ambitious students strive for that title of "doctor" in fulfillment of personal, yet more superficial reasons. Along with the use of artful wording and adequate interviewing skills, perhaps such superficial reasons can help aspiring students gain admission into their desired doctoral program. However, superficial hopes and ambitions are easily swiped clean by other, more influential life matters and their level of top priority soon becomes a fading element of the past. The passion, in those cases, was most likely never present. Deep, burning passion is what will drive doctoral students to, and even past, the finish line. Whether it is hate, love, anger, or sadness that fuels the passion, it is permanent. Passion has led numerous leaders to success, armies to victory, and has changed the world one single accomplishment at a time.

Candidates of informed change. Those individuals who do have passion should consider taking the appropriate steps to achieve their so called "passion related ambitions." For example, a person who ultimately plans to change the current healthcare system of the U.S. by implementing the key working aspects of international social healthcare systems would require more than just hopes and dreams to realize this goal. A potentially qualified individual (one who may be able to make a reasonably informed series of decisions) may present with 3, 5, or even 10 or more years of solid healthcare experience. This healthcare experience may be as a doctor who treats patients and deals directly with malpractice insurance and law suits, or may be a physical therapist who unwillingly has to turn away a small child due to inadequate health coverage. A strong, well rounded understanding of the system of healthcare and its history will serve as this person's Core Knowledge Base.

It may be argued that years of college can compensate for lack of work experience in many fields. As a settlement to this argument, all one needs to do is review the job requirements of some of the highest paid, highest profile, and most important corporate openings. The U.S. military abides by the rule of awarding merit for both years of experience and/or years of college. Too many times have companies suffered some level of failure for placing the wrong "college graduate" in a position that demands a strong Core Knowledge Base of work experience.

So, our qualified, ambitious "changer" of the U.S. healthcare system must have his/her share of solid, reputable healthcare related work experience. This does not automatically qualify him/her to be the right person to change the system. After all, part of contributing to knowledge and change to society involves social acceptance. People will research and assess your level of reputability, in addition to work experience, education, goals, and criminal record amongst other things. For example, let us say that a candidate of change has a clear criminal record and a widely accepted general goal that appears to make sense. Where is the passion? What is it that would help to rally the support of society and to make any person believe this candidate will follow through 110%, or even for that matter, finish the job that was started?

The birth of passion. The passion of a candidate cannot be thought-up or figured out, it must be born intrinsically through reflection and experience. There must have been a monumental moment or emotionally altering experience that makes that person feel a certain way. True passion can be rare. Even those who do possess true passion for something, but lack other attributes, will make no significant difference because of it. For example the physical therapist, has his/her established daily routine of treating physically and developmentally disabled children. His/her routine entails 30 minute direct patient treatment sessions 12 times per day, contacting and communicating the needs of these patients to insurance companies for approval of services, then relaying data back to the parents of the children. Although sometimes very routine, this therapist loves the job of helping children and has been doing it for about 10 years. Ten years ago, one may argue, the healthcare system was so different than the way it is today. With experience he/she can pinpoint specific positive and negative differences over the years within the system. For instance, one can explain that today's insurance companies actually hire other companies to help "unjustify" the need for therapy and other health services so they can cut corporate costs.

One's passion is born on the day when he or she has performed an initial evaluation on a young six-year old girl who had fractured her elbow. The patient's insurance company reviewed the paperwork, and then submitted it to their "cost saving review" unit. Their response was received in the form of a denial of services letter. This was absurd and unbelievable as expressed by the therapist. The justification of their decision would state such issues as "she can use her hand," "she is still growing and will grow out of it," and "low levels of pain reported." The moment this therapist had to communicate this response to the patient and parent is when his/her passion was born. He or she would feel "had by the system," embarrassed, and ashamed. It was at that moment that a vow was made to step up and make a difference.

Well-rounded skill set. Our candidate, now with the passion and the Core Knowledge Base, realizes that in order to implement change in this highly complex arena of healthcare, there are still many necessary skills he/she is missing. In order to make informed decisions and be respected with regards to her suggestions for change, she would have to learn how to properly conduct research, utilize resources, develop relationships via networking, and learn the basic business principals of society. Our candidate decides to return to school.

The set of skills that may be deemed necessary to make informed decisions can be generalized as follows: A- Pertinent General Core Knowledge Base; B- Passion; and C- Continuous Education/ On-Going Base Growth.

A. Pertinent General Core Knowledge. As discussed within the case example, the Core Knowledge Base is all of what one knows of an industry as a result of work experience. This does not mean that a person should occupy the same position for 20 years; quite the contrary, in fact. Well-rounded, more diversified experiences within the same industry would provide the richest source of lessons to the Knowledge Base.

B. Passion. Passion, possibly the primary driving force behind many significant accomplishments, was explained as being born. Within passion, as a general term, comes determination, sacrifice, patience, and persistence. This overall passion represents the emotional driver of the person. Without it, there is no will or reason to use your Core Knowledge Base.

C. Continuous Education/ On-Going Base Growth. Continuous Education and On-going relevant work experience is that skill set which consists of what may justify obtaining higher degrees of education, specifically terminal degrees. The fast paced, dynamic business and healthcare world requires more in-depth knowledge today than merely a bachelor's degree obtained 15 or 20 years ago can provide. Terminal degrees teach students those lasting skills of how to teach themselves. The research, resources, and practice it provides can be combined with simpler skill sets such as time management, self discipline, organization, and perseverance that will ensure that the "learning" aspect is continuous. Healthcare, and all the systems it consists of, changes so rapidly that people who dare alter or suggest change to the system must remain current with regard to affairs and practices- on a day-to-day basis. Terminal degrees are never ending and are becoming increasingly sought after by those individuals especially engulfed in passion and adequate Core Knowledge Bases.

As can be seen from observations and literature, "the need for healthcare reform in the United States continues to be high on the public agenda" (Hayes, 1997, p. 288). This section is part case example and part justification of the motivation and simple skill sets necessary, not only to complete a "doctorate degree," but on a wider scope, to implement well-informed change. The subject of this section of the book actually is a therapist by profession, with ten years of relevant healthcare work experience whose passion was really born as explained. His intentions and strategies for completion of a doctorate degree in business administration with specialization in management is merely a sacrifice of time and a form of preparation for a lifetime of implementing what he calls "well-informed decision making and change." This type of passion for advanced education can certainly help in making informed decisions for successfully earning a doctorate degree.

Techniques Used to Complete the Degree[5]

To obtain a doctoral degree, doctoral students need to have and focus on three important factors: attitude, drive, and strategy. This section will explain each factor.

---

[5] Coauthored with Natcha Limthanakom, Nova Southeastern University.

Attitude. A student's attitude when entering a program of study is a critical factor in his/her success. Additionally, a strong internal locus of control – the belief that you, and not outside forces or the environment, have primary control over your results and achievements – may be critical. Bandura (as cited in Tuckman, 2004) identified the link between attitude and motivation as self-efficacy, the beliefs of ability to accomplish their task. Students who have self-efficacy tend to successfully complete their academic goals since they will attempt to use all kinds of strategies such as self- regulatory cognitive engagement and persistence (Linnerbrink, 2002). Tuckman (2004) and Cole (2004) also believed that self-efficacy will enhance students' motivation to achieve their objectives. If students have a strong positive attitude toward obtaining a doctoral degree, their attitude will lead them to pursue challenging and satisfying studies.

Drive. If students have a strong positive attitude to pursue their doctoral degrees, they should have sufficient energy to motivate themselves to work on their doctorate. To drive their attitudes, there are several approaches and motivation theories that can help explain the drive of their attitudes.

1. *Achievement goal theory.* Achievement goal theory can be applied to the academic achievement as the desires of students motivate themselves to achieve their particular goals (Seifert, 2004). These future goals can motivate doctoral students to finish their research. Perceptions of future goals can encourage doctoral students in self-regulation and engagement of their tasks (Miller & Brickman, 2004). Students must have intrinsic-directed goals to attempt and complete their own efforts. Students who have intrinsic-directed goals will try to complete their tasks and evaluate their performance against some internalized standard of excellence (Petri, 1991).

2. *Intrinsic motivation.* Deci and Ryan (1985) stated that "intrinsic motivation is in evidence whenever students' natural curiosity and interest energize their learning" (p. 245). The most significant factor that determines if a student will complete a doctoral degree is that the student has a strong interest in earning a doctorate. Both personal and situational interests have the potential to influence academic achievement, as these interests can enhance achievement by engaging students in the task or activity (Linnenbrink, 2002).

Strategies. Beyond having a high level of intrinsic motivation, other factors that play a role in successful completion of a terminal degree include effective time-management, emotional maturity or management, networking, and gathering relevant resources are important factors to achieve a doctorate degree. This book provides numerous strategies that have worked for others. We recommend you adopt those techniques and strategies that you feel will work for you.

Time management. Having an effective plan is a critical step to successfully completing a doctorate degree. Many doctoral students give up their study because they do not have a good plan. For example, if doctoral students do not have a detailed plan, their research may easily move to a lower priority causing not only delays, but may negatively affect each student's motivation. Adopting a research plan is further discussed in Chapter 7. Planning and scheduling time are two of the most significant factors for doctoral students and cannot be overstressed. Initially, students should create an overall plan highlighting the length of time over which they would like to complete the degree. The school you are attending (or planning to attend) should be able to provide you with some general guidelines of how long it takes students to get through the program and earn a degree. See Chapter 4 for more detailed information about selecting a doctoral program. Once a plan is created, students should schedule their time accordingly. After planning time, students should schedule tasks that need to be accomplished in the order of their priority or importance. Students need to plan effectively and conscientiously in order to perform effective jobs (Spitzer, 1995). The overall plan, at a minimum, should include coursework, general dissertation research time, time for writing the proposal, feedback from committee members, Academic Review Board (ARB) and Institutional Review Board (IRB) approval, data collection, writing up findings, and defense of the dissertation. More detailed advice on creating and updating your doctoral plan will be given in Chapters 6, 7 and 8.

Working on a doctoral degree has a sense of self-control. Doctoral students need to devote their time to study and do research daily. The earlier students select a research topic for their dissertation, the more time they will have to conduct research and target their coursework, to the maximum extent possible, toward their research topic. Moreover, doctoral students have to eliminate time wasters which are divided into two groups: internal and external. External time wasters are uncontrollable, and while they may not be predictable, they should be expected over the time spent in a doctoral program. These external factors may include job changes, deaths in the family, downsizing, or illnesses. Whereas internal time wasters are the serious personal habits that need to change such as excessively surfing the internet or watching television. Changing these habits will allow students to spend more time on their academic work. Unpredicted events can always happen when working for a doctorate degree. Moreover, the writing process often takes students more time than they expect (Graves & Varma, 1997). Especially for English as second language students, they tend to spend more time in writing and editing their work. Students should allow plenty of time for writing, editing, and a critical analysis of their work by colleagues. Writing every day and getting help from expert writers until it becomes a habit can greatly improve the writing process.

Emotional management. To earn a doctoral degree, students will face significant stress, boredom, and frustration. Students will have to learn to concentrate on their project from a long-term perspective. To manage their feelings, doctoral students need to control their emotions in order to "survive." It may be difficult to avoid negative thinking over the course of a doctoral program, especially when different obstacles and delays beyond your control get in the way; however, to the greatest extent possible, students should avoid negative thinking and focus on the end goal. Working consciously and analytically will help students figure out the problems they are facing in the course of their studies. Also, setting interim goals like reading several journal articles each week toward your dissertation topic may also help reduce other frustrations.

Building support. While preparing to work on dissertation, doctoral students should establish good relationships with the departmental offices, the graduate school staffs, librarians, and student union personnel to make work go smoothly (Leonard, 2001). Also, having friends who are studying for their doctorate degree can lend moral support and assist one's success in academia. For international students, having some friends who are native English speakers, and who can proof-read one's writing, will be very helpful. For students starting a doctoral program who have families, a spouse's support during the long hours away studying is of immeasurable help to succeeding in a program.

Resources. Many resources can provide helpful information as well as facilities to assist students. For example, many schools in the United States provide writing centers, which can be useful for English as a second language students or those students with poor writing skills. In addition, libraries offer great information, such as services to assist students find articles. A school may also offer sessions on how to write in American Psychological Association (APA) style and how to access relevant journals from academic databases.

Continuous improvement, known as Kaizen, is the strategy that can lead doctoral students to finish their education as per their original plan and with better results. Using the Plan –Do –Check –Act (PDCA) cycle approach can help develop the needed discipline for improvement and reflections as well as better learning ability. The PDCA cycle can eliminate unwanted behaviors such as boredom and laziness. The PDCA cycle can also develop and motivate doctorate students while working on the dissertation. Working for a doctorate is different from previous education in its intellectual and psychological demands. As a result, doctoral students need to have the intrinsic motivation to encourage them in completing a terminal degree. To get the doctoral degree, students need to manage their time, emotions, networks, and other relevant resources. Also, they need to use a continuous improvement strategy to change and develop their behaviors in order to successfully complete all the requirements for this monumental terminal achievement, known as the doctorate degree.

The Psychological Contract and Framework of a Doctoral Program[6]

This book provides an illustration of the mechanics and requirements associated with starting and completing a doctoral program. It is abundantly clear that the doctoral program fully engages the student at all levels and in every manner imaginable. One of such engagements is the psychological contract in terms of the doctoral program framework, which many potential graduate students fail to quickly appreciate in the doctoral program.

A doctoral program is first a theoretical endeavor and often less of a practice-based program, built on arcane constructs, concepts, theories, and ideas. This framework does require a significant degree of rigor and mental stamina in order to sustain. Potential students are rarely ever prepared for this framework. Only after several months into the program, do doctoral students wonder about the meaning and purpose of the theoretical framework. Students, being pragmatic creatures, are sometimes apt to make a direct connection between classroom exercises and its significance in the real world. When such direct connections are unavailable, students are apt to call into question, the essence of their participation in the doctoral program. It is usually at this point that a doctoral student may experience some level of cognitive dissonance in the program, which they must overcome, if they are to successfully complete the program.

The truth of the matter is that sometimes, research must be carried out for its sake because it is through such means that we understand the world around us. In

---

[6] Contributed by Ikwukananne I. Udechukwu, Georgia State University.

such a situation, there may not be a direct connection between theory and real life. However, after the concepts and theories have been fully validated or extensively discussed in the field, they mostly tend to be tested, and then applied in the real world in order to determine their viability and purpose for managers, consultants, and executives. Would you buy a product that has been well tested under controlled conditions or not? Just as in the natural and physical sciences, the management science, for example, tries to adopt a rigorous system of philosophies in support of conclusions in the field of study.

How doctoral students accept this way of life and thinking is very important in their academic development. This framework is in essence, the basis for the cognitive ability and potential desire of students who pursue research objectives either as a means to an end or an end to itself. Because the much-sought-after faculty tenure system is built on the premise and conclusion of active research, the wisdom of engaged cognition in a theoretical framework for students, if they are to aspire to the ranks of fully tenured Professors during their academic career, cannot be over-emphasized.

While most students believe consultancy as being the aim and focus of the doctoral program, even then, consultancy is also partially based on observations, concepts, framework, hypothesis, and conclusions, perhaps, in less rigorous terms than in academia. Thus, the student, whether in traditional or non-traditional doctoral programs, has nowhere to escape this level of rigor, for in it lies the cognitive foundations for those who will ultimately become world-class consultants or revered researchers. The true test of this psychological contract begins with providing evidence of referred publications or the completion of the dissertation process. Therefore, institutions of higher learning, while grappling with the dwindling numbers of available doctoral students, also have an unsaid obligation in providing students with the psychological basis for entering a doctoral program, based on the amount of resources (time, money, energy, etc.) students typically expend in completing a doctoral program. As with many jobs and job previews, a realistic doctoral program preview would be highly encouraged for students. However, the overall burden of improving the psychological contract of students in the doctoral program does lie on the door-step of the student itself.

It should be realized that merely obtaining affirmation of a student's optimistic comments about being able to complete a doctoral program, does not necessarily translate into a completed program. The thought process and appreciation of the essence of doctoral work is also very important. The sooner the student accepts this psychological process and change, the better off they are. With increasing comfort and confidence in the psychological contract, students are able to test the referred publication waters before they even complete their dissertation and overall doctoral program. Thus, the doctoral program does change a student's thinking and perception of the world around them. It provides students with the tools of inquiry and resolution of important problems.

Whether or not a student decides to overcome the psychological inertia or resistance in accepting the theoretical underpinnings of a doctoral program, may in fact be one of the fences that separates successful doctoral students from unsuccessful ones. For some students leaving the doctoral program to a more practitioner-oriented program may seem like the most appropriate option. However, the peer-review process almost always requires the type of theoretical rigor long advocated by most terminally-degreed professors. So, the student might as well accept this way of life and thinking if they are to experience the dawn of a new day in their future academic career.

From Practitioner to Pracademician - Audrey Ellison's Journey [7]

My life is coming full circle. I started my career working in the public schools as a library media specialist with a Master's in Library Science. At the ripe old age of 27, I became the manager of all the school libraries. I had people on my team older than my mother…needless to say getting their respect was not easy. I also served as President of the Simsbury Education Association for four years where I implemented a new performance management system, negotiated contracts and resolved grievances. I was on the Board of Directors of the Connecticut Education Association for four years where I chaired several committees, lobbied the state legislature on educational issues, and served as an elected state delegate to the National Education Association Convention. During this time, I also managed a successful state senate campaign and worked on a successful US Senate campaign.

After 11 years, it was time for a change. The transition to educational consultant and move from Connecticut (CT) to Massachusetts (MA) was relatively easy. Almost immediately after embarking on a new career, I learned of the Simmons College MBA program for women. It seemed like the perfect program for someone with limited business experience and a desire to learn. I started my MBA when I was 35 and working full time. I went to school four nights a week, for two years with a one-week break at Christmas and a two-week break in August. It was grueling. No books, no movies for two years—and I love to read and go to the movies. But it is the best thing I ever did for me. And I learned two new methods for learning—involving the student in the process and working in study teams. Finally, at the age of 37 I was ready for the business world.

I realized that my two passions were marketing and organizational development (OD). A wise professor steered me towards doing marketing in a firm that consulted in OD. It was a great match. I spent eight years steadily moving up in the marketing department at Organizational Dynamics, Inc (ODI). At ODI, I learned a great deal about business, marketing, quality (was trained as a Baldrige examiner), managing people and processes, OD and customer service. I also organized the annual Executive Study Tour to visit Deming Prize winning companies in Japan and managed the customer advisory panel. At ODI, I received the Corporate Vision Award and the Marketing MVP Award.

After eight years, I was recruited by Kaset International (now AchieveGlobal) to lead the marketing communications and events team. Despite my initial reluctance to leave the northeast for FL, it seemed like a good opportunity. I told friends I was beating the Baby Boomer rush and trading in a bad winter for a bad summer. At Kaset, I orchestrated their premier international customer service conference and launched a new international brand (merger of Kaset, Learning International and Zenger Miller). When a new president was hired who wanted his own marketing team, it was time for another change.

---

[7] Contributed by Audrey Ellison, Nova Southeastern University.

Starting my own marketing business was a scary and challenging move. As a marketing strategist and consultant, I work with organizations to develop and implement marketing strategies, enhance corporate image and brand, create marketing materials and collateral, organize tradeshows and marketing events, launch new products and services, market conferences and events, and develop direct mail and email campaigns. In addition to marketing, I am a business coach working one-on-one with managers to improve their communication, performance management, conflict resolution and business planning skills. I also coach entrepreneurs in creating their business.

I have spoken at industry conferences on creating winning marketing events, getting the most of out tradeshows, developing an effective marketing mix, marketing on a shoestring, making the most of your brand (brand-aid), internal marketing and creating a business. I recently spoke at my first academic conference, which is a totally different experience. I served as communications chairperson for the Tampa Chapter of the National Association of Women Business Owners for two years and received the Chapter's 2003 Unsung Hero Award. I am currently on the leadership council. I am a volunteer and member of the Speakers' Bureau at the Ronald McDonald House in Tampa, and on the Board of Directors at the PACE Center, a school for at-risk girls.

Once the business was started, I decided I wanted to go back to my first love: teaching at the college level. The University of Phoenix (UofP), West Florida, provided an opportunity as a practitioner to teach business students. I started teaching marketing and management courses on campus and online classes. I am currently lead faculty for online marketing courses and lead faculty in Tampa for the blended learning program. In May 2002, I received the Outstanding Faculty Award, voted on by graduating students and in 2004, the Faculty Academic Excellence Award for the College of Graduate Business and Management. In 2002, I also started teaching marketing and management classes at Nova Southeastern University (NSU), Tampa.

The campus college chair at UofP started encouraging me to go back to school for a doctorate. At first, I resisted another degree, then I realized I had earned a degree in every state I have lived (NY – high school diploma, CT – BS and MLS, MA – MBA) except Florida, I decided I had better go back to school for another degree, despite not finishing the degree until I turn 60! So, in July 2004, I started a Doctorate of Business Administration (DBA) program at Nova Southeastern University. Switching hats was difficult. I could not wrap my mind around theory being more important than practice. The term "empirical" had become my least favorite word. I had trouble understanding why something was not valued until it was studied empirically, despite having been used by practitioners for years.

Somewhere along the line I realized I had become better teaching my own classes because of what I was learning taking classes. Business schools today are changing. Traditional programs compartmentalized by discipline are moving to teaching about the complexities of management. Leadership and communication skills are critical in solving the multi-discipline problems in organizations (Lavelle, 2006). Critical thinking, problem-solving, and decision-making are the skills needed today. As a pracademician with business experience and academic discipline, I can bring more value to students to help them understand more than one academic discipline or managerial function. Problems in organizations do not play out in disciplines. The loss of a customer is not a sales or marketing problem, it is an organizational problem. Education and management, knowledge and practice can be aligned.

The business school curriculum is becoming more relevant for business. As a pracademician, I have the balance between scientific approach rigor and practical relevance. I can help students collect, use and integrate data for decision-making (Bennis & O'Toole, 2005). There is a growing demand for business school professors to be able to integrate theory and practice. Academics wonder why practitioners do not value their work. Practitioners wonder why academics do not value their experience. The pracademician can speak both "languages" and help bridge the gap. The time is right...and earning a doctorate degree at 60 no longer seems as crazy!

Summary

It is been said many times and believed by philosophers and great leaders that the only thing that often stands between people and what they want from life is merely the "will" to try it and the "faith" to believe that it is possible. As the Roman philosopher Seneca once remarked, "It is not because things are difficult that we do not dare; it is because we do not dare that they are difficult." Most doctoral candidates and graduate scholars tend to have both the will and faith that it is possible for them to complete the degree; and once this is fully internalized, then it is only a matter of understanding the process and its requisite steps, strategizing, and working each step until the degree is earned.

Motivational speaker, Lou Holtz, in his program entitled "*Do Right! The Plan,*" mentions four main points for doing right and achieving success and they are: 1) *Attitude* - The path to success begins with a positive attitude; 2) *Focus* - Focus on what is important at the moment; 3) *Dream* - Dreams inspire, challenge, encourage and dare us; and 4) *Passion* - Passion is more important than talent. So, on your way to achieving your doctoral dream, have a great attitude toward your studies, stay focused on your priorities of life at the moment and keep a good balance, realistically dream big, and have a passion for what you do and what you want to do.

Mary Kay Ash, the founder of Mary Kay Cosmetics, said "A mediocre idea that generates enthusiasm will go further than a great idea that inspires no one." Perhaps the key to success can partially be explained by attitude and enthusiasm since without them, even great ideas may not get too far. With regards to aspirations, author Louisa May Alcott wrote that "Far away there in the sunshine are my highest aspirations. I may not reach them, but I can look up and see their beauty, believe in them, and try to follow where they lead." Not only can aspirations be achieved but they can also inspire others. Sir Winston Churchill has been quoted as having said "If your actions inspire others to dream more, learn more, do more and become more, you are a leader!" The key is to strive to contribute something to the world that is best done by you and your talents. Sometimes, a major contribution can be made in academia, but one must do it "one bite" at a time. "Whatever you're working on, take 'small bites.'" The task will not be overwhelming if you can reduce it to its smallest component," said author Richard Russo. Put your natural and obtained talent to work since the real tragedy of life is not in being limited to one talent or specialization, but in the failure to use that one talent or specialization one has earned.

It is true that if you treat people as if they were what they ought to be, then you will help them become what they are capable of becoming through their natural talents or obtained expertise. The same applies to the achievement of aspirations and major life objectives, such as earning a doctorate degree. Treat yourself as if you already are a terminally-degreed individual and let such feelings sink in deep in your subconscious mind. Initially, the feeling must come before anything tangible can be realized and if you have a deep inner conviction that you will always have all that you need or all that you can be, then it will be so with patience and persistency. First, you must determine what it is that you want and what you were meant to be in this life. Abraham Maslow, the popular psychologist, once said that "A musician must make music, an artist must paint, a poet must write, if he is to be ultimately at peace with himself. What a man can be, he must be." Determine what you can be and then become it. While patiently waiting to become what one is meant to be, it is best to show gratitude and appreciation to all those who made it possible. Buddha's philosophy is as follows: "Let us rise up and be thankful, for if we didn't learn a lot today, at least we learned a little, and if we didn't learn a little, at least we didn't get sick, and if we got sick, at least we didn't die; so, let us all be thankful." Be thankful and do less talking and take more calculated actions to achieve your destiny. Confucius, the philosopher, believed that "The superior man [person] is modest in his speech, but exceeds in his actions." Focus on continuous improvement and on becoming more than you currently are through worthwhile contributions. Muhammad Ali, world champion boxer, said that "The man who views the world at 50 the same as he did at 20 has wasted 30 years of his life." So, be goal-directed and use your time purposefully. Earl Nightingale, speaker and author, stated "Don't let the fear of the time it will take to accomplish something stand in the way of your doing it. The time will pass anyway; we might just as well put that passing time to the best possible use." Before you can be, you must see yourself as an accomplished academician and human being. In order to come to be what you must be, you must have a vision of being and becoming and eventually you will become what you can believe and perceive. For example, if you want excellence in your life, then dream it, see it, envision it, and work toward it. Aristotle, the early Greek philosopher, told us a long time ago that "Excellence is an art won by training and habituation; we do not act rightly because we have virtue or excellence, but we rather have those because we have acted rightly; we are what we repeatedly do; excellence, then, is not an act but a habit." Ultimately, it is the highest level of excellence in one's trade and profession where true and lasting happiness actually lies. Frank Gelett Burgess, artist and poet, stated that "There is work that is work and there is play that is play; there is play that is work and work that is play. And in only one of these lie happiness."

Make sure your work is play, and your time is spent purposefully toward meaningful activities and projects that are important in your life. Thomas Alva Edison, the inventor, said that "Being busy does not always mean real work. The object of all work is production or accomplishment and to either of these ends there must be forethought, system, planning, intelligence, and honest purpose, as well as perspiration." The big secret to achievement is goal-orientation, persistency in taking action toward one's goals, and making sure one's goals benefit others. Walt Disney, businessman and dreamer, said that "Somehow I can't believe that there are any heights that can't be scaled by a man who knows the secrets of making dreams come true. These special secrets -- curiosity, confidence, courage and constancy -- and the greatest of all is confidence. When you believe in a thing, believe in it all the way, implicitly and unquestionably." To believe, you need reflection and information from various sources and those who are impacted by what you do. The British Prime Minister, Benjamin Disraeli, once said that "As a general rule the most successful man in life is the man who has the best information." So, gain the relevant information by reading, reviewing, skimming, integrating what you learn in your writing, and taking actions that make sense for your purpose and life. With regard to action, the popular psychologist and philosopher, Dr. William James of Harvard University once said that "Action seems to follow feeling, but really action and feeling go together; and by regulating the action, which is under the more direct control of the will, we can indirectly regulate the feeling, which is not." For example, to feel better and more confident, one can take action by physically exercising and enrolling into a doctoral program for mental growth. Be a goal-oriented person, and make sure your goals are directly linked to your life goals and overall purpose in life. Furthermore, clarify your feelings regarding your goals and make sure your goals are driven by your deeply-held values. In other words, your feelings and values must also be aligned with each other. If education and knowledge attainment matches your values, then a doctorate certainly supports your dream of achieving a higher level of academic excellence.

Regardless of the circumstance, and when taking action, you must remember to be yourself; and author Theodore Seuss Geisel (Dr. Suess) recommends that you "Be who you are and say what you feel, because those who mind don't matter, and those who matter don't mind." Determine your goals, set the course, begin the journey, and continue on the road while adjusting when needed as well as enjoying the process and "smelling the roses" along the way. As Chinese philosopher Lau-tzu remarked "the journey of a thousand miles begins with a single step." So for many, especially those who have been out of academia for a long time, taking that first step may be a daunting and scary proposition, yet we recommend you take that leap – don't look back and wonder "what if." But most of all, if you want to have both success and happiness, remember what Albert Schweitzer, Nobel Prize winner, said that "Success is not the key to happiness. Happiness is the key to success. If you love what you are doing, you will be successful."

2 – Issues for International and Minority Students

M inority and international students face some unique challenges in obtaining a doctoral degree. According to Smallwood (2004), minority students in the United States drop out of doctoral programs at a higher rate than white students and women drop out at a higher rate than do men. While international students may face additional challenges, they actually have a lower attrition rate than do U.S. students (Smallwood, 2004). One of the issues with higher attrition rates for the U.S. students could be the lack of peer support. According to a recent report by the Association to Advance Collegiate Schools of Business (AACSB), about 63% of doctoral students were males and 76% were white. Matching the lower attrition rates, the numbers of U.S. versus international students were almost equal with 50.2% U.S. citizens and 49.8% international students.

Increasing the number of minority students graduating with doctoral degrees is important so that they may become academic mentors and role models for the next generation of both undergraduate and graduate students. According to the Council of Graduate Schools (2004), almost "80% of the growth in college-age students will come from minorities." We believe that effective mentors are critical to the overall success of students graduating from doctoral programs and may have similar affects in other programs as well (see Chapter 7 for more information on mentoring in doctoral programs). Not having enough role models who can effectively empathize with minority students may have a significant effect on the decreased graduation rates of minority students. There is some good news for minority students on the horizon. For example, according to NSU's statistics, the number of African Americans enrolled in their doctoral programs almost doubled from 1988 to 2002. The increase is due to the popularity of the program among students of diverse racial/ethnic backgrounds. According to the Black Issues in Higher Education (June 5th, 2003 – Volume 20(8)), NSU's Business School is ranked number 2 in the nation for the number of doctorate degrees in business awarded to all minorities. Furthermore, Nova Southeastern University awarded 645 doctoral degrees in 2004, ranking it fourth for the largest number of doctoral degrees awarded during that year. In the first place was the University of California at Berkeley with 769 doctoral graduates, second was the University of Texas at Austin with 702 graduates, and the third ranking was held by the University of California at Los Angeles with 664 doctoral graduates.

International students' needs. Students from less developed countries and some from developing nations are likely to diversify their degrees by attending one school for their undergraduate degree, another to obtain a masters degree from one's own nation or a foreign country, and, yet, a third institution or country to pursue a doctoral degree. This diversity can better equip the student to gain different skills and knowledge from a diverse group of faculty members. Some students are also able to get their degrees from multiple nations and countries, thereby leading to learning about a new culture and language. International students are likely to face distance, diversity, and cultural issues when obtaining a doctoral degree in foreign nations. They are also likely to face conflict, stress, change, and time management challenges. Going into a new culture might bring a number of changes in one's life and daily routines. Some changes can be severe and may cause culture shock, while others might be minor and can initially cause some discomfort. As such, mentors and advisors should be aware of such needs and help international students effectively integrate into the new culture while showing them how to manage their time, stress, and conflicting demands.

Stress is a normal part of life in higher education as there are deadlines and critical feedback from one's colleagues, teachers, and advisors. Most working adult doctoral students are likely to be busy professionals who hold stressful positions, take care of one or more family members, volunteer in the community, and remain focused on a specific academic route to stay abreast of the latest findings. Such pressures can be very challenging and stressful. While all students are likely to experience stress, it may be greater for international students. As such, time management, stress management and change management skills become even more important for internationals students. Another important element of a doctoral student's life is to initially focus on what is important and then work on other tasks that appear urgent but may not necessarily be important. Furthermore, one must prioritize among various activities and concerns and only focus on high leverage activities. Some international students might have a difficult time saying no to different faculty members and advisors' who overloads them with research project responsibilities. As such, they should be conditioned to learn to respectfully say no to projects that might cause them too much stress or those that keep them away from their main priorities, which is to successfully complete the doctoral program. Mentors can help national and international doctoral students remain abreast of such challenges, stresses and conflicts and guide them in the right direction.

International students, especially those from developing economies, should pursue their objective of getting an advanced degree to fulfill their own dreams, help their country's higher education institutions compete more effectively with other universities around the globe, and teach others in the country to become terminally-degreed. Besides many other reasons, having a doctoral degree can also secure one more fulfilling jobs and ranks at prestigious organizations. Having an advanced degree is not "an end-all" or a panacea and should not be seen as such toward world peace, financial stability, or even wisdom. Having an advanced degree simply means one is passionate about a specific subject area and has developed a mastery of a few topics in that field of study. Nonetheless, it is an achievement that should be respected and admired by others in society. It is not the degree that makes one an expert or a better philosopher; but rather, it is one's level of effort and how one uses the gained knowledge to create an identity for oneself.

Trials and Tribulations of Earning a Doctorate for Albert Williams[8]

My name is Albert Williams and I am from a beautiful little country in Central America, called Belize, formerly known as British Honduras. Belize, referred to as the 'Jewel in Central America', is sitting between Mexico and Guatemala and borders the Caribbean Sea. Belize has the second largest barrier reef in the world and has thousands of acres of lush tropical rain forests.

I grew up in a small coastal town in southern Belize called Punta Gorda. Presently, Punta Gorda has 28,000 people with an ethnic mix of Gariganu (African and Carib), Creoles (Whites and Blacks), Mayans, and a few Chinese and East Indians (Indian ancestry). I am East Indian. I am from a big family. I am the second eldest among four sisters and six brothers. My sisters were Frances (eldest), Linda, Margaret, and Julie. My brothers were Solomon, Alexander, Douglas, Chester, and Henry. My father, Alexander Williams, was a hardworking man, who drove a bulldozer to make a living for his family. He cleared roads in the jungle for the Government of Belize. My mother, Ellane Williams, was much younger than my father. She was a housewife and cared for her ten children. We were poor but had abundant family support and love.

Primary and Secondary Education

From 1961 to 1968, I went to Punta Gorda Methodist School for my elementary education. This was a school by the sea and was a great setting for children. I was a typical child. I played at the beach and many times came home late. Like my eldest sister, Frances, I got a high score on my primary school leaving departmental exam and won a scholarship to attend high school. I went to Claver College, the only high school in town. At this high school, I was exposed to many different subjects but had a natural interest in mathematics. I was good at it. This turned out to be the best gift that was ever bestowed upon me. Challenges for high school were typical. I had to study and at the same time enjoy playing with my friends. Joel Munoz, Peter Vasquez, and I ended up forming a little study group of three that played together and studied together. We got the three highest GPAs in our class for the entire four years. Joel was first and gave the valedictory address at our graduation. I came in second and gave the salutatory address at the same graduation. Peter was a really smart guy. Our GPAs were very close.

The joys included all the fun time that we had in class as well as in the society. We enjoyed going during recess to purchase buns (sweet bread) from Mrs. Paulino. We had many teachers from the U.S. including Papal Volunteers and Peace Corps. We enjoyed having them. I learned a lot. I had two favorite teachers. One was Mr. Jim Knutson (a Papal Volunteer) who was a mathematics teacher from the U.S. I

---

[8] Contributed by Albert A. Williams, University of Georgia.

learned to play the guitar partly because of wanting to be like him. The other teacher was Mr. Hugh Joseph, an English and Spanish teacher from Trinidad. He pushed us to do well. He was tough but we liked him a lot. I did well on my high school departmental exams and was awarded a scholarship to attend St. John's College Sixth Form in the 'big' city (Belize City) to pursue an associate degree in mathematics and economics. This was a challenging experience for a young fellow from a small town. My parents were poor and could not make consistent monthly payments for my room and board. I stayed with Peter (my high school buddy) at his aunt's house. I enjoyed staying there but my scholarship money was so little and my parents could not afford to pay the difference. After three months, I had to move in with a first cousin (Lindsford Parham) and his family (Elvira (wife), Deon, (son), Rensford (son), and Arlene (daughter)). Their second daughter, Avriel, came later. They were also struggling to make ends meet. I was very pleased that they were willing to allow me to stay a year and a half with them. The little allowance from the scholarship was not enough to take care of me. I pitched in to help out with whatever I could. I am forever grateful to my cousin and his family.

After two years in the big city, I then returned to my home town and taught Mathematics at Claver College, my high school. In those days, an associate degree was all that was required to teach in a high school. I loved it. It was strange for a nineteen year old to be teaching classes that had some nineteen year olds. I also made a good income and contributed to the education of some of my brothers and sisters.

At this point in time, a doctorate degree was the last thing on my mind. I was just making a living and helping my parents.

Bachelors Degree

After two years of teaching, I was awarded a scholarship to pursue a bachelor's degree in mathematics education in Calgary, Alberta in Canada. I was told that I got the scholarship and that I had to travel in a week. This was exciting but also intimidating. I remembered how my parents, my brothers and sisters, and some of my cousins were so proud that I was going off to study in a far-away country! This was BIG news. I especially remembered my big sister, Frances, smiling (beaming). She was so proud of me. She was really smart and had similar dreams, but did not get the opportunity to pursue them.

I knew that this was very important and I wanted this so badly! However, I also had to leave my wonderful and beautiful fiancé, Miss Juana Engleton. This was really hard to do. I partly justified my going to study as a way of making life better for both of us as I had all intentions of marrying her sometime in the near future. I got everything ready in a week and hit the road. I had to hitch a ride with a cousin to Belize City. His car broke down several times along the dirt road (150 miles) but we fixed it. Juana tried to meet me before I left but that was not to be. This was the hardest thing to do – to leave her. I took off on this bitter/sweet adventure to study. This was my first ride on an airplane. I was going into the great unknown. A gentleman from Florida sat beside me. He and his sons were vacationing in Belize. I told him about my situation and he 'held my hand' all the way throughout the U.S. immigration process and took me to a hotel at the airport. I said thank you but was so overwhelmed that I did not get his phone number or his address to send him a thank-you note. When I relaxed a bit in the hotel room, I searched the phone book looking for him. I called a few numbers trying to reach him. His help will never be forgotten. The next day, I left Miami and headed to Ottawa then to Calgary. I took a taxi from the airport to the University of Calgary. The taxi driver heard my story and was also kind. He took me to student housing and waited until I got a room.

The whole experience was a culture shock, a technology shock, a total shock! All in two days! The next day, I met a few other Belizeans studying at my university and this eased the alien feeling. At the University of Calgary, I was not given any credit for my associate degree earned in Belize. I had to repeat many courses and ended up taking four years to complete this degree. I did not mind. I actually did extra courses in mathematics which turned out to be a great thing. There were many challenges to get the bachelor's degree. It was hard living in a foreign land and knowing only a few people. The first Christmas was so hard. I cried. I went with some friends for Christmas dinner but it was not the same. I missed my family and especially my beautiful fiancé, Juana.

The courses were hard but I was able to get through them. I had to study hard – a part of the deal. Also, I had to get used to living in so much snow. This was not that bad. I shoveled a lot of snow in my time. I had to learn how to live in a big society where people were very conscious about the color of their skin or their race. The amount of terrible things that I read in the campus bathrooms made me realize that the society had issues with ethnicity. However, I did meet some great Canadians. Two years later, I got married to Juana and we moved to Calgary. We lived there for two more years until I finished the degree. She did babysitting for someone at the international student office on campus. We appreciated the extra money that she made. I regretted that she was not able to attend college as she was very intelligent.

The joys of getting this degree were many. I had the opportunity to live in a new setting. I experienced snow. I met many interesting people. I gained an education that was going to make a difference in my life and in the lives of others that I touched. This education opened more doors for me. My earning power also increased. This scholarship was bonded, implying that I had to return to Belize and work for five years or else pay the Government of Belize for the education. I returned to Belize and taught at the Belmopan Comprehensive School for five years. Belmopan is the capital of Belize and is 150 miles from my home town. I taught Mathematics to several classes and I took part in many school activities, including educational trips, school projects in the community, sports, and choir. I played my guitar for many school events, including graduation ceremonies and weekly service. I could still remember receiving my first paycheck. The other teachers, who were teaching for many years but were not qualified, were staring at me. They could not believe that a young person with no experience would get more income than they did. The system reinforced education and few people had the chance to pursue a bachelor's degree, which was only available outside of the country. I was very fortunate.

Juana and I had our three children, Kenrick, Oscar, and Diane, during the period between the bachelors and masters degrees. Our responsibilities increased many folds. I felt that I had arrived and was making a good living. I had no interest in getting a masters degree. However, after a few years of working, I felt the need and drive to pursue a master's degree. I applied to the Ministry of Education to get a scholarship to study educational administration but was turned down many times. I was told that I was good at what I did and so there was no need to change. The scholarship papers were 'lost' in the bureaucracy and never made the deadlines. I got tired of the situation and switched jobs. On the recommendation of the then Prime Minister, Honorable George Cadle Price, I was given a job at the Development Finance Corporation. I was a project officer in the economics division at this development bank. I did project analysis. I supervised the student loans program and occasionally managed the home improvement housing loan scheme. The mathematics background was certainly a plus at the bank. However, I was always looking for an opportunity to continue my education.

Masters Degree

While assisting with an Agricultural Census, I met a great lady, Mrs. Marge Ramdares, who told me about a scholarship in agricultural economics that was sitting at the Ministry of Agriculture and had no takers. I told her that I was interested and she suggested that I visit the project leader, Dr. Fred Mangum, a USAID consultant. Dr. Mangum had a doctorate degree in agricultural economics and was in Belize supervising a livestock improvement project. He liked the fact that I had a first degree in mathematics and that I showed a passion for what I wanted to do. He went to speak to the persons in charge. After a bunch of politicking and some pressure from Dr. Mangum, I got the scholarship to attend the University of Georgia in Athens, Georgia. I am forever grateful to Dr. Fred Mangum for his willingness to take a chance on me. I was told that when he got my first semester grades (all As), he personally walked the results over to the Permanent Secretary of Agriculture. Dr. Mangum was proud of the results! This put a lid on any doubts that the administrators had about my ability to finish the masters degree.

My master's degree was challenging. At the University of Georgia, I had to do prerequisites in economics, and accounting. I worked real hard the first semester and did well. I had to increase my basic knowledge in economics in order to enter the masters program. After completing the prerequisites in the first semester, I got in without any problem. In order to succeed in the masters program, I had to use both undergraduate and graduate text books to study and to do the assignments. I was changing fields and had to get the foundation. This was really hard. When the regular students were using the prescribed text, I had to pull out many others. I did not have the background but I did not give up. Also, I was only able to afford an old car that broke down often. I had to fix this car many times in order to save some money. My wife and children came up after the first semester. We were living on the scholarship money. The kids were small so she took care of them. She could not go to school. She ended up taking correspondence courses. Money was real scarce. Juana understood. The kids were young and did not care about income.

The joys of getting the masters degree were many. I was able to gather a wealth of knowledge. This was empowering. This knowledge was also a confidence builder. I met many great people at the university and in the community. This master's degree opened many more doors for me. For example, I was able to return to pursue the doctorate degree. Furthermore, I held a top position in the government and was well respected in the society. Also, I made more money and was able to increase the standard of living for my family. I was able to contribute more to society. During my master's degree, I worked very closely with my faculty advisor, Dr. Bill Miller. He was a great mentor. I will be forever grateful for all his help to get me through the program, especially for his advice to help me to complete my technical paper, which turned up to be as good as a master's thesis. I was the first student in the department to get a masters degree in agricultural economics (MAE), which was basically an MBA degree in agriculture business. I finished the master's degree in agricultural economics with about 21 hours extra. My department gave me the opportunity to continue with the doctorate degree but I had to return home to serve my bond. I wanted to take this opportunity to continue studying but I had a bond to serve so I had to return to Belize.

On return to Belize, I took up the post of agricultural economist at the Ministry of Agriculture. I did project analysis. I managed the agricultural statistics collection, processing and dissemination. In addition, I taught agricultural economics and management at the Belize College of Agriculture, acted as policy analyst, and attended weekly management meetings. I was always thinking of the opportunity to return to Georgia to get that doctorate degree. I knew that I had done all these extra courses which would reduce the time to complete the doctorate degree.

Doctorate Degree Education

After two years, I applied to the University of Georgia and was again awarded an assistantship to pursue the doctorate degree in agricultural and applied economics. This time, I was able to get the administrators in Belize to approve the study leave. I had to sign a bond for five years to take up this training. I had absolutely no problem signing this bond.

In September of 1989, I returned to the University of Georgia to pursue a doctorate degree in agricultural and applied economics. I started out with Dr. Lewell Gunter. I took my courses and assisted him with research in labor economics. I downloaded tons of data. However, I did not have a fundamental passion for labor economics. I was more interested in market economics. After a year, I shared this information with the dean and a marketing professor, Dr. Jack Houston. I approached Dr. Gunter and told him of my dilemma. I could still remember him looking across the desk from me and said, "Albert, I was in that same situation, and I will not block your way." I am forever grateful to Dr. Gunter for his willingness to assist me. I then went to work with Dr. Jack Houston. Dr. Houston was also a great guy to work for! He had high standards. He had a quiet disposition but was very talented. I will never forget the many times that he advised me and reread my dissertation. I am forever indebted to Dr. Houston for his dedication, kindness, and care to get me through this huge project of getting a doctorate degree.

I was very ambitious and embarked on doing a double major. I took all the course requirements for both agricultural and applied economics and finance. I then wrote my dissertation on a topic that transcended both fields. My dissertation topic was, "Forecasting Volatility of Futures Prices: An Application of GARCH Models Incorporating Volume and Open Interest." This topic included agricultural marketing, finance, and advanced time series modeling. Writing this dissertation was a full time job. I had to get data from computer tapes, and from the Wall Street Journal stored on micro fiche. I then had to write my own computer program in SAS to do exactly what

I wanted to do. There was no software at that time that could do ARCH and GARCH models. In this process, I also worked closely with four other professors. Dr. Steve Turner assisted with agricultural marketing. Dr. Jeff Dorfman helped tremendously with model specification. Dr. William Lastrapes was also instrumental. He was very familiar with these types of models. Dr. Louis Scott was also very instrumental in assisting with the finance component of the paper. I had visited these professors many times to seek their assistance. I appreciated all that they had done to assist me with this challenging research. During the last year, my family returned to Belize in August to get the children in school for September. Being alone was hard for me but I was determined to get the job done. I worked even harder to complete the dissertation. By December, I finally finished the dissertation. I was proud of this project.

The challenges of completing a doctorate degree were many. Most courses were very intense. The papers were very involved. The preliminary examinations (prelims) were very challenging. Many people failed at this level. I studied real hard to take these exams. The dissertation by itself was a huge project. This was another phase that many failed. I worked diligently for more than a year to get it done. Next, I had to defend the dissertation. This was a total defense. You had to show that you understood your research. Printing the dissertation and trying to put it in before the deadline was also challenging. I barely made it. A key challenge was to follow up after completing the dissertation. This was hard to do. I took corporate jobs and did not continue my academic career at the same intensity.

While pursuing the doctorate degree, the economic challenges were many. Income was minimal. I had the assistantship money and a stipend from Belize. It was challenging for all five of us to live on this income. The children were older and had more expenses. We had to put on blinders (like the horse) and just focus on going to school. With young children there were medical bills for sickness and accidents. Someone at school fell on top of Oscar, my second son, and fractured his arm. Again, I had to purchase an old car that I had to fix many times. I learned a lot about cars during this time. My wife could not go to school and ended up doing her education by correspondence. She finally got her AA degree in accounting. The joys of getting the doctorate degree were many. I had acquired a great wealth of knowledge that few people had. I was able to do a creative piece of work that was unique. I had accomplished a goal that few people had ever done. This was extremely empowering and a great confidence builder. Again, I met many great people at the university and in the society. Many doors were opened. I held an even more prestigious job in the government. I earned more respect in the society. I also made more money and I was able to provide more for my family. The sacrifice was well worth it.

I promptly returned to Belize to satisfy my bond requirements of working in the country for five years. With the help of the then Prime Minister, Honorable Dr. Manuel Esquivel, (my mechanics lecturer in junior college), I got a job as chief executive officer of a quasi government marketing company. I was responsible for the marketing of agricultural products produced primarily by small producers. I did all that I could to make the lives of the small farmers better. This was a great job in many respects but it was not challenging academically. I was basically underemployed. I was able to get some academic stimulation by teaching undergraduate courses in economics and finance at the University of Belize in the evening program. I volunteered to be on committees to work on economic policy and planning for the country. Also, I gave many presentations to different groups of people and was also a guest on national radio and television shows. Even though I was not able to find that level of academic discourse, I contributed as much as I could to improve the quality of rice and other agricultural products for the country.

Life after the doctorate was greatly improved for my family and me. I was a small town boy coming through school and worked my way up to one of the best positions in the country. I attended many regional and international conferences. I was a director of the Caribbean Rice Association for five years and traveled all over the Caribbean looking at rice research, production, and marketing. Also, I went to meetings sponsored by the World Trade Organization in Jamaica and Guyana. I was sponsored by the Taiwanese government to attend a three-week working tour of small businesses in Taiwan. With the change of government, I was 'reassigned' to another position. I decided to look for other opportunities. At least 12 years prior, my sister, Linda, applied for a U.S. immigrant visa for me. The visa was approved not too long before my reassignment! My family and I were very thankful to Linda for this. The timing was right as our children were of university age and my wife and I wanted them to get a good education.

A few months after, my family and I migrated to the United States and experienced both sides of having the doctorate degree. I applied for many management jobs but was never considered for many reasons, including being overqualified. This was frustrating. I ended getting an analyst job at a fast food corporate office due partly to the fact that my mentor, Dr. Fred Mangum, knew the chief executive office, who also had a doctorate degree in agricultural economics. After a year, I left as I was not managing but crunching numbers for others. I had people doing this for me for years.

I then put the doctorate to use again by applying to teach at different colleges and universities. I started at the University of Phoenix. The coordinator, Mr. Eric Block, was very eager to get me in. Since then, I taught economics, finance, business statistics and marketing in both the graduate and undergraduate business programs. I have been able to contribute and make a living at the same time. I was awarded professor-of-the-year twice and undergraduate business professor-of-the-year once at the said UofP in South Florida. I also went to Broward Community College in South Florida and taught economics. Furthermore, after meeting with Dr. Preston Jones, Associate Dean, I became an adjunct faculty member at Nova Southeastern University. I am currently teaching business statistics, economics, and corporate finance in the MBA program. I have also taught many courses in the undergraduate business program. In addition, I have also taught a few undergraduate economics courses at Miami Dade College.

The doctorate degree has opened many doors for me. However, it did not come easily. I worked extremely hard to complete the program. As I reflect, I do not regret getting this degree. I am presently contributing more to my society and am making a decent living doing so. My wife was able to complete her undergraduate degree in business from the University of Belize. She did another bachelors degree in accounting at Florida Atlantic University. My eldest son completed a bachelor's degree in finance at University of South Florida. My second son, Oscar, is completing a bachelor's degree in mechanical engineering and my daughter, Diane, is completing her bachelor's degree in chemistry.

It is critical to remember that obtaining this doctorate degree was only possible due to the assistance from so many people and institutions along the way. I am truly grateful to all of them. This overall journey was a humbling experience. These are gifts that I received from God. I continue to share them with as many people as I can. My students appreciate my passion and willingness to share. I am sure that I have made some difference in their lives. My job is to make the world a better place. I am doing my share and am always looking for more ways to contribute.

Bahaudin's Journey to Higher Education

Everyone faces challenges in entering and completing a doctoral program. Changing from one culture to another increases these challenges. However, education can play an important role in one's adjustment process. To give a clear picture of some of the challenges faced by both minority and international students, it may be helpful to identify some of the trials others have gone through. This section of the book relates Bahaudin's journey from Afghanistan to obtaining a doctorate degree and a faculty position at Nova Southeastern University (NSU).

Bahaudin was born[9] in 1966 at the village of Khoshie, which is in the Logar province adjacent to Kabul--the capitol state of Afghanistan. Khoshie was a small village made-up of about a thousand families and a population of four to five thousand people. It was surrounded by mountains and high hills. Khoshie is located right in the middle of the valley. I lived in Khoshie until I was six years of age. When my father came back from the United States of America, after completing his two years of graduate studies at the University of Cincinnati in Cincinnati-Ohio, we moved to Kabul, where he was teaching at the College of Engineering, Kabul University. I started first grade at age six, and was considered and perceived to be "different," in terms of language, from others according to most of my classmates and teachers. The kids in Kabul used to laugh about my accent and the way I talked.

In 1983, due to the heavy fighting between the Russian forces and the Afghan Freedom Fighters, as a family we packed up and left for the village of Rahm-Abaud (officially known as *Rahm-Abaud*) in the Logar province in hopes of leaving the country. Rahm-Abaud is where my mom's brothers and cousins could help us move to Pakistan. A myriad of considerations went into our decision to move to Pakistan and proceeding with circumspection was a necessity to everyone's survival. We could not tell many of the relatives, family friends, classmates, and neighbors at Kabul about our plans of leaving the country, as that would put them in danger with the Communist government. Not only would we have put their lives in danger by telling them about our plans to escape, but we also would have put our own lives in danger as well. So, we had to leave and disappear once and for all without anyone knowing what happened to us. We came to Rahm-Abaud to my grandmother's house, where the government did not have much control over the people or their activities at all times. Freedom Fighters came, lived in the city, and passed by almost everyday. People basically lived by their own rules of respecting others, respecting the environment, and practicing the Golden Rule.

---

[9] For the complete version of this biography, see "*Afghanistan: Realities of War and Rebuilding*" (2nd ed.) by ILEAD Academy, 2007.

The next few days and nights went well and we finally got to a province called Teri-Mangal, which is a liberated province in Pakistan located on its border to Afghanistan (it never has had government control and decisions are made by village elders and chiefs). Looking from the top of the mountain down into the valley showed a crowded, noisy, dusty, and an old ancient city that was full of people throughout the valley. The picture was not pretty at all. The walk from top to the bottom of the valley was a very slow process because the camels and horses could not travel well down the hill. Also, the route which we were traveling on was a very narrow trail along the mountain, zigzagging left and right, which had the appearance of continuously making U-turns down the hill. This is basically where we left our guides, since we were able to take the bus from here, and the guides would go back to Logar while carrying weapons on their horses, camels and donkeys for the Freedom Fighters.

We stayed in one of the hotels on the border of Afghanistan-Pakistan during the fourth night, and the next morning we rode the bus to Peshawar which took about ten to twelve hours or so. In Peshawar, we met more friends and relatives who helped us find a house to rent as we settled in the city. The people of Peshawar were very nice, and many of them spoke Pashto which was our second language. So, we could communicate well with them. We stayed there as refugees and eventually were accepted as immigrants to the United States.

About one year later in 1984, from Islam-Abaud of Pakistan, our plane left for the United States, and we switched planes in London. Then we were in New York, where our immigration paperwork for coming to the U.S. was finally completed. After four hours of waiting in New York's airport, we flew to Atlanta, and then to Fort Myers, Florida where we finally met with my Dad after three and half years of being apart. Finally, we got home to Cape Coral which is near Fort Myers.

A week later, we started going to school, starting in April of 1984. My two oldest sisters and I started going to Fort Myers High School, where they had a special English as a Second Language (ESL) Program for students who came from non-English speaking countries. Mrs. Vanna Crawford was the head instructor in the program and she had a very good way of getting her students to learn English. The first day we all went to our homerooms and didn't know what was going on or why I was in that classroom. I went where they took me and sat where the teachers told me to sit. I spoke very little English and understood even less. About twenty minutes later, the principal, Mr. Wiseman, came and took me to my sister Anisa's homeroom, where she was a little upset and crying because she wasn't sure what to do or what was going on. I tried to be supportive to her because she was young (fourteen years old) and this was a totally new experience for her. I stayed with Anisa for about one hour, and we tried to figure out what the teacher was saying, but not much was registering in our minds. After about a week or so we knew where to go and who to listen to and who our teachers were. It took me about two months to figure out what to say when the teacher in the homeroom called our names. Of course, most of the time when he got to my name, he said "OK you are here" so I knew that my name was very difficult for them to pronounce just as theirs' were to me. For the first two months, when the teachers called my name, I answered "yes," and later I figured out that the common word was "here."

Learning to Speak English

Nonetheless, it has been said that English is a complex, yet crazy language as the following examples which have been gleaned from the sayings and writings of many creative individuals (colleagues, writers, teachers, trainers, and friends). For example, it was a hard lesson to learn that there is no egg in eggplant, neither pine nor apple in pineapple, and no ham in hamburger. For the first several months when we came to the United States, we avoided eating hamburgers thinking it had "ham" in it. Of course, ham is pork and hamburgers are made from beef which is eaten by Muslims. Besides, there is no dog meat in "hot-dogs" which do not look like dogs nor are they made for dogs. I also learned that English muffins weren't invented in England and French fries did not originate in France. However, I think the "French Kiss" which is practiced in every nationality may very well have come from France...we can certainly give them credit for romanticizing it. Sweetmeats are candy, while sweetbreads, which aren't sweet, are meat. Most native speakers in the United States tend to take English for granted and don't necessarily think of such complexities. You see, as someone once wrote, when a person explores the paradoxes present in the English language, one finds that quicksand can work slowly, boxing rings are square, public bathrooms have no baths, and a guinea pig is neither a pig nor from Guinea. Bathrooms are refereed to as "John" by some Americans and as "Box" by some of the British while others call it "lady's room," "powder room," "little boys room," "washroom," or even "restrooms." I don't know too many English speakers that actually "rest" in the bathroom. Somebody posted the question of "why is it that a writer writes, but fingers don't fing, grocers don't groce, humdingers don't hum, and hammers don't ham?" Why is it that one can tell a baker that his bread is tasty but can't really tell him that his "buns" are to die for? How is it that the word "read" can be used with the same spelling for both the present and past tense?

Of course, I have seen other interesting aspect of the English language but, like many native speakers, I don't think much about it now as I speak much more fluently. Doesn't it seem loopy, someone wrote, that you can make amends but not just one amend, that you comb through the annals of history but not just one annal? If you have a bunch of odds and ends and you get rid of all but one, what do you call it? Someone said that "sometimes I wonder if all English speakers should be committed to an asylum for the verbally insane." In what other language do people drive on a parkway and park in the driveway? Fly on a runway and run on a highway? Recite at a play and play at a recital? Ship by truck and send cargo by ship? Have noses that run and feet that smell? How can a slim chance and a fat chance be the same, while a wise man and a wise guy are opposites? How can overlook and oversee be opposites, while quite a lot and quite a few are alike? How can the weather be hot as hell one day and cold as hell the next? Are you curious yet? Well, you will certainly notice more of such nuances as you hear them each day. How is it that one can keep a record of files in the court of law, buy a record to play a specific song, and make a record to do something tomorrow? You have to wonder at the unique lunacy of a language in which your house can burn up as it burns down, in which you fill in a form by filling it out, and where your alarm clock goes off by going on. These examples which are gleaned from various sources and authors show that English, like other languages, was created by people over time; and it reflects the genius and creativity of the human race (which, of course, isn't really a race at all). That is why, when stars are out they are visible, but when lights are out they are invisible. And why, when I wind up my watch I start it, but when I wind up this paragraph I end it?

Besides such complexities of the English language, pronunciation makes a huge difference as well. Many of the little differences in how words are vocally said can be difficult to notice when one is initially learning English. Words like bread, breed, breath, and breadth can all be perceived to be similar in sound unless one is pronouncing it slowly to a new English learner. For example, I had a classmate in Edison Community College that I kept calling "Dog" for about the first two weeks. Finally, he said "are you calling me Dog? I said "yes." He said "why" and I said "you told me that was your name." He replied "it is not dog, it is Doug." I couldn't really tell the difference in pronunciation between "dog" and "Doug" but knew there was a slight difference. Another student at the calculus class in Edison Community College once borrowed my calculator during the start of the class. About ten minutes later, I asked another classmate his name and, since the teacher was lecturing, with a low volume I said "Hey Dick, I need my calculator back." He asked "What did you call me?" I answered "Dick." He said "Why?" I said because that is your name. I was wrong because his actual name was Seth and the classmate (named Vonn) had just set me up to call him a bad name. I feel more confident now, but during my first few years in the United States, I must have been pretty gauche. However, my ability to converse easily, although sometimes without perspicuity, about mundane matters, with friends and classmates has helped me considerably in pronunciation of words in the English language. Some of the challenges today for me are to figure out the true meaning of such phrases as "partly cloudy" or "partly sunny" skies that meteorologists tend to use on a daily basis. I still wonder why is it that people named Robert are called Bob and those named Richard are often called "Dick"? What is even more confusing is that many of the nicknames are gender neutral that can be used for either boys or girls. For example, names such as Pat, Chris, Leslie, Carol, Morgan, Kelly, Terry, Jerry, Sam, and Jamie are used for males and females. Of course, it takes some enculturation before one finds out that "Pat" can come from Patrick (male name) or Patricia (female name). Similarly, "Chris" can come from Christopher (male name) or Christina (female name). I am still confused why so many people name their dogs "Spot" which usually is a synonym for a mark, location or dot. Then again, such curiosity and its fulfillment are the essence of life and it must continue based on priority and importance.

While the use of the same names for both genders can confuse one, there are also many stereotypes and biases attached to the daily interactions. A colleague at a diversity workshop in Washington D.C. once said the he is often picked first for basketball teams due to his height advantage and ability to "steal," "shoot," and "run." Of course, he said, as an African American male people often assume that I am good at "stealing", "shooting" and "running" simply because of the color of my skin. The reality is that the best basketball players are great at "stealing" the ball, "shooting" the ball to the basket, and "running" the ball up the court, and these skills are the result of hard work, practice and talent (and not necessarily a person's ethnicity, gender or skin color). The same thing is true for higher education; the best doctoral students will eventually become known for their talent, hard work and practice by reading, writing and teaching a specific topic that is their area of passion. Overall, one must remember that the improper use of language and words often convey stereotypes which can lead to confusion and miscommunication.

From Cleaning Up to Management: The Importance of Mentors

Hope is one element of growth, and action is another. While hope can keep one's spirit high toward a brighter future, it is one's actions that take a person from the real to the ideal. The term "action" is a verb and requires doing something. When one's actions are geared toward a specific goal, then chances are very good that sooner or later he or she is going to achieve that objective. Getting one's first job or even a second job is a major initiative and life event. However, most individuals in developed economies are likely to move on to something else as per their goals and experience.

A few months after arriving in the United States, I got my first temporary job doing landscaping work earning minimum wage which was $3.25 per hour in 1984. This job was basically farming and required digging the ground all day long in the summer days of nearly 100 degree weather and planting trees to make the streets of "hot" Florida beautiful. I was able to do a good job while I was employed there for a short duration and I learned that farming and physical labor was not easy. At the first day of the job, I had previously made an appointment to get my written driving license exam. I started my job at seven o'clock in the morning and worked very hard until four in the afternoon. At this time I knew my Dad was coming to pick me up for the test, so I started washing my hands to be ready. The pain of hard work and manual labor was present in my arm muscles as they kept cramping up each time I moved them. I was tired and thought that I was definitely going to fail the test, so I told my Dad that maybe I should take this test some other day. He said, "Oh, don't worry about it, it is just a test." Anyhow, I took the test and luckily passed it on the first attempt. My Dad was very proud and he let me drive the car for about one-sixth of a mile as soon as we got out of the police station. For the first time, I really felt happy, because Dad made me feel like I didn't let him down and even not passing the test would have been all right with him.

After about a month, my temporary employment at the landscaping job was over since they had hired me temporarily as a replacement for a vacation and I had to start looking for other employment opportunities. Within a month, I got a job at the Jefferson World Stores (retail outlet) working in the garden section to assist customers and keep the plants fresh every day. They probably offered me the job since I had some experience with landscaping and because the garden section did not require as much interaction with customers as other parts of the store. This job paid $3.50 each hour and I had to dress up and wear a tie to work every day. So, I went to high school at about 7:00am in the morning and packed my work tie and clothes in the school bag so I could go directly to work after school each day. I would take the city bus from the Fort Myers High School neighborhood to go to work and then Dad would pick me up from work at about 10:00pm. I enjoyed working indoors learning about the various plants, taking care of the plants, and helping customers with their gardening needs. The managers were very customer-oriented and showed great leadership skills. My colleagues were very nice and helped me to learn English words and phrases since they liked my work ethic. I sort of grew to like this job and had aspirations of eventually going into retail management when I finished college. This job lasted three months because the company went bankrupt and we were all laid off.

Then I was unemployed for about another month, but I was able to study more for school since twelfth grade courses had more homework and I was preparing for college entrance examinations as well. So, the month went by very quickly and eventually I was hired at the Danish Bakery of Publix Super Markets at their Cape Coral Parkway Store in Cape Coral. Once again, I began going directly to work everyday after school. This job was paying $3.75 each hour…the lesson I learned then was that with every job change I was making more money per hour. I reported to work on the first day at about 3:30pm and a beautiful female salesperson by the name of Tricia Grover said "Welcome, you must be the new clean up boy." So, now I knew my new title was "clean up boy." She wrote my name on a time card and asked me to "punch in" and start working. She took about five minutes to show and tell me that I had to wash the dishes (there seemed to be several "tons" that needed washing), take the trash out to the dumpster, and mop the floors. As such, my official training was over in about five minutes…of course, I could go back and ask any questions and she would check on me later to make sure I was doing things right. Taking care of the sanitation in the bakery department was basically my daily routine, which often took about five to six hours each day to complete all the tasks well. I was able to finally meet Wayne, the Assistant Manager at the Bakery Department. Wayne showed me how to do a few other jobs besides washing the dishes and mopping the floors on Saturdays and Sundays. So, on Saturdays and Sundays I was able to work about eight to twelve hours since there was more work that could be done. Since I needed the money, I welcomed all the extra work and responsibilities. Two weeks later I met the department manager, Bob Manfredo. He turned out to be very impressed with my flexibility, work ethics, commitment, and performance over the first few weeks. So, he gave me a 50 cent raise as I was going on my fourth week of work at this Bakery.

I was very happy and really impressed with the manager's style of management and leadership. Anyhow, since I did not receive much training I did not know when I would be paid. During week six, Bob asked me if I had received my checks yet and I said no. He said I could go and pick them up from the front office cashiers as they keep everyone's checks. So, he took me to the front office and they had five checks for me and Bob said "wow, what are you going to do with all that money?" I said I was probably going to give it to my Dad for household expenses. He said "if your Dad does not need it, then don't spend it all in one place or on girls because you can invest your money on Publix stocks." As it turns out, that was the best financial advice anyone could have given me at that time. The next month, I did invest one thousand dollars on Publix stocks and if I had continued that trend each month during my employment with the company, I would have become a millionaire much faster. Anyhow, that is the strategy that Bob and his brother John Manfredo used, while working with Publix, to become rich and retire as multi-millionaires before they were fifty years of age. Today, as young men, they enjoy their retirement while watching their money grow every year. John Manfredo was also a Bakery Manager with Publix Super Markets and was promoted to Supervisor in the Central Florida region. I ended working with Mr. Manfredo as well in the Orlando area when I moved there to attend school at the University of Central Florida (UCF).

I continued working with Publix and learned many new skills besides washing dishes and mopping the floors. I learned customer service, management and leadership skills with my colleagues. I was given a full time job in the company as a Baker and began receiving full benefits. Three years after starting to work with Publix as a "clean up boy," I was promoted to an Assistant Bakery Manager earning a good salary each year. The salary was great and much higher than college graduates although managers often worked very hard, some weeks putting in as many as 70-80 hours. After four weeks as an Assistant Manager, once again, I was promoted to a Bakery Manager at the Altamonte Springs Publix Store (#194) in Central Florida while receiving around a thirty percent increase in compensation. Once again, this was a great increase in salary because managers needed the skills of ethics, service and value delivery, management, showing high commitment, and leadership skills to make the department a success. I managed a team of 23 employees, reported to several bosses in a matrix structure, and we produced nearly one million dollars in revenue each year. I was responsible for hiring, development, retention, and performance appraisals of employees in my department.

During my first year as a manager, my team and I, in the bakery department, were able to increase sales by over 30 percent and net profits by over 220 percent from the prior year. I had an experienced Assistant Manager, Ed Zebraski, who had previously been a manager with the company for many years. He had chosen to step back to the assistant level due to health reasons. Also, I had a full-time employee name Marlene who had been a manager with Publix for many years and had now chosen to step back to forty hours of work to spend more time with her family members. Beside these two experienced individuals who were of tremendous assistant to me as their new manager, I had many other experienced bakers and dedicated employees who respected me as a manager and worked very hard to produce quality products and provide superior service to our customers. Also, with John Manfredo as my immediate supervisor and mentor in Orlando I had access to great leaders when I had questions or concerns. Mr. John Manfredo was always kind enough to provide "the tips" I needed to be an effective manager and leader. Mr. Manfredo was a skilled analyst of people's likes and dislikes who listened to employees and observed their behaviors to effectively motivate them as per their needs and desires.

Education, Career Changes, and Mentors

I had worked my way up the hierarchy from a "clean up boy" to a "manager" in less than three years with this organization which employed nearly 100,000 individuals at that time. I worked as a manager in different locations taking different regional responsibilities for the training of other managers whenever opportunities presented itself. At this time, I was completing my masters and doctorate degrees at nights and on weekends besides working about 50-60 hours each week as a manager. After the completion of my doctoral dissertation in 1995, I was promoted to a Training Specialist in the Management Development Department of Human Resources at the headquarters of Publix in Lakeland. In this position I was responsible for the development, designing, and delivery of leadership and management training for all Publix executives and managers. Over the years at Publix, which has been repeatedly ranked as one of top 100 best companies in America, I had the pleasure and honor of working with some very honest, kind-hearted, and intelligent corporate entrepreneurs who have made the company one of the premier companies in the world. Once again, I attempted to study the most successful people on the support side to see what traits made them great trainers and leaders for thousands of employees in the company. While asking for the advice of my previous mentors when needed, I also became an admirer of the skills demonstrated by many new individuals who were there to make sure I was a great "management trainer and developer." Each person served as a teacher or mentor to me in his or her own way since I observed their behaviors and listened to their advice. I capitalized on their wisdom and avoided their mistakes or traits that did not match my style. For example, Frank taught me that we can have a good sense of humor and integrate fun into the classroom in order to increase learning and retention. Annisa and Anthony (known as Amp) taught me that diversity management requires more than just seeing the physical differences in people by getting to know the needs, desires, wants, and challenges facing each person because of his or her unique characteristics. MaryLou, Max, and Ruth showed me how to facilitate emotional issues of leadership and management with a high level of professionalism by being a living example of what we preach. David (whom we lovingly called Gator Dave since he was a huge fan of University of Florida's football team) taught me the art of story telling to keep the audience hooked and active on the material. David Richard showed us the impact of brain-based learning, blooms taxonomy and how various adult learning skills can be used to effectively teach and facilitate based on higher levels as per the learner's level of readiness. Similarly, many other colleagues had great lessons for me either by their wisdom, by what they said or simply by how they acted to various aspects of adult education and leadership. For nearly six years working in the improvement systems and human resources departments of Publix, I worked on different long-term projects to develop and coach company managers or executives so they can be successful leaders in their departments and regions. I eventually retired from there as a senior training specialist and a coach to executives at different regions. I stayed with Publix Super Markets for over sixteen years and very much enjoyed it.

I had begun teaching as an adjunct college professor in 1996 for Nova Southeastern University and thoroughly enjoyed it as I was dealing with working adults graduate students. The retirement from the retail environment in 2000, was planned as a transition into academia by taking a job as a Campus College Chair for Undergraduate Business Programs in the city of Tampa which ended up being very fruitful.

So, in a matter of about twelve years, I had gone from being a "clean up boy" to becoming a university professor, a college chair, and then a college director a few years later. I am not telling you all of this to impress you but I am discussing it because it impresses me as I went from a person who was not sure about his abilities as a young boy in a new culture to a person who progressively kept going toward his dreams by taking advantage of every opportunity that was afforded to him over the years. A person does not have to be a genius or a "rocket scientist" to achieve his or her dreams. However, a person has to learn that taking full advantage of available opportunities as they become open, and having an interdependent relationship with others can have huge dividends for all parties. Such progressive success also goes to show that good guidance from parents and colleagues as well as persistency, patience, and value-based goal setting do make a difference. Of course, I am humbled to have had great colleagues, friends, mentors, bosses, and parents who showed confidence on my commitments and trusted my abilities to live up to their expectations. Academically, there were many individuals at Fort Myers High School, Edison Community College, University of Central Florida, and at the Nova Southeastern University who left great impressions on me and helped me get where I am today. At the university level, I didn't get to an academic director and professor's position simply due to my own abilities, although that is an important part of it, since many individuals guided me to get there through their mentorship. Of course, getting there is one thing, but staying there is a totally another variable. Staying there requires doing a good job and helping others discover their hidden talents while providing them opportunities to apply them toward worthwhile endeavors. One cannot achieve his or her dreams without helping others while capitalizing on their talents and efforts through interdependent relationships and candid expectations. Hundreds of other great individuals helped me as colleagues, employees and faculty members in the programs and departments I was responsible for making sure students were treated with respect and dignity and that they received the highest quality education in the most effective manner. These are the great heroes that provided thousands of undergraduate and graduate students quality education, and I thank them for their commitment to the education industry.

Education is one of the best industries to work in since there are great opportunities for learning and for helping others learn. For example, at Nova Southeastern University (NSU) students, staff, and faculty members are offered many opportunities to personally develop their management and leadership skills. Everyone can attend lecture sessions by some of the leading authorities in the local community as well as nationally and internationally known speakers. Everyone has many great opportunities to attend sessions on Life Management, Stress Management, Leadership, Entrepreneurship, etc. while meeting some of today's leaders. "Life 101...Personally Speaking Welcomes Max Weinberg" is one of such opportunities for learning how to manage life and its conflicting goals. Max Weinberg, drummer for Bruce Springsteen's E Street Band and music director for *Late Night with Conan O'Brien*, was the guest for NSU's "Life 101...Personally Speaking" on Monday, Dec. 6th 2004 at 7:00 p.m. This informal interview and question and answer session was held in the Rose and Alfred Miniaci Performing Arts Center on NSU's main campus. Of course, tickets were free to NSU students, staff and faculty and staff members. Also, in the past few years, at NSU we have had the opportunity to personally meet people like Jack Welch, Clarence Thomas, Larry Bossidy, Paul Hersey, Richard Wagoner, the Dalai Lama, L. Paul Bremer III, and many other world renowned leaders. Each leader brings a message of hope, leadership, strong values, and/or a great character in society.

For example, the Dalai Lama brought a message of hope and compassion to us at NSU. His Holiness the 14th Dalai Lama of Tibet, Tenzin Gaytso, came to Nova Southeastern University on September 18th 2004 to address students, faculty, and members of the public. Approximately 10,000 students and people from the local community attended the event which was held in front of the Alvin Sherman Library, Resource and Information Technology Center. NSU President Ray Ferrero, Jr. conferred an honorary Doctorate of Humane Letters on the exiled Tibetan leader, citing his unflinching support for human rights. The Dalai Lama spoke movingly on "Universal Responsibility," addressing the crowd in English with occasional assistance from his translator. His theme was simple: "Human affection and loving kindness, I believe, are the most important values." He urged us to keep compassion in out hearts, "because in the long run it's the only way." After his speech, the Dalai Lama took questions from audience members, and then blessed a Tibetian prayer wheel donated by philanthropist Albert Miniaci, Jr. The prayer wheel is now on display at the Alvin Sherman Library, Research and Information Technology Center. At his request, the Dalai Lama met personally with five NSU students after his speech. "You are of the 21st century and this century belongs to you," he told them. "Do what is necessary to make a difference."

NSU's Farquhar College of Arts and Sciences invited L. Paul Bremer, III as their distinguished Speaker Series on Thursday, February 17ᵗʰ 2005 to speak about and discuss his experiences and thoughts on "Iraq and the War on Terrorism." Mr. Bremer was the former civilian presidential envoy to Iraq and he left his position once the interim government selected their Iraqi cabinet members. Speakers such as Paul Bremer, Dalai Lama, Richard Wagoner, and Paul Hersey tend to show, through their presence, the impact of great leadership and how students can make the best of their education while attending the H. Wayne Huizenga School of Business and Entrepreneurship and after their graduation. These distinguished lecture series and other events are offered to all those who are a part of NSU and those who seek growth in a variety of areas such as leadership development, ethics, and diversity. So, it is great to be involved with the education industry…even though the income generation opportunities are limited and not always as good as the private sector.

Summary

People decide to get advanced degrees for different reasons. To discover one's true motivation for it, it is best to reflect upon where one has been, where one wants to go and how one can actually best get there. Living in poverty can provide a person a different perspective about the achievement and meaning of wealth than not having this opportunity. Generally speaking, some people seem to work, take care of their family members, and attend school during the evenings and weekends. Why are these individuals going to school, while many others who are financially in good position so that can devote their full energy to education often ignore it? Of course, this is not true of everyone since some of the wealthiest people seem to get the best education and most advanced degrees that society allows one to formally achieve. The point is that having a different point of view can often mean stronger commitment to one's predetermined goals and milestones. Having an advanced degree is usually one excellent way to financial stability or better jobs in today's competitive world of work. Another strong motivation for having an advanced degree is the credibility that it brings to one to make valuable contributions to society in ways that would not otherwise be easily possible. Reflect on your past, know where you have been, clarify where you are going, and create a strategy for getting there efficiently.

Going from washing dishes to management and eventually to academia was a huge challenge for Bahaudin, but it was achieved one step at a time through action, goal setting, committing to those goals, persistency, and interdependency. Interdependency means overcoming biases and stereotypes to rely on others and enabling others to rely on you. Through interdependency, we have learned that there are many stereotypes in this society and they are often hidden in the languages we speak. So, it is important to enhance one's speaking ability and communication skills through continuous education. Overall, if you can perceive and believe it then you can definitely achieve it. We often ask new doctoral candidates the following question: Can you see yourself as a doctor of philosophy? If so, then go for it with a full commitment and in a balanced strategy.

3 – Teamwork and Transitions to Academia

D ependency is a normal part of life and growth as all children are born depending on their parents for their physical safety as well as mental, spiritual, and psychological growth. Some individuals "mature" earlier in life and are able to move away from this dependency sooner, while others tend to enjoy this process a longer period of time than the average person. In the education arena, most programs and courses up until the masters program can probably be completed successfully through independent work by the student. However, independency begins to merge into and include interdependency when a student is required to study a specific population through a scientific methodology, and to work with a committee to finalize the data analysis into a dissertation format. At a minimum, such interdependency requires interpersonal skills, teamwork, cooperation, and good time management. The same applies to groups, organizations, and nations. All individuals, groups, and organizational leaders must understand that they can move forward toward their goals of becoming independent and work their way toward interdependency. This chapter emphasizes goal-setting, and being able to both independently and interdependently work with others to achieve one's personal and professional goals.

Interdependency and Being Forward Looking

The past cannot be changed, but one can change what happens now and in the future. The belief that you can change the future is referred to as an internal locus of control. Having a strong internal locus of control suggests that change is most effective when it starts from within; and each person should take personal responsibility for his or her success as well as professional growth and development. Regardless of our chosen field, we must all be productive individuals in order to effectively contribute to the team's goal toward the creation of a peaceful environment for all. Of course, being productive individuals, and becoming effective leaders, is a good start for everyone, since individuals have the most control over their own behaviors. Through their behaviors and vision, individuals must be able to leave a positive mark in history by enhancing the welfare of others. It is not only the quantity of the various life enhancing resources that matter, but the quality of each.

Instead of being too focused on the past, we need to be forward-looking and with single-minded intensity toward the future that we desire for ourselves. Productive individuals and effective leaders are future-oriented and, at challenging times, use professionalism to create synergy with people of diverse backgrounds, ethnicities, faiths, and languages. *Professionalism* can be operationalized at all localities at the individual level by putting the needs of others in the community, organization, society, and country above one's own through accountability, compassion, integrity, and mutual respect for all human beings. In any case, diagnosis must come before prescription if leaders, managers, educators, and workers are to bypass much "rework" and wasted efforts. As such, one can begin by understanding him- or herself and his/her desires for "independency" and transitioning vehicles toward obtaining interdependency. This will require creative alternatives and "brainstorming" to select the right prescriptions. Individual and team creativity can solve most problems; the creative act, implemented with audacious and aggressive resolve can overcome every challenging task one faces.

Becoming "Independent": The Case of a Developing Economy

Successfully completing a doctoral program requires independent thinking to generate new knowledge and new theories. Throughout one's education process, students go from being dependent to independent and eventually evolve to interdependent mindsets in order to synergize. This process cannot be minimized or marginalized as the transition to independent thinking is a critical step in completing a doctorate degree. Because the focus of a doctoral degree is so different than previous degrees, those that cannot move from dependency on professors to an independent mindset will more than likely leave the doctoral program prior to earning the degree and at a large personal expense. Furthermore, such a monumental task also requires interdependency to work with others in the community, the institution and one's profession toward worthwhile objectives. Independency of thinking is a requisite to interdependency and doctoral students must understand that their research and work can be best achieved through effective interdependent relationships with their family members, peers, advisors, practitioners, and other experts from around the world that are currently working in one's profession and on similar research. To demonstrate the philosophy of independent thinking and the necessity of interdependent relationships, let us look at the application of these two concepts in terms of a developing economy, Afghanistan.

The term "Afghan" stands for love, courage, devotion, dignity, commitment, loyalty, and the desire to make sacrifices for one's country and people. It further symbolizes endurance, patriotism, dedication to the Afghan land and flag, and the freedom to soar in the beautiful mountains and deserts which are considered to be their ancestors' gleaned and protected backyards. Afghans are known to be people of honor, great hospitality, and are committed to being masters and architects of their own destiny. Afghans are also known for their stubbornness (hard-headedness) or animosity to "get even" with those who interfere with them, even if it is other

Afghans, a characteristic which has been shown by the civil war. Afghans have long been committed to being free of outsiders' influence at all costs. This type of patriotism and conditioning to keep the country independent has been weaved into the culture. As the world becomes smaller, or as some have said "flatter," Afghans need to realize that independency is not the solution to all of the country's challenges, and in today's environment all people need to work through "interdependent" relationships with other countries and allies. As a matter of fact, being independent (or isolated from the real world) can mean becoming dependent once again on foreign countries, or donors, which is actually the case now and it has been this way since the invasion of Afghanistan by the former Soviet Union (Russians) forces. So, dependence is not a good stage especially when the nation relies on other countries that are less developed. "Dependence" must be converted to "independence" and then to "interdependent relationships" with other countries so Afghanistan and its neighbors can benefit from certain comparative advantages which are afforded to it through its natural resources.

Unfortunately, the continuous conditioning on "independence" can also lead to ethnocentricity, as well as xenophobic thinking and paradigm, particularly when one is thinking or reflecting only at the "surface level" with regard to receiving international assistance and help from foreigners in the rebuilding process. High illiteracy rates in the country may be causing some individuals to only think at the surface level since they may not have access to more material for inductive and deductive reasoning for cause and effect analysis. It appears that the Afghan government is encouraging capacity building by making literacy a top priority while building the workforce's capacity for more effective decision-making. High literacy rates, continuous education, training, and equipping the workforce with the right skills to become industrialized through interdependent relationships with the global world are critical elements to Afghanistan's progressive development and growth. Efforts geared toward such personal developments of the workforce generations can speed up the process of economic development and independence of Afghanistan from foreign aid. All such efforts should be accompanied strategically with effective management and leadership of interdependent relationships.

Many Afghan experts tend to agree that one major change in today's corporate and political environment in Kabul might be the transformation and creation of a culture with regard to honest "service" to customers, suppliers, employees, and one's colleagues through interdependency. While transactional leadership can play a role, it is transformational leadership that creates the vision and changes the culture toward a vision of excellence, integrity, and high moral standards through interdependent relationships with diverse individuals.

The Citadel: A Case for Interdependency

The Citadel is a military college located in Charleston, South Carolina. Michael graduated from The Citadel in 1983 with a degree in Business Administration after which he spent eleven years as a officer in the United States Army. While entering the military upon graduation from The Citadel is not a requirement like the service academies, all students must take four years of military training. This training begins freshman year when students learn discipline, moral and ethical standards, as well as subordination of individual goals to that of the organization. While these are the obvious outcomes of a military education, others include creativity, audacity, and interdependency. Those that have never spent time in the military might question each of these as they may seem counterintuitive and run against stereotypes of the military. Yet officers in the military quickly learn that battlefield environments are extremely chaotic where things rarely go according to a specified plan. To succeed on the battlefield, officers must learn to trust their instincts, be creative in extraordinarily stressful situations, use surprise and audacity to their advantage, and interdependency. The pressure put on officers is tremendous when compared to managers in corporate environments as a mistake can cause people their lives. Regarding interdependency, military officers quickly learn that they must count on everyone within the organization, regardless of rank or position, to be a success. In fact, once a plan is in place, the lowest ranking individual in the military organization, like in business, may have more to do with the overall success of the operation than higher level officers or managers.

Education and Job-Fit

It is encouraging to see that educated and visionary individuals are paving the way for brighter futures in so many areas. As Heraclitus said, you can never step into the same river twice. In the same way, the education required by our parents or grandparents is not the same as that which will be required of us. Charles Handy suggests that we should all become continuous learners and what he calls portfolio workers. Like artists, portfolio workers are those that are persistently learning new skills to increase their individual portfolio. Because the promise of employment for life is long gone, Handy (1996) suggested that individuals focus on jobs that increase their individual portfolios (skills). Once a skill has been mastered, individuals should be looking to expand the scope and responsibilities within their current position, or be looking for other opportunities either internal or external to their current company to increase their portfolio. In this way, individuals can increase their value in the marketplace and don't become stagnant or outdated.

While education is a critical aspect of success in the new economy, it is not the *end all* answer to every issue. It is an important initial step toward the development of each person's capacity to produce knowledge, make better decisions, and live in a more qualitative manner through collaboration and interdependent relationships with others. However, education and advanced skills without the element of job-fit does little to advance one's career. For example, Bahaudin has a doctorate degree in business administration with post-doctoral specialties in human resources and international management which academically qualify him to work and teach in these fields. These degrees and over twenty years of management experience and training also qualify him to manage departments, companies, businesses, and non-profit agencies. However, none of these degrees and years of experience qualify him to effectively function as an engineer, a nurse, a soldier or commander in the armed forces, a doctor, or a counselor to individuals with mental disabilities. So, he functions best and has the best opportunity for success in the fields of consulting, directing, training, teaching, managing, speaking, leading, and coordinating small or large projects related to governance and management.

Nobody has ever gotten too far simply by the sheer force of his or her own muscles. Somebody was there to advice, nurture, coach, and teach them how to effectively make the best use of their talents and capabilities. Even sports champions and movie stars need other people to keep them stars and in the public eye. Education is important and higher education means further developing interdependent relationships to gain the right guidelines, support, and knowledge. The need for several key people throughout a doctoral journey will be discussed further in future chapters of this book. Besides having the right education, the right candidates should be continuous learners since knowledge doubles every five to ten years as new information is being generated at an enormous pace.

From Real to Ideal: Managing to Teaching

Educational advancement and the attainment of knowledge have always been a normal part of life, and perhaps more so today than ever before. Thousands of years ago, for a modest fee for their services, Sophists used to teach people how to formulate an argument and win a debate in order to become successful in life, politics, and business. Some people use this same process today. However, to maintain and sustain success in today's work environment, people are realizing that they need to become continuous learners if they are to achieve continuous employment and realize their dreams. Because the world is changing so fast, employees, executives, and educators must be open to new and creative ideas from different perspectives. The achievement of one's dreams cannot be realized solely through independent thinking, but it is highly dependant on the development of interdependent relationships. One can best achieve personal goals and objectives by helping others achieve their dreams. In other words, society rewards one's level of service to the same extent that one's services are beneficial to the society and its members.

Educational institutions and faculty members can best achieve their dreams if they actually assist learners in obtaining their goals of advanced degrees. Higher education is one avenue for the achievement of one's dreams while assisting others to do the same. However, higher education institutions are facing a critical shortage of qualified terminally-degreed faculty members and must resolve this challenge by encouraging more students and practitioners to obtain doctorate degrees in various fields of business and management in the coming decades. The next section focuses on the authors' personal trials as they transitioned from corporate America into academic environments.

Our Reasons are All Different: Michael's Journey

Our reasons for pursuing additional education are probably as varied as each one of us. This may be particularly true at the baccalaureate and perhaps master's levels. As one begins contemplating a doctorate degree, these reasons may begin to merge into a smaller population of motivations – although there are still a number of reasons people pursue a doctorate degree. During my very first doctoral class, the professor had each student introduce themselves and explain why they were there. In other words, why pursue a doctorate degree. Out of a class of 13, the two largest reasons were to go into teaching and to add a credential to their name as a consultant. These were not the only reasons identified in the class. For one, it was the life-long goal to be called a doctor, for another it was to "force" them into conducting research on their passion, and another wasn't sure why he was pursuing the degree, he just knew this was the next step in the learning process and knew that he would figure out the "whys" along the way.

Peter Senge, the director of the Center for Organizational Learning at MIT's Sloan School of Management, discussed the idea of personal mastery in his book *The Fifth Discipline*. According to Senge (1990), one of the first steps in personal mastery is creating a personal vision of where you want to be in your life. The second step is to take a hard look at your current reality and identify the steps needed to get to where you would like to be. In other words, where are you today and how big a gap is there between your current reality and your vision. Jim Collins (2001) calls this confronting the brutal facts of your current situation. While confronting the brutal facts is important, Collins also stated that a critical component of success is never losing faith with the vision you want to create. While there may be a huge gap between your vision and current reality, "truly creative people use the gap between vision and current reality to generate energy for change" (Senge, 1990, p. 153). Senge called this gap creative tension. Creative tension is the tension or stress involved in the gap between your vision and reality. If you are still contemplating going back to school, this tension might include questions of how you will pay for school, the unknown amount of school work, the potentially unknown process of creating a dissertation. Each of these may spur you into action to finding creative ways to overcome this gap.

My own journey toward earning a doctorate degree began a couple years after the birth of my son. Up to that point I had two major careers. One as an officer in the U.S. Army and the other in various management positions with MCI in Atlanta, Georgia. As is the case with most positions, as you rise up the corporate ladder, the stress and amount of travel required tend to increase. While in a senior management position within corporate America allows one to live an extremely comfortable lifestyle, the time spent away from family – both through actual trips and the number of hours spent at work when not traveling became a concern. The vision of working at a college where my schedule could more closely match my son's as he grew became increasingly appealing. Confronting the brutal facts included the issue that to be successful in higher education I needed a terminal degree. In hindsight, this seems like it should be an easy decision, yet the potential loss of a significant portion of income was disquieting. While obtaining a terminal degree is not cheap, the largest concern was the loss of time. It almost seemed counterintuitive that I would have to spend so much time studying – thus time away from my family – in order to gain more time with my family. The final concern I had prior to entering a doctoral program was if I was bright enough to complete a terminal degree program. To use Senge's terminology, I felt that there was a great deal of creative tension between my current reality and my future goal of obtaining an assistant professor's position.

I used to tell my staff at MCI *even if you fall on your face, at least you were moving forward* meaning that it is far better to try and fail than to never try. As I looked at this gap, the only way for me to know if I could accomplish this dream was to try. And what is the worst thing that would happen if I failed? Really nothing, other than perhaps a few thousand dollars spent taking a class that would not lead to a degree. But even that may not be a complete loss as I may actually learn something useful. As Roman philosopher Seneca (5 BC – 65 AD) wrote "it is not because things are difficult that we do not dare, it is because we do not dare that they are difficult." So as Collins recommends, I took a critical look at my current reality, confronted the brutal facts, yet never lost sight in my personal vision, or lost faith that ultimately I would succeed.

While not the main purpose of obtaining a doctorate degree, I did learn a great deal of management and leadership theory which was immediately useful in my current position within MCI. For example, throughout the management, organizational behavior, and leadership classes, I conducted research into corporate culture, ethics, groupthink, and various management theories that I was able to put into use in my job. Additionally, because I was learning about proper research techniques and had practical experience, I was able to get a couple of articles published in peer reviewed journals while I was still a student.

Through some hard work, internal focus, and determination I was able to close and eliminate the gap between my current reality and my future goals in a relatively short number of years. However, had I let fear of the unknown impact my decisions I would have never been able to achieve my goals. My advice is to not allow others or your own self-doubt influence your decision to jump in and achieve your dreams. You can do it—never lose focus on your goals!

From Corporate America to Academia: Bahaudin's Transition

Upon the successful completion of the doctorate degree and since I was often invited by previous doctoral faculty members to lecture on the subject of ethics to their doctoral students, I submitted a resume for part-time (adjunct) teaching opportunities to two universities in the state of Florida (Nova Southeastern University (NSU) and the University of Phoenix-Tampa Campus). Both schools called me and said that a few classes would be available for me to teach. Since during weekdays I was busy with my full-time work responsibilities at the Publix Super Market headquarters I began teaching master's level courses at NSU. My first assignment was to teach a master's of business administration (MBA) course entitled "*Delivering Superior Customer Value*" and ninety percent of the students were middle to top level managers, including two vice presidents. I was a little nervous with my first academic assignment and spoke with several of my academic mentors (including Dr. Art Weinstein, Dr. Frank Cavico, Dr. Timothy McCartney, and Dr. Preston Jones), who provided me the benefits of their experience regarding teaching adults as well as staying focused on the course outcomes while being student-oriented. Their advice, guidance and mentoring went along way in reassuring me that things would go well. They reassured me that as a faculty member who had over a decade of experience in the service and value delivery industry, I was fully qualified to be the professor. The semester went well and I could not have asked for a better group of students or a more enjoyable teaching experience.

In the coming terms, I became a regular faculty member and often taught two or more courses each semester at NSU's School of Business and Entrepreneurship in the master's of business administration program. Some semesters, I would be teaching every weekend and sometimes I would be teaching two different courses to make the topics a bit more interesting for myself. In the course of my first four years at NSU, I taught eight different courses in the master's program (two in the master's of business administration program, three in the master's of international business administration program, and three courses in the master's of science in human resource management program). I was flexible and open to teaching various courses as they became open and available to me. The program office knew that they could count on me to teach a course for them when there were too many students registered in a section and needed to split it into two sections. As a result of my flexibility and qualifications to teach in the three different programs, I was given the opportunity to teach in Brazil, Bahamas, Jamaica, and various states and cities within the United States (including Fort Lauderdale, Miami, Kendal, Tampa, Orlando, Jacksonville, Atlanta, and many others). This led to the opportunity to begin teaching online classes at the Graduate School of Business and Entrepreneurship at NSU. In 1998, the graduate program was starting the online program and they asked me if I would like to receive the training to begin teaching online classes. Teaching online courses added more flexibility and learning opportunities to my repertoire of teaching skills. Teaching online not only brought more flexibility in my schedule and added a little extra income to my annual salary, but it also opened a new world of distance facilitation, learning and education. What is even more interesting is that I was on the cutting edge of cyberspace education, and besides learning myself along with other professionals I was always making history in the creation of knowledge about online facilitation and learning assessment. Furthermore, while online teaching required more time dealing with the classes on the course newsgroups (aka: bulletin board) and evaluation of submissions on a regular basis, it also allowed me to spend more time at home instead of having to travel to the physical classroom.

While teaching as an adjunct professor and eventually teaching two masters' courses for students in the Tampa Campus of University of Phoenix, I was encouraged to apply for a College Chair position for the Undergraduate Business Program. The College Chair is responsible for all academic and operational issues related to students, faculty, employees, and every curriculum offered by the college. Taking this position meant leaving my very comfortable job in corporate America and being able to live with a reduced salary. After much thinking and deep reflections about the pros and cons of moving to academia on a full-time basis, I decided to retire from my full-time job at Publix Super Markets and took the College Chair position.

Despite the fact that I had to talk myself into making the switch, since I was very comfortable with my colleagues in one of the most admired companies in America, the transition was not stressful, nor difficult. Besides being an administrator, I was also teaching undergraduate and graduate business courses for students at the University of Phoenix in the Tampa Campus. Almost all of the students were working adults who brought many years of work and management experience to the classroom. During my second year in academia, an opportunity opened up and I was promoted to the College Chair for the Graduate College of Business and Management at the Tampa Campus. While working as a College Chair, I was able to teach, serve on various curriculum committees, assist in the creation of courses for the university's doctoral programs, measure learning outcomes of various curriculums, and assist the university successfully achieve a ten-year reaffirmation of regional accreditation through the Higher Learning Commission. In 2002, I was offered an opportunity to join Nova Southeastern University as the academic director of undergraduate business administration programs with the Farquhar College of Arts and Sciences with an Assistant Professor rank. So, I moved to Fort Lauderdale and, since then, I have traveled to various countries around the globe for lecturing opportunities. All in all, the transition to academia was fun, exciting, and a good learning experience.

Since I enjoy thinking, writing and coming up with new ideas I have been able to continue my academic experience and the transition to higher education on a full-time basis has been fun. The academic environment has allowed me to gain many new and exiting network of friends and colleagues around the globe through conference attendance, publications, teachings, training, and guest lecturing. The transition into academia has also provided me with sufficient flexibility to where I have been able to assist in the reconstruction and development of my country of birth, Afghanistan. Since 2002, I have participated and spoken in various conferences geared toward the rebuilding of the country and I have been able to Chair two major international conferences in Kabul, Afghanistan. So, besides earning enough money to live happily, I have also had plenty of opportunities to help various agencies in local and international communities. While all these activities are fun and exciting, the core job in academia has been teaching in the classroom. As long as you enjoy teaching or facilitating to "open minds" and adjusting to their learning needs, academia should be a good journey and transition. While I enjoy doing a number of activities, one must keep in mind that as administrators and educators, we must stay focused on students as they are the reason we are all in academia. One must be very cautious and never allow anything to interfere with the achievement of student learning and the assessment of course and program level outcomes. In academia, the student and his/her learning is the highest priority and every other activity is simply part of the agenda or politics associated with it.

Transitions to Academia

As can be seen from the above-mentioned personal and professional experiences, the transition to academia has been fun, exiting, and full of developmental opportunities. We can all be grateful for the opportunities we have had and we recommend preparing yourself for new opportunities in the future. As motivational speaker Les Brown once remarked, it is far better to be prepared for the opportunity that never comes, than to be unprepared for an opportunity when it arrives. The point here is that with some flexibility and openness to new ideas and guidance from experienced colleagues, you can enjoy your transition to academia and fulfill many of your professional dreams. Moving from corporate America into academe will test you and can potentially get you out of your comfort zone, but there is also tremendous flexibility and openness within academe to test new ideas and create new knowledge. Before moving to academia, we recommend learning as much as you can about higher education and academia and attend conferences that provide the latest trends. This will better equip you to deal with prospective challenges and, in some cases, turn them into opportunities for you, your students and your colleagues in academia.

Higher Education and Academia

There has been an increasing trend with schools using part-time (adjunct) faculty members to teach in their master's and doctoral programs. One reason for this is lack of sufficient funding to hire full-time faculty members and another reason has to do with the fact that there is a shortage of qualified candidates. As such, the cost of recruiting the right individuals with the right credentials has dramatically increased. Nonetheless, while many schools are dealing with the current shortage of qualified terminally degreed faculty members, others are taking advantage of this opportunity to offer new doctoral programs to fill this need. The Doctor of Philosophy (Ph.D.) or Doctor of Business Administration programs in various fields of business can be a quality niche specialization that can generate new enrollment for both traditional and non-traditional schools of higher education. According to the information provided by the U.S. Education Information Center (2004), "Historically, the DBA provided a more general perspective on management, while the Ph.D. emphasized research in a specialized area of management. However, the difference between the two degrees is no longer so precise and varies from institution to institution. The Ph.D. is the more commonly offered degree." According to a report by the Association to Advance Collegiate Schools of Business (AACSB) in 2003, there is a need for more than 1,100 doctors in Business within the next 5 years and more than 2,400 new doctors within 10 years. This equates to a huge opportunity for those thinking about pursuing a terminal degree. As demonstrated from the survey of 85 doctorate alumni at Nova Southeastern University's School of Business and Entrepreneurship in 2003, about 66% of the respondents stated that they started teaching at a college level after graduation from the doctoral program and that their NSU degree was a factor in receiving teaching opportunities. Many non-traditional schools tend to offer doctor of business administration (DBA), doctor of public administration (DPA), doctor of international business administration (DIBA), doctor of management (DM), doctor of organizational leadership (DOL), etc. instead of the more research based Ph.D. program. However, according to many colleagues, the quality of accredited DBA, DIBA, DPA, DM, DOL, and other such programs are just as good, if not better, than many of the traditional programs offering Ph.D. degrees. While the title of the degree may not make much of a difference in the outcomes achieved, the Ph.D. title seems to be more popular because it has been around longer than other equivalent programs offered through distance education for working adult professionals and many older faculty may have difficulty in accepting these new degrees. Because of these concerns, and based on personal interactions, discussions, and visits with many non-traditional doctoral students at two different accredited universities in the United States, it is apparent that many of them have been asking for a Ph.D. Program that can be completed while they work full-time since they are willing to get more involved in research and teaching both during and after their corporate and government careers. This demand provides another great marketing opportunity for both traditional and non-traditional schools that can fill this need for working professionals. Business Week (March 2004) noted that "The business Ph.D. is an endangered species. In 2002, a mere 1,095 people earned the degree versus more than 6,600 Ph.D.s in social sciences and 5,300 in humanities. And, some 40% of all business PhDs head directly from B-school to Corporate America. That leaves only about 650 to fill faculty slots at B-schools. The schools have been coping but some 500 spots for doctorate-holding faculty went vacant in 2003—more than double the number two years earlier." Again, for those contemplating a terminal degree in business, this is extremely encouraging as the demand far outweighs the supply. However, those not interested in a business degree should not fret as shortages will occur in other disciplines as well.

A doctor of philosophy program can be a quality research-oriented degree that can fill the need for more Ph.D.s, create new enrollment, and enhance a school's brand. Non-traditional schools can use their existing model and unique delivery format to prepare Ph.D.s that will be able to fill the educational needs of twenty-first century institutions. While the traditional schools are finding it very difficult to enroll and successfully graduate doctoral students due to the high cost associated with such programs and lack of sufficient public funding, a non-traditional school's unique delivery format enables it to deliver this program much more efficiently than the traditionally operated institutions. A Doctoral Program can prepare students for positions such as researchers, faculty members, university administrators, and practitioners in government, not for profit institutions and for profit organizations. With the projected increasing demand for doctoral graduates, these professionals will be able to differentiate themselves through their specialized fields of expertise from other professionals. The graduate of specialized Doctoral Programs should be able to compete globally with both research and teaching oriented institutions.

According to the Association to Advance Collegiate Schools of Business (AACSB) report titled "*Overview of U.S. Business Schools 2002-2003*," there were 5,598 doctoral students at the 99 schools that responded to their survey. So, the market has a huge potential for student enrollment at schools that have flexible delivery formats for doctoral courses and the overall program. The same report by the AACSB concluded that about 63% of the enrolled doctoral students were males and 37% were females. Furthermore, it was concluded that 50.2% of the enrolled students were American citizens or permanent residents of the United States while 49.8% were Non-U.S. citizens without permanent visas. From the 50.2% (2,835 students) that were either U.S. citizens or permanent residents, 76% were white (non-Hispanic), 3.7% were Hispanic, 7.1% were Black (non-Hispanic), and 7.7% were Asians or Pacific Islander.

The Communicator: Council of Graduate Schools (2004) stated that "with attrition from Ph.D. programs averaging 30% to 50%, the nation is losing an important resource of highly trained personnel" while the demand is rising. The article further mentioned that the attrition is much more severe for women and minorities since they tend to leave doctoral programs at a greater rate than the majority and international students. Furthermore, this is a concern because projections show that about 80% of the growth in college-age students will come from minorities. The Council of Graduate Schools statistics showed that 39,955 students graduated with doctorate degrees in 2002 and this number was the lowest total since 1993. Because many schools are cutting back their doctoral programs, fewer percentage of qualified students get the opportunity to enter and successfully complete doctoral degrees. In an article entitled "Is There a Doctorate in the House" written by Tricia Bisoux at the March/April issue of BizEd (2003), the author stated that "replenishing the world's supply of doctorates in business has become imperative." While there is an increase in the demand for more terminally degreed educators, many traditional schools have been downsizing their programs for cost-cutting purposes. As cost rises, "many Ph.D.-granting institutions are shrinking their doctoral programs in business, especially those in the U. S." (BizEd, 2003). As business schools reduce their Ph.D. Program enrollment, fewer qualified educators enter the pipeline. As the number of qualified candidates decreases in the doctoral programs, salaries will rise in the United States thereby attracting terminally degreed faculty members from other countries. As such, schools throughout the world will find themselves in a "salary war that many will likely lose" as stated by BizEd (2003). Non-traditional schools or traditional schools with on-line formats are in a good position to offer doctoral programs and to economically fulfill society's needs for more research-oriented graduates. With today's internet age and advanced technology, making such programs available with a great quality should be much easier than ever before.

The twenty-first century is the first century of comprehensive worldwide cyberspace education through distance learning both academically and for workforce development. Higher education students in this new millennium can and should be selective in choosing a doctoral program (be it a Ph.D., a DBA or other terminal degree programs) for enrollment since a doctorate of business administration (DBA) program can cost anywhere from $35,000 to over $100,000 depending on the program and school offering the degree. There is also the four to five years it will take to complete the degree with its opportunity cost as well. The business of higher education has become very competitive as schools move far beyond their main campuses to offer programs nationally and internationally. Many of the schools involved in distance education also use cyberspace technology as their students complete the doctoral program while remaining employed full-time. If you are considering a non-traditional school, you may wonder about the education you are receiving. You should not be overly concerned about this, assuming you will be attending an accredited institution, especially since many of the same faculty who facilitate in the traditional programs are also now teaching at distance education programs. As such, the quality and outcomes achieved are likely to be similar for all programs. All doctoral students are likely to complete some form of comprehensive exams or produce peer reviewed publications as part of the requirement for graduation. Therefore, the quality of the education is likely to be the same when students are achieving similar outcomes as a result of their degree and perform equally well on the exams.

A Systems Approach to Education

Higher education institutions are one of the longest lasting organizational systems that society has created for the purpose of developing experts, practitioners and researchers (Carr et al., 2004). The formal educational system, dating back to the thirteenth century, has changed dramatically from its beginnings to today. According to Jacques (1996), as late as the mid 1800's a degree obtained from Harvard University was primarily a recognition of attendance, and the suggestion to implement grading, structured curricula, and standardized testing was considered radical. Today, universities are "standard producers of knowledge." Nova Southeastern University and University of Phoenix have been pioneers in making higher education available to working adult students through innovative distance education mediums. They have been successful because they have a holistic view of education rather than limiting themselves to just doing what has always been done. Rather, they made education available through non-traditional methods by thinking holistically and seeing how working adults can impact the society if they are given quality opportunities to advance their education without having to quit their jobs and attend the traditional schools.

In order for people within an organization to build and grow the skills and competencies needed for increased employee participation, Hesselbein, Marshall, and Beckhard (1997) asserted that organizations need to create learning communities. The creation of learning communities is easier in traditional academic environments. Many non-traditional programs have attempted to fill this gap by creating learning teams which stay together for the entire program. These learning teams may also help elevate some of the isolation that may be felt when taking classes on-line and/or away from the school's main campus. Even with learning teams, some students have reported feeling isolated. This potential should be fully explored by each individual prior to enrolling in a completely off-campus or internet based program. You can find additional information on selecting the right program in Chapter 4.

Summary

According to Eastmond (1998), the term "distance education" has become synonymous with instruction and facilitation provided through face-to-face interactions as well as cyberspace technologies. As a result, many programs are commonly referred to as off-campus or online education. For example, some colleges are exploring the use of podcasts for lectures and asynchronous discussion boards as a future method of content delivery to help students make a better connection with the faculty member facilitating the off-campus-based course.

Terminally-degreed professionals who want to transition from the "real world" into the "ideal world" of academia can do so by obtaining the relevant knowledge and learning to stay focused on students and their learning. If you enjoy working with students and facilitating concepts in creative and, at times, uncomfortable manners, you are probably going to enjoy the academic environment. Teaching working adults is not an easy task as each session can be a challenge of balance when dealing with diverse and knowledgeable audience. It is the faculty or facilitator's job to balance his or her interest in the topic, students' knowledge and willingness to participate, in addition to the student's perceived need to only stay focused on earning a good grade with the realities of time limitations, assessment and being focused on the objectives of the curriculum, course, and the specific session.

While being able to teach is one outcome of the terminal degree, serving as an educator may not be for everyone. As such, one must enjoy teaching and interacting with students in order to fully realize the intrinsic satisfaction of educating learners. If educating is not one's "cup of tea," then terminally-degreed candidates can certainly make a name for themselves in research, serving as academic administrators, and working in the government and corporate arenas. The key is to match your goals and skills in pursuing the right career.

4 – Selecting and Beginning a Doctoral Program

P rior to beginning a terminal degree program and during the first few classes, and this may be difficult to believe, but completing the coursework is probably the "easiest" part of a doctoral program. However, you can save yourself a great deal of heartache and additional work by selecting a dissertation topic early in the coursework process so that you can focus your class research in the general area of your dissertation. While this may not be possible in every instance, there are many opportunities to do this. There will be more information on the dissertation topic in Chapter 7.

Before completing anything, one must choose and enter a doctoral program. When selecting a doctoral program, one must make sure that the school is regionally accredited. A college or university is not required to be accredited; however, without accreditation through a regional accrediting body, the degree is not worth much to outsiders such as state officials, colleges or universities when it comes to getting a job. So, make sure to choose a school that is regionally accredited. When choosing a university for your doctorate degree, make sure that the school is accredited by a regional accrediting body, such as the Southern Association of Colleges and Schools (SACS). The six regional accrediting bodies in the U.S. are the New England Association of Schools and Colleges (NEASC), North Central Association of Schools and Colleges (NCA), Middle States Association of Schools and Colleges (MSA), Southern Association of Schools and Colleges (SACS), Western Association of Schools and Colleges (WASC), and the Northwest Association of Schools and Colleges (NWCCU). Regional accreditation is very important and cannot be overemphasized. In the United States, you should not attend a program that is not accredited by one of these accrediting bodies. In addition to the regional accreditation, schools may also choose to pursue programmatic level accreditations by various bodies such as the International Assembly for Collegiate Business Education (IACBE) or the Association to Advance Collegiate Schools of Business (AACSB) International.

Some school administrators and leaders, due to their institutional mission and target audience, may purposely choose not to pursue programmatic level accreditation if the achievement of this goal does not allow them to effectively achieve their purpose and serve their students. For example, generally speaking, the programmatic level accreditation bodies have been focused on the traditional age students and research-oriented programs which are not necessarily always suitable for working adult professionals and institutions that serve them using formats such evening, weekend, hybrid, and online technologies. Most traditional doctoral programs tend to require students to attend school on a full-time basis, serve as a teaching assistant, grade papers, teach one or more classes under the supervision of his/her advisor, conduct research, and serve the school on other capacities as appropriate to become a "serious," credible, and skilled researcher in academia. Such requirements, while appropriate and needed for traditional-age and full-time students, may not be necessary for most working adult doctoral students who are already successfully teaching or working in professional positions in the private or public arenas. Most of these working professionals want to pursue their doctoral education at their own pace and time in the evenings, weekends, and their vacation time with institutions that offer such flexible programs and faculty, so they can achieve the same outcomes as students in traditional terminal-degree programs. Most of these professional working adults do not always need to work under the close supervision of a full-time faculty or advisor to learn research skills, teamwork, teaching skills, or to secure a sample population for their dissertation research. Since these working professionals are already in the fields and industries of their choice, they are likely to conduct research with these populations as they have access to the data or can easily get the samples when needed. Furthermore, many of these working adult students might currently be consumers of data and are already conducting research, or they are hiring professional firms to conduct research for them in their industries. Therefore, they can independently and interdependently perform many of the tasks that traditional students conduct with the guidance of, and/or through, their faculty advisors. So, schools that serve these working adult populations of students do not necessarily require their learners to be full-time students, to teach classes at their school to become skilled teachers, or conduct research on a full-time basis. However, for those that do not already have such skills, they do offer programs that can help them meet such requirements if and when needed. As such, these schools' format of going about producing doctoral candidates do not always match those elements of the programmatic level accrediting bodies which are geared toward the needs of traditional institutions and students. If they were to achieve this programmatic level accreditation through an accrediting body that is focused on traditional schools and institutions, then they too would become more traditional and, thus, would not serve their mission or target market which might very well be non-traditional working adult professionals. Consequently, since programmatic level accreditation is not a necessity, and its achievement can prevent them from effectively serving their audience, many of these modern and non-traditional schools choose not to pursue such program level and field-related credentials.

While programmatic level accreditations can be great for credentialing of a school's brand, faculty members and students in the United States, it is not necessary since the most important factor for enrollment consideration is that the school is regionally accredited through an agency such as NEASC, NCA (or the Higher Learning Commission), MSA, SACS, WASC, and NWCCU. Other variables to consider in choosing a school might be that they need to have top-notch faculty members who provide personal attention to students, have real experience along with academic credentials, extensive academic choices, flexible programs, a diverse student and faculty ratio, academic resources, such as online journals and student assistance, as well as successful graduates.

Enrolling into a Doctoral Program

Higher education, where one can complete a degree without having to leave one's full-time position, is a reality; and it is not going to be disappearing anytime soon. While adult education, through flexible schedules, is the buzz of the decade, it is not for everyone and requires getting used to the technology. Adult students can and should be selective in choosing a graduate program for enrollment as today's doctoral programs at a private school can cost anywhere from $35,000 to over $100,000 depending on the program and school offering the degree. The "business" of higher education has become very competitive as schools move far beyond their main campuses to offer programs nationally and internationally. Just in South Florida, students can choose from over ten different doctoral programs and universities to complete various degrees

Many of the top schools involved in higher education offer complete programs through weekend and evening formats or an online modality. As previously mentioned, students need not be concerned about the modality of the distance education programs since many of the same faculty members who teach in the traditional programs at the main campuses also teach at distant sites and online programs at different universities.

The term "distance education" has become synonymous with instruction and facilitation provided through cyberspace technologies via the Internet. As a result, these programs are commonly referred to as online education. There are different types of Internet-based courses: *first*, there is the distance learning programs which are supplemented by use of the Internet technologies as a support mechanism as opposed to being the primary medium of delivery; *second*, there is the computer conferencing medium where Internet is the primary means of delivery utilizing asynchronous discussions and emails; *third*, there are the synchronous virtual course where all or most aspects of the course are delivered online. This third option is similar to traditional face-to-face courses where students log on to the class at a specific time and attend along with other students and the professor. The one issue with this delivery method is that it requires the students to have a high speed Internet connection. Regardless of format, adult students are expected to be actively involved in the knowledge generation process while regularly interacting with the instructor and their colleagues each week about the material to be learned as guided by the faculty. Faculty members make the difference in student learning as their facilitation skills can be either exciting or boring (pretty much the same as on-ground courses). Online faculty members tend to involve the learner through their formal and informal facilitation, since that is what leads to real learning. As such, the faculty serves as a facilitator in the learning process as is the case in the on-ground sessions.

Student involvement is even more important in the online environment if the material is to be learned, utilized and retained by the graduates of a course in the long-term. When choosing a graduate online program, prospective students should:

1. Assess their learning styles, their preferences and their interests.
2. Assemble a list of various programs that are likely to best meet the aforementioned needs.
3. Check each school's accreditation. If the school is not regionally accredited by one of the accrediting bodies (SACS, NEASC, NCA, MSA, WASC, or NWCCU) eliminate the school as a choice. Do not consider schools that are not regionally accredited.
4. Learn about the credentials of the faculty and their teaching philosophy to see if they match or accommodate a student's dominant learning style.
5. Interview the school's administrators, advisors, and determine their student services offerings and their level of technical assistance for online students.
6. Determine each program's graduation and employability rates after graduation as well as the program's overall rankings.
7. Spend more time with the programs that look the most attractive to gain a deeper understanding of the school, its culture, and their overall quality.
8. Once you have narrowed the search down to a couple of schools, ask the university for several references from recent graduates. These individuals can tell you how it was to be a student in the prospective program. At a minimum you should contact a couple of references. Remember, you are planning to invest a significant sum of money with the school, you should be sure your investment will pay off. Some potential questions you could ask recent graduates:
   a. How was your overall experience at (name of school)?
   b. How long did it take you to complete the degree?
   c. How many of the students that started with you completed the degree?
   d. Was the administration helpful once you were enrolled in the program?
   e. How helpful was your dissertation committee in ensuring you completed the degree?
   f. If you had to do it all over again, would you still select (name of school)?
   g. Any further advice you can give me?
9. Select a program that best matches your needs, learning philosophy, and a school that provides helpful information to make sure students are able to finish the program in a reasonable time period.

Since students have many choices in today's competitive environment of higher education, schools must also understand their needs and offer them the appropriate tools so they can be successful using today's cyberspace technologies. When it comes to doctoral degree programs, there are number of choices and one must be very selective. Choose a program that best matches your needs and schedule. Although there are many others, Table 4.1 presents a list of universities that awarded the most doctorate degrees in 2004 (as reported on August 25, 2006 by the Chronicle of Higher Education, p. 22).

Table 4.1 - Universities Awarding Most Earned Doctorates, 2004

School / University	#s	School / University	#s
University of California at Berkeley	769	Harvard University	579
University of Texas at Austin	702	University of Illinois at Urbana-Champaign	574
University of California at Los Angeles	664	University of Minnesota-Twin Cities	565
Nova Southeastern University	645	Ohio State University – Main Campus	560
University of Wisconsin at Madison	627	University of Florida	522
Stanford University	591	University of Washington	506
Pennsylvania State University at University Part	580	Texas A&M University at College Station	492

These schools have been able to be part of such a prestigious number of institutions because they are mission-driven and consistently stay focused on creating long-term value for their faculty members, staff and students. Of course, universities that are successful often go "beyond the classroom" to "bring life to learning" and create long-term value for all their stakeholders: faculty, staff, students, and the community. Dr. Randolph A. Pohlman, author of the *Value Driven Management* book and Dean of the H. Wayne Huizenga School of Business and Entrepreneurship at NSU, stated the following in his welcome message to the faculty, which we believe is the essence of communicating a clear vision for the school and, then, living it:

> Nova Southeastern University's H. Wayne Huizenga School of Business and Entrepreneurship does not just talk about the need to transform business education—it lives it. In an era when business schools are struggling to keep pace with the trends and challenges faced by the business world, we are pioneering the development of an integrated approach to leading and managing that will place our graduates at the forefront of management application and theory.
>
> As our business world continues to become more complex, advanced levels of technology are utilized; creating a market that has truly become global in scope. The H. Wayne Huizenga School of Business and Entrepreneurship of Nova Southeastern University (NSU) is committed to preparing students at bachelor's, master's, and doctoral levels to be strong competitors in this challenging environment. The Huizenga School degree programs stand apart from others for several significant reasons: First, the programs emphasize entrepreneurial, innovative, and creative applications taught by professors

who bring to the classroom a mix of excellence in teaching, research, and business experience. Second, the flexible delivery systems are designed to meet the needs of the working professional, full-time student, and individual organizations. Finally, although we have grown large in size, we continue to provide individual attention to ensure the success of our students.

We are committed to working as a team in partnering with students to serve the global business community...We join together to provide students with the foundation of knowledge, skills, and experience on which they may build their future (Welcome Message, Faculty Handbook, 2005).

Completing the Doctoral Courses

Besides actual coursework, there are other requirements for a doctoral student. Most doctoral programs tend to require a certain number of courses that a student must complete, as well as to take a comprehensive exam, complete a dissertation study, publish an academic paper, and successfully finish an oral defense for the dissertation project. Besides these main elements, some doctoral programs that have full-time students may also require them to serve as graduate assistants (or teaching assistants) for a number of terms as well as to teach one or more courses during their doctoral study program. Serving as teaching assistants can certainly provide students the basic skills for teaching, while giving them the opportunity to be a mentee under the direction of their chair (mentor), who is normally an experienced educator. This requirement can encourage more terminally-degreed graduates to pursue teaching careers rather than going into the government sector for professional positions or the corporate arena. For many, more traditional programs may not be an option because they normally require one to be a full time student. This option may not be acceptable for many adult learners with full time careers and/or family obligations.

Once a student is enrolled into a doctoral program, he or she can immediately begin completing the required courses. Of course, some of the courses need to be completed in the order specified in the school's catalog based on their prerequisites. However, there may be other courses in the doctoral program that can be taken in any sequence that a student wishes to complete them or as convenient based on time and course availability. Just because a course is available and its term dates match one's schedule does not obligate one to take it. Especially if it has been some time since you have attended school, it may be worthwhile for you to take one of your favorite topics first to get back into academia and to familiarize yourself with the process and program expectations. This should be followed by several research courses to understand the dissertation process, and specifically how a primary study with a specific population can be initiated, statistically analyzed and finalized for the dissertation or a journal publication. You can find more information on this topic in Chapters 7 and 8.

The good news about doctoral courses is that they are the easiest part of the program and most students end up successfully completing all of them. If at all possible, one must try to complete the coursework and immediately take the comprehensive exam while the content is still fresh in one's thoughts. Successfully passing the comprehensive exam is a major part of the program and it should be done soon after the required courses are completed. During the first few terms or first year of enrollment, one must seriously reflect upon what his/her dissertation topic and research question(s) will be. Try to determine this before going into the second year of the doctoral course work. If the school you are attending requires a prospectus (concept paper), you should start working on this as early as possible or during your second year of study. Once the topic and research question are determined and the concept paper (prospectus) is approved by one's advisor / chair, then one can develop various portions of the dissertation as part of his/her coursework requirements. Working through this process (starting the dissertation work during the first two years of enrollment and doing the work along with the required courses) can greatly enhance one's chances of successfully completing the journey. We can't emphasize this point enough – the sooner you find a topic and begin your research, the higher the probability of completing the degree. What increases the probability of not completing the dissertation (and not earning the doctorate degree) is the process of completing all the courses and not having done any reflection, thinking, or work on the dissertation. Not only can this lead to abandoning the program and giving up the idea of finishing the doctorate degree, but it can also lead to more stress and headaches while one is finalizing the dissertation. An important "rule of thumb" to remember can be to start the dissertation process and research once one has fully reviewed all the literature in one's area of interest. For some individuals this might take a few semesters, while for others this process can require several years of course work and readings.

The goal of each student should be to finish each course and understand the literature in the area of one's concentration while reflecting on completing part of his/her dissertation work in it (if the content and course outcomes lend themselves to meeting the outcomes of the course). If one's dissertation work and topic does not match the specific course, then one's goal should be to finish each course with a quality publishable term project that can be submitted to an academic conference or a journal for publication consideration. Using the suggestions stated above will not only increase the probability of successfully finishing the program, but it can also lead to having several good papers published while the student is enrolled in the program. Many students have used this process, and everyone else can, and should, as well. The key is to plan to take the courses slowly, while doing the dissertation work alongside of it. In the mean time, some of the term projects completed for the courses should be sent to academic conferences and journals for peer review and potential publication acceptance. If you are too busy to complete all the edits required to improve a paper for publication, there is nothing wrong with asking other colleagues to take your paper, edit it, add it to, and make it better while trying to get it published as a co-author. Some faculty members may also be interested in co-authoring with you if you submit a quality paper for their review and assistance. Since faculty members often attend academic conferences annually, they are likely to be able to get it published as a co-author without you having to attend the conference. We recommend you attend the top conference(s) in your field as a doctoral student. Not only does it give you an idea of what is required to publish, but it may give you additional topics, directions, or methodologies for your own research. If you have written a quality term paper that managers, professionals, or academicians might find useful and practical, try to get it published by yourself or with a co-author. Avoid the tendency of only finishing the coursework, the dissertation, or getting only publications as quickly as possible (while ignoring the courses and the dissertation). They all can be done, and should be worked on in a balanced manner simultaneously during each year you are in the program. Of course, one area will need more of a focus during the term than the others but the key is to not go too long without working on the others as well. For example, during the term one may spend more time on the suggested course readings, articles, and the preparation of the coursework and the term project. Once those are completed or when the semester has ended, then one can work on the dissertation process and submit the course's completed term project for publication to a journal or conference. Overall, remain focused on completing the doctoral courses while doing part of the dissertation work, and submitting quality term projects for publication consideration. You can do all the required works in a balanced manner as you move forward toward achieving the doctorate degree.

Outcome-Orientation and Networking

An important aspect of successfully finishing the doctoral program is to know the outcomes or the graduation requirements from the outset. Similar to faculty members or facilitators, doctoral students need to become "outcome-oriented" and figure out exactly what is expected, and how to successfully achieve these expectations in order to earn the terminal degree. Typically, as mentioned above, a doctoral program will require the successful completion of the following elements as prerequisite for graduation:

1. *Courses*. Completion of the required core and specialized courses in one's area of study.
2. *Comp exam*. Receiving a passing score on the comprehensive examination.
3. *Publication or academic presentation*. Publication of a blind peer-reviewed paper in a refereed journal or conference in one's area of study or academic specialization.
4. *Dissertation*. Writing of the dissertation, using a valid and scientific quantitative or qualitative methodology for the research and its analysis.
5. *Defense*. Completing the oral defense of the research presented in the dissertation. Oral defense can at times be substituted by a publication or an academic presentation if the results of the dissertation are published in a refereed conference or journal where the presenter answers questions regarding his or her research, the soundness of the methodology used, and the overall conclusions and results.

The outcome of each course in the program is not necessarily just a good grade, but rather it is the area-specific knowledge and skills that better equip you to research and publish in your field of study. So, stay focused on the major outcomes (such as knowledge acquisition of the latest concepts, research papers and publication opportunities) and not just the grade. Since completing doctoral courses and meeting the faculty's requirements are a natural part of the process and most students can successfully handle them, this book does not focus too much on this requirement. This book has devoted many chapters on the successful completion of the later four elements mentioned above as they tend to be new to most graduate students who are experiencing such requirements for the first time in their educational journey. Overall, it is the successful completion of the required courses, passing the comprehensive exam, publishing at an academic conference or journal, writing the dissertation, and going through the oral defense that earns the candidate a doctoral / terminal degree. While the aforementioned elements are almost always the major necessities, some doctoral programs might also require other elements such as researching with a faculty member for one or more semesters, teaching one or more courses during the program, grant writing, serving as a graduate assistant and grading papers, etc. as part of earning the terminal degree. While some of the requirements might vary from school to school, it is the student's responsibility to know exactly what needs to be done, and how to successfully meet all of the requirements for this prestigious terminal degree at the conclusion of his or her first semester in the doctoral program. Doctoral students should note that they are not alone in this journey as many other students are going through the same process and requirements along with them. The key is to get to know and network with these individuals so you can have a team of friends and coaches that can be of assistance to you at various times in the doctoral program.

During the first few semesters of the doctoral program, it is best to develop at least one, two, or more great relationships with someone who is just starting the program, someone who is in the middle of the program and another person who is just about finished with the degree. You should commit to a great partnership with at least one person or several individuals who are just starting the program. It helps if you like the person's character and work ethic, as well as live in close proximity of each other. However, you do not have to like each other and can be as diverse as "day and night" since you are not committing to a life-partnership, but rather to simply help and coach each other in the doctoral program. If you do not like the word partnership or teamwork, then maybe you can serve as coaches to each other in the doctoral program, where you can call one another when you face an obstacle, when you need a second opinion, when you need someone to review or proofread your work, and when you need a shoulder to cry on during the higher education journey. Doctoral students who are in the middle or at the end of the program can also serve as great coaches since they can help you avoid certain challenges and successfully finish the program using their suggestions and wisdom. So, get a good network of people who can guide you, direct you in the right path, and someone that you can research with for academic publications. Overall, be outcome-oriented, and develop a network of academic friends and colleagues that you can work with interdependently during your doctoral journey.

Michael's Advice for Getting It All Done

Everyone that has made it through a doctoral program has his or her own story and advice on how they made it through. My advice is to listen to as many of these stories as possible and adopt those hints and strategies that you feel will assist you and discard those that you don't feel fit into your learning style or personality. With that in mind, you may find these recommendations of modest value or "true gems."

During my doctoral coursework two professors gave me some key advice which turned out to be of critical importance in my completing the degree on time and finding employment afterwards. After six months of classes, one of my professors recommended two things. The first was to pick a topic as soon as possible, and then attempt to use the courses I was taking to assist me in furthering the research on my dissertation topic. Throughout my coursework I found that most professors, if you ask them up front, were more than willing to modify the direction of course papers to meet my research needs and interests. This allowed me to complete a substantial amount of background research on my topic during my coursework. The second recommendation this professor had was to work on my dissertation every week, regardless of what else was going on. At the time I thought *easier said than done* or *that's easy for you to say!*. Yet, as I really took a hard and critical look at my time, I did find some *spare* time in my schedule. For example, for the next two years I spent almost every lunch hour reading journal articles for the dissertation. I also kept articles in my car in case I was stuck in traffic and I read journal articles if I arrived at church or to the movies 15 minutes early. In other words, I filled all the downtime in my life with dissertation research. It is amazing how many articles you can read filling the 15 or 20 minute gaps in your life waiting for meetings or other appointments to start. For many this method will add too much stress – and it did – and should be discarded. I will admit that it did add a significant amount of stress to my life because I started to feel that I didn't even have a second to breathe – I was *constantly* doing something. I was, however, able to deal with the added stress by keeping my eyes focused on the end goal. Knowing that there was an end – albeit years in the future. What I feared worse than the added stress was knowing that I didn't want to look back on this time in my life and wonder *what if.* What would have happened if I really focused and concentrated on this goal? What would have happened if I'd really focused on my dissertation? What would have happened if I'd delayed other things?

To a much lesser extent I have continued this process beyond my doctoral studies. For example, I always make sure to have a pen and paper with me to jot down notes during my *down time.* In fact, I am writing the first draft of this section of the book while sitting in church waiting for the service to begin. So my first bit of advice is to find time in your busy schedule to work on your dissertation each week throughout your studies. In the grand scheme of things, a couple years goes by relatively quickly, so focus now to get your research done on time. There will be time to relax once you are done, push to the finish line!

The second piece of advice came from another professor who encouraged all of the students to use our experiences in "corporate America," along with the theories we were discussing in our courses to prepare possible papers for publication. This professor's thrust was that very few people have years of corporate experience coupled with a doctorate degree. He highlighted that each of us in the program had a unique perspective that very few had and that we should use the opportunity while we were taking classes to express (and publish) our voices. This advice led me to expand two papers I wrote for two different courses and submit them for possible publication. Within the next two years, I had two articles published in peer reviewed journals. So my second piece of advice is to not waste your time solely writing papers for your coursework. Look for opportunities to *double dip* and use the research you are already doing for your courses to write articles for academic publication. Some may not fit exactly, but look beyond the requirement to something that others may be interested in reading or learning about.

Educational Leaders Left Behind[10]

Attrition in doctoral programs has remained in a crisis state for many years. The attrition rate of doctoral students remains at 40-60% and approximately 65,400 doctoral students quit from U.S. educational programs during 2000-2005. The attrition of doctoral students is a critical societal issue as the U.S. is rapidly losing the dominance as being the world leader in doctoral-degreed citizens. Civilizations with a highly educated workforce experience higher economic and living conditions than societies with less educated citizenries, therefore, continued high attrition rates might have future impact on the U.S. economy. The innovation that results from doctoral dissertations enriches the body of knowledge within a country and thus the economy.

The one area of the doctoral program success rate that should be reviewed and enhanced is the role of the *"Protector of Wisdom"* and how some faculty members, professors, and institutions make the process nearly impossible for their students. It appears that some individuals and institutions take the role of "protector of wisdom" a bit too seriously and purposely try to prevent others from joining the academic club. You may have heard stories of students who were and remained at an ABD status because their chair died and no other faculty members were willing to take them on. While such instances are rare and exceptions to the norm these types of circumstances are highly unfair and the institution is to be blamed for it. Higher education institutions must have contingency plans to make sure talented students who are working hard and deserve to finish their doctoral program are able to do so in a timely manner. Having appropriate contingency plans for exceptional circumstances can greatly assist those students who leave the school system without completing their doctoral degree.

Doctoral Attrition Remains a Crisis

The literature supports that academic failure of doctoral students' accounts for only a small percentage of those that leave doctoral programs; therefore, program and graduate culture issues might benefit from leadership interventions. While high attrition rates appear to be *normal* in academic environments, we contend that they should not be. Can you imagine a business remaining competitive in the marketplace with a 40-60% loss of customers? Yet educational leaders continue to accept this as a cost of doing business. Multiple reasons for doctoral attrition have been identified in the literature including health, finance, and family issues, however a portion of the issue may be attributed to the program design and the culture within the schools.

Introduction to the Challenge

If each five of ten drivers were involved in a fatal traffic crash on a specific road, citizens would demand strategies be implemented to eliminate conditions that

---

[10] Contributed by Freda Turner, Grand Canyon University.

caused this highway hazard. If five out of each ten individuals admitted to a hospital for treatment died, the institution would be investigated for malpractice. If an air traffic controller safely landed only five of each ten incoming flights, this situation would be labeled a national crisis. If five of ten drivers were unable to purchase fuel for their cars, immediate investigations would be launched to resolve the issue. If five of ten babies were dropped during birth deliveries, lawsuits would abound! Yet, this type of statistic exists in the American educational system for over 40 years with no improvement and worse, it is viewed as a price of doing business (Lovitts, 2000).

The Washington Post (2006) identified the rate of attrition of doctoral students as 40-60% and Malmberg (2000) found that approximately 65,400 doctoral students will depart from U.S. programs during 2000-2005. Civilizations with a highly educated workforce experience higher economic and living conditions than societies with less educated citizenries, therefore, this continued 40-60% attrition rate might have future impact on the U.S. economy. Interestingly, Lovitts (2000) noted that academic failure of doctoral students' accounts for only a small percentage of those that leave programs.

While educational leaders have yet to identify interventions to reduce attrition rates, The Council of Graduate Schools reported that Pfizer, Inc., and the Ford Foundation has donated a $2 million grant for a three-year study to investigate on how to increase doctoral degree completion rates (Denecke, 2005). The attrition of doctoral students becomes a broader and critical societal issue as the U.S. is rapidly losing the dominance as being the world leader in doctoral-degreed citizens. China, India, Germany, and other countries are conversely, growing their doctoral student pipeline (Strauss, 2006). The innovation resulting from doctoral dissertations is needed to enrich the body of knowledge within a country and thus the economy.

Multiple reasons for doctoral attrition have been identified and include health, finance, and family issues. However, the focus this paper is to suggest how educational leaders might use technology as an intervention strategy to reduce doctoral attrition. Incorporating technology strategies as an element of the doctoral experience might increase the survival rate of doctoral learners. The following suggestions are provided:

Problem 1 related to attrition: Since Lovitts (2000) found that 30% of those that attrite out of doctoral programs do so in the first year, this appears to be a critical time to implement an intervention effort. In 2000, after surveying 816 doctoral students, Lovitts concluded that attrition often arises from the failure of programs to integrate students academically and socially. This socialization may be even more difficult in non-traditional type schools and should be taken into consideration prior to beginning a program of this type. Most doctoral students return to school after a long absence from the classroom. A possible solution is to create a web page for doctoral students that include links and tips from former students, recommendations for success in the academic world, information relating to professional conferences, publishing opportunities, and a doctoral chat room. Additionally, forming learning teams which remain consistent throughout the coursework may alleviate some of the attrition during the first year of a doctoral program. These recommendations might also help traditional doctoral students move from psychological apprehension and procrastination stages to engagement and socialization in the early critical stages of their studies. Additionally, the forming of permanent student teams and a chat room for these students could facilitate increased feelings of involvement.

Problem 2 associated to attrition: According to Nelson (2000), the single most important factor in a student's decision to continue or withdraw from a doctoral program relates to the student's relationship with the dissertation chair. Additionally, another common concern expressed by doctoral learners is their inability to contact their dissertation chair. After a student completes the comprehensive exams and course work, doctoral students may not see or hear from their classmates once they enter the "*all but dissertation* (ABD)" status. Many report feelings of isolation and loneliness. A possible solution is for educational leaders to create a culture that requires the dissertation chair and the student to log in frequently – perhaps weekly, into an online class or communicate electronically relating to progress and/or problems. Such fostered communications might help avoid inertia during the ABD phase. This might allow students to maintain contact and involvement with the academic world during this critical phase. ADBs also should have access to a web page that provides guidance relating to experience and tips from former graduates; dissertation preparation; conducting research ; links to the university librarians; and information on how to contact counselors, academic advisors, and technology technicians. For more information on selecting a dissertation chair see Chapter 7.

Problem 3 related to attrition: Selection of the dissertation committee is very important and often problematic for educational leaders to manage. A committee assigned by the university to a student may result in the faculty member not having the interest or time in the dissertation topic. A possible solution is to establish a web page that lists dissertation-interested faculty, their credentials, and area of research interest. Then the doctoral students can view and invite listed faculty to be part of his/her own dissertation committee. This can enhance the compatibility of personalities and scholarly interests. If the relationship does not work, the student and the committee members should be allowed the opportunity to remove themselves from the academic relationship after notification of all involved parties. Educational leaders should provide additional compensation to the committee members and contract that committee feedback must be provided to the learner within 10 working days of the student submission. Providing *compensation to the faculty is less costly than the attrition of a student.* For recommendations on selecting dissertation committee members, please see Chapter 7.

Problem 4 related to attrition: Lack of focus on the dissertation topic has been addressed as a reason for attrition during the ABD stage. A possible intervention to reduce attrition at late stage is to require doctoral students to select the dissertation topic, which addresses a societal problem, the method of data collection, and dissertation chair/committee during their *first year* in a doctoral program. The earlier the committee selection occurs along with a specific topic/methodology, the more engaged the student may become throughout their doctoral work and the more applicable many of their courses become to their research.

The Reality of Michael's Doctoral Group's Completion Rate

I started my doctoral studies early one January morning. As I walked into my very first doctoral level class, I saw some confident expressions on student's faces as well as some that looked more like I felt. I was scared, unsure, and insecure about my ability to complete the coursework at the doctoral level. I remember thinking to myself, why did I get myself into this and why not quit now and avoid facing failure later. However, not being one to give up on any challenge, I ignored these feelings and entered a new phase of my education. In hindsight, I was fairly ignorant about what was entailed in obtaining a doctorate degree, the amount of research required, or much at all about the amount of work involved in completing a dissertation. For this first class, as well as for others to follow, the room was set up in a horseshoe configuration and I selected a seat at one of the spokes or legs of the horseshoe near the middle of the classroom. As we went around the room to introduce ourselves and give a brief description of our backgrounds, my feelings of self-doubt did not subside. Other students had impressive academic and work credentials. Students had graduated from such prestigious schools as Washington and Lee, Bucknell University, Lehigh University, Virginia Polytechnic Institute, Massachusetts Institute of Technology, and the United States Naval Academy. From a work perspective, there was a CEO of a multimillion dollar corporation, an Army Colonel, a Vice President at JPMorganCase, and a former U.S. Ambassador.

It was during this first class when I heard the abysmal completion rates for doctoral degrees. I was not alone in being shocked by these statistics. It is certainly not a statistic that is emphasized by the admissions department at schools! At the beginning of my program our class consisted of 14 students. The 14 of us got together and agreed that we would do whatever it would take to break the poor completion trends and see that everyone made it through to the end. In retrospect, this was very naive. After the very first class we were down to 13 students, after the second course to 12, and after the first year down to 11 students. The good news was that, within a couple of years, the 11 of us made it through all the course work and passed the comprehensive examinations – moving into All But Dissertation (ABD) status. This gave us an impressive 78% completion rate from the beginning of the program through passing the comprehensive examinations. Unfortunately, as often happens, without the stress and pressure of constant deadlines of coursework, many students lose focus toward completing their dissertation – life gets in the way and it is easy to put off the dissertation when other matters appear more pressing. This may be especially true for those with families that had to suffer through years of school and now need some additional attention. After nearly three years of being in the ABD status, 7 of the original 14 (or 50%) have completed their dissertations. The remaining four students are still in various stages of working toward completing their dissertation proposals. While it is likely that not all will finish, the group has already achieved the average completion rate for doctoral programs with the potential of achieving as high as a 78% completion rate.

One issue that had a dramatic impact on our overall success rate was the use of permanent learning teams. During our very first course, we got together and divided ourselves into 3 work/learning teams each consisting of 4 or 5 students. The purpose of these teams was to act as a support mechanism and study group for each course. We were able to keep these teams consistent throughout all the group projects required by various courses. By keeping the teams consistent we were able to build a strong bond between students and help support each other throughout the coursework. This group bond was particularly important when a life changing event occurred with a student (death in the family, loss of a job, or a deployment to Iraq) because there was a built in support mechanism for a student and other students willing to pick up some of the "slack" when events occurred. To a lesser extent, once the coursework was completed the larger group of 11 has stayed close and we produce a monthly newsletter via email to update each other on professional and academic successes as well as requests for help. The hope is that this newsletter will help keep the learning team bonds stronger, lessen potential feelings of isolation, and help spur more students on to completion.

Summary

Denecke (2005) published, "Research has shown that the vast majority of students, including minority students, who enter doctoral programs, have the academic ability to complete the degree" (para. 4). Therefore, attrition appears to be a cultural or a programmatic issue. High attrition losses are of no benefit to the students, the educational institution, or the nation. Educational leaders might benefit from the thoughts of Smith, when he stated the refusal to change can be liken to expecting a person to be comfortable wearing the same item of clothing that fitted him as a child. So should national energies be focused on *no child left behind* or might more benefits be gained from educational leaders viewing the organization as a business. Few businesses could survive long-term with high rates of attrition. The first step in reducing high attrition is awareness and interventions within one's own institution.

In the ideal world, each doctoral student should plan to complete the required courses while he/she is working on the dissertation process simultaneously. Beginning the dissertation work during one's first year in a doctoral program can greatly enhance the probability of successfully earning the terminal degree. So, begin your dissertation research before moving too far into the course work.

5 – Don't Sweat the Little Things

S tress is a normal part of life in higher education, as there are deadlines and critical "feedback" from one's colleagues, teachers, and advisors. Much of the felt stress seems to come from the "little things," and, of course, they are all "little" compared to one's health, life, and family. The truth is that most working adult doctoral students are likely to be busy professionals who hold stressful positions, take care of one or more family members, volunteer in the community, and remain focused on a specific academic route to stay abreast of the latest findings. Such pressures can be very challenging and stressful. As such, time management, project management, stress management, and change management skills become important. An important element of a doctoral student's life is to focus on what is important first and then focus on other tasks that appear urgent but may not necessarily be important.

Some doctoral students who begin teaching while still in their doctoral program end up enjoying teaching and, unfortunately, ignore their goal of finishing the dissertation and end up falling short of their ultimate goal. While teaching can be fun and it should be enjoyed as it can be financially and psychologically rewarding, one must remain focused on the task at hand, and balance teaching (or any job responsibilities) along with the dissertation project. Furthermore, one must discriminate among various other important tasks and concerns and only focus on high leverage activities in order to successfully finish the doctoral dissertation. Remember that not completing the dissertation is the same as not having a doctorate degree. So, if you began the doctorate program to earn the degree, then it is an obligation to actually complete it and earn the terminal title.

Should One Worry About Grades?

The obvious answer is "yes." However, grade is not the ultimate objective or outcome of each course; learning is the goal. The major outcomes of each course tends to be area-specific knowledge, as well as becoming skilled in research methodologies and possibly getting a publication as a result of one's work in each course. However, it must be acknowledged that grades are one way to move forward and show credentials of success for a degree; therefore, it should not be denigrated. Grades are often seen as a measure of one's success or understanding of the content in a specific course. Your goal should be to be outcome-oriented to understand the content, which in return often helps one earn good grades. A professor once said that education is the one thing people are willing to pay for, and not get anything for their money. This can happen when the pursuit of higher grades takes precedence over reflection and truly understanding the material. In a graduate program there are many successful and intelligent people who are driven by high standards and many of them may be experts in a specific topic. So, in certain classes the experts are going to earn the top grades and everyone else will have to settle for the near top grades as per their performance. The grade will not always appear fair or in fact be fair; your focus should be to successfully move on to the next step and not necessarily "ace" each course. A person who has ten "B" grades will still be called a doctor, the same as a person who earned all "A" grades. They will both have the same privileges and rights as a result of their earned terminal degree.

Arguing over a grade that was based on the perception of the faculty is not always smart and, at times, just "down right" stupid due to its short-term orientation. This is not to say that one should not ask why a certain grade was awarded. Each student should know exactly where he or she stands for each assignment submission so he or she can improve in specific areas as per the recommendation of the faculty or other experts in the education profession. However, arguing over the fact that one should have earned a "B +" instead of a "B" or one should have earned an "A-" instead of a "B+" is not fruitful nor a good use of one's time. Remember that networking and interdependency means that one should focus on maintaining a good relationship with every person in one's profession. You may very well need this faculty member's assistance, vote, or guidance on the dissertation process or at a future date. You may need a reference in the future to secure a faculty position or you may need some coaching for a teaching assignment as a first time teacher or as a first-time administrator, such as a director, an Associate Dean or a Dean in the coming decades.

Project Management Considerations

Doctoral students should have excellent time and project management skills as they are the driver of their dissertation research. It is important that a doctoral student be outcome-oriented with any of the doctoral projects and to begin with the end objective in mind. Project management workshops can help doctoral students develop skills that will ensure that the dissertation project is completed on schedule and meets all requirements. Generally speaking, *project management* is the process of assembling and leading a team of people to plan, estimate, monitor, and drive the progress of a number of related tasks that result in a specific deliverable that must be accomplished on time, with approved resources, within budget, and in accordance with predetermined specifications. *A Project* is a set of related tasks designed to produce a particular deliverable within the boundaries of specified constraints on time, quality, and other resources. Of course, a dissertation by itself is a major project that requires a number of resources, including people on the team. Project managers generally complete the following tasks:

1. Define the project
2. Plan the project

3. Implement
4. Evaluate
5. Celebrate.

A project (such as a dissertation) is goal-oriented, consists of a set of deliverables, has connected and interrelated activities, and has some elements of uniqueness that can be implemented step by step and objectively (quantitatively) or subjectively (qualitatively) evaluated. Therefore, it is important to determine your project time requirements and exact deliverables; and remember that each task within the project should be:

- *S*pecific and focused.
- *M*easurable with regard to quality and quantity.
- *A*greed to by everyone on the team.
- *R*eachable, given the available resources.
- *T*imely and needed to achieve an end.

There is no need to get involved in tasks that appear interesting but have no overall value to your project or mission in life. The late father of modern management, Peter Drucker, is quoted as having said that "There is nothing so useless as doing efficiently that which should not be done at all." So, set SMART goals for each project and be sure to first complete those tasks that provide progress and movement toward the achievement of your objectives.

If you are a visual person, then you may holistically see the doctoral program as a set of projects and tasks using a Gantt chart. A Gantt chart is a bar chart that shows the relationship of a list of tasks to a calendar located at the top of the chart. A Gantt chart, which is a visual report, can further show tasks and dependencies, progress on each task, and it is easy to use. One can also visually determine the critical path toward the achievement of the doctoral degree for oneself. The critical path is the longest sequential series of tasks and deliverables from the start of the project to the end. Usually, a delay to a task or deliverable on the critical path will cause a delay to the project completion time. The Program Evaluation Review Technique (PERT) and the Critical Path Method (CPM) are network planning tools that can help one see how activities are interrelated. As a project manager, you can use the Work Breakdown Structure concept. Work Breakdown Structure (WBS) helps organize your project by breaking down the overall project into "chunks" or specifics tasks that can be done in a specific period of time.

Inevitably, regardless of what process one uses to manage a project, work on any project that requires the direct and indirect cooperation of many individuals is likely to cause some conflict somewhere in the process. Conflict is the struggle that results when two or more individuals perceive a difference or incompatibility in their interests, values, or goals. Due to the politics involved, you do not want any of your committee members to be embarrassed or lose face in the achievement of your dissertation process. The goal is to have a win-win outcome for all. Of course, every interaction has a potential for conflict. So, as a doctoral student, you need to become an effective conflict manager as well. Conflict management is the process of dealing with conflicts in an effective manner by considering the long-term consequences and moving forward as appropriate to achieve a win-win solution. Try not to make a short-term decision at a cost of long-term benefits. Most conflicts will be "little issues" that may appear to temporarily get in the way of your progress in the dissertation completion process, and there is no reason to make them "big issues." However, if problems and challenges do occur, consider the following problem-solving steps and apply them as needed:

1. Identify the problem.
2. Generate alternative solutions.
3. Evaluate alternative solutions in terms of their long-term consequences.
4. Make a decision.
5. Implement the decision.
6. Follow-up or evaluate the results, if necessary.

In the conflict resolution and problem-solving processes, try not to offend anyone or cause undue stress or harm to anyone since such consequences are never effective for gaining everyone's cooperation. Regardless of the level of difficulty in the project, conflict or problem, remember to have fun, be positive, exercise good time management skills, thank and reward people for their cooperation, be a team player, be moral, and be exemplary. These are great qualities for any project manager and doctoral student.

Time Management Principles[11]

You have the talent to create your own future (first mentally and then physically through action). Author Thomas Wolfe tells us that "If a man has talent and cannot use it, he has failed. If he has talent and only uses half of it, he has partly failed. If he has a talent and learns somehow to use the whole of it, he has gloriously succeeded and has a satisfaction and a triumph few men ever know." A mission and vision of your future must be first created mentally before it can be created physically through action. Of course, the mission and vision should be achieved one project and one step at a time. The achievement of a doctoral degree is one objective made up of many projects and interrelated tasks.

Just "Because You Can" Syndrome

Beware of the *"because you can"* syndrome, as it can rob valuable time away from your day, week, month, and year. Many people become victims of the "because you can" syndrome because either they cannot say no to people or they do not have anything else to do that is worthwhile or purposeful. For example, let us say that your job is to manage the activities and efforts of 300 people (faculty and staff) to provide "quality education and excellent operational service" to 2,200 students. You are a very busy individual and this huge responsibility keeps you very busy. However, you also have ten years of corporate training experience in diversity and time management workshops for executives. Your "peer" colleague at the institution asks if you would be able to take some time to prepare and facilitate several training

---

[11] For more information about topics in this chapter, see *Cross-Cultural Change Management*, 2007 by Bahaudin G. Mujtaba; Llumina Press.

sessions for faculty members and a few for outside members of the community. You and your peers know that currently you are the best person at this institution for this type of a project due to your experience and this project must be a success. However, it is best to keep in mind that you do not have to take on this extra responsibility since this is not part of your job and your "peer" has no direct impact on your success at the institution. You enjoy training but also understand that preparing this material and facilitating them will take many valuable hours away from working with your own departmental tasks and colleagues to provide "quality education and excellent operational service." Furthermore, being involved in the preparation and facilitation of this training will not assist in your professional endeavor with this institution in any way, regardless of the success rate for the program. You also know that you will enjoy this project and the facilitation while pleasing another colleague by doing this huge favor for him/her; but you are also fully enjoying your own current responsibilities and the purposeful interaction with people in your department as well. Even though you can take on extra projects, you should say "no" since it will take much valuable time away from your important professional role in life. It would be nice to be involved if you had "free" time, but your priority is not in training anymore and it does not advance your professional role. "Just because you can," due to your past experiences with it, does not obligate you to be the person to take on this challenge. The same is true of "babysitting" for family members, driving friends to the airport, picking up nephews and nieces from soccer, going to the late night parties with friends simply because you don't want them to go alone, etc. when you don't have the time to do so. Remember, "just because you can" does not obligate you to do so. Bill Gates, one of the richest men on earth, can probably eliminate poverty and hunger in many small countries, at least temporarily, by donating a few billion dollars for resources. However, "just because he can" does not mean that he should if such a cause does not match his purpose in life. Mother Teresa, on the other side, devoted her life to assisting the elderly, poor and disadvantaged individuals in India because that was part of her mission in life. So, do not become a victim of "just because you can" syndrome by only taking on activities that add to your life's mission and important roles.

The moral of these examples is that just because one has the opportunity to do something does not mean one should do it. Instead, one should do only those things that match his/her mission in life. It is certainly okay to help someone who needs assistance, and it is perfectly fair to volunteer as a coach or as a mentor; but one should not do things that do not match one's values and purpose in life. Creating a mission statement for your life, identifying your five to six important current roles, identifying activities that help you progress toward your life's mission and important roles each week, and scheduling as well as implementing those activities each day will be the key to effective time management and avoiding the "just because you can" syndrome. Of course, one must use politically correct means of effectively avoiding it as to not hurt others' feelings while not becoming a victim oneself either. Harriet Woods, the American Politician, once said that "You can stand tall without standing on someone. You can be a victor without having victims."

Time Management Model: Important and Urgent

Generally speaking, "there are two days in the week about which and upon which I never worry. Two carefree days, kept sacredly free from fear and apprehension. One of these days is Yesterday... And the other... is Tomorrow" said author Robert Jones Burdette. Many individuals spend a large percentage of the days and nights worrying about either the past or the future and achieve very little in the present. The past is gone but it can offer learning when one reflects upon it consciously for a limited amount of time. The future has not come but one can plan for it accordingly. However, actions must be taken in the present and these actions should be geared toward what is important in one's life.

In effective time management, activities can be categorized and understood as important, urgent, not important, and not urgent. The following definitions and concept are foundational in time management and effective decision-making.

◊ *Urgent* – Urgent is defined as activities that have the appearance of needing immediate attention.

◊ *Important* – Important is defined as all those activities that contribute to life's goals and mission.

Activities that are important will always produce better outcomes in the long-term. However, some activities are both important and urgent so they must be completed first. Activities that are neither important nor urgent can be left alone if they do not hinder your mission in life. The German philosopher, Johann Goethe, said "every man has only enough strength to complete those activities that he is fully convinced are important." So, discover your important activities in order not to waste time on the unimportant things. Some discipline is required when it comes to time management. When it comes to discipline Jim Rohn, motivational speaker and author, states "We must all suffer one of two things: the pain of discipline or the pain of regret or disappointment." Properly planning for doing what is important leaves no excuses for not achieving them. With regard to excuses Bob Burg, author and speaker, once said "One trademark of successful people is that they don't let excuses deter them. They determine what it is they need to do - and then do it." So, focus on what is important by going in that direction one step at a time.

Conscious thinking, deep reflection, prioritizing according to one's mission, and planning improves time management skills which is all about managing the needed activities in the allotted time. Most of us have experienced the difficulties of balancing available time with the many commitments and opportunities we would like to fulfill. Each day, managers are bombarded by a multitude of tasks and demands in a setting of frequent interruptions, crisis and unexpected events. It can be easy to lose track of objectives and fall prey to what experts identify as "time wasters." For many of us, time is probably dominated by other people and/or by nonessential activities rather our own "big rocks." Through the personal benefits of improved focus, flexibility, coordination, control, and planning everyone can become better time managers. The following are quick tips on how to better manage scarce time:

◊ Do say "No" when others' requests will divert you from more important work toward your "big rocks" that you should be doing.

◊ Don't get bogged down in details and routines that should be left to others.

◊ Do establish a system for screening your telephone calls.
◊ Don't let "drop in" or unannounced visitors use too much of your time.
◊ Do prioritize work tasks in order of their importance and urgency.
◊ Don't become "calendar bound" by losing control of your schedule or other important opportunities that surface. Need to adapt daily.
◊ Do work tasks in their order of priority by focusing on the important first.
◊ Do take the time to laugh often with your friends and family members. Valerie Bell, author, says "Shared laughter is like family glue. It is the stuff of family well-being and all-is-well thoughts. It brings us together as few other things can."

Time management is important because more time for research on complex problems may equal better decisions. In some cases, having more time for proper research can prevent problems and disasters from taking place.

There is a wise statement about misuse of social time and it says: "great minds discuss ideas, average minds discuss events, small minds discuss people, and very small minds discuss themselves." There is no reason for anyone to waste time complaining about others. For busy researchers, educators, and managers, understanding the concepts behind the following terms is important in effective time management.

◊ *Murphy's Law*: What can happen, will happen. Take the time to plan and provide plenty of opportunities for activities that you want to happen in your life. Invite those activities and tasks that will drive your purpose of life and your mission in the right direction.
◊ *Pareto Law*: It states that 80% of the results flow from 20% of the activities. So, some activities have much more impact than others and we can call them "High leverage activities" or "big rocks."
◊ *Parkinson's Law*: It states that work expands to fill the time available to complete the job. The safeguard for this is to set realistic deadlines, to train people appropriately and trust them to do their jobs the right way and to be ethical about its completion.
◊ *True North*: The North Star at night helps pilots see the north direction. Faith, thinking, hope, and education are our true north star, our yardstick, our ruler, our inspector, and our guide, which can measure our effectiveness to see whether we are on the right path or not. So, organize your life and execute your actions around your priorities according to the mission and purpose of your life, and that objective becomes the essence of time management.

Change Management Skills

Change, in its simplest form, is the art of making things different. It is a modification to the way things are, or how things are done. In other words, change is a modification to the status quo. *Change* is the process of turning things from one state to another. *Change management,* then, is the art of effectively and efficiently making things different. Change is not something that only top executives or community leaders decide to bring about. Change is brought about often by outside forces that are beyond one's immediate control. It is driven by technological advancements, a better workforce, globalization, diversity, natural environmental forces, and other variables that one may not be able to fully control. Therefore, human beings are pressured into adapting with these changes and making the best of each change. There are at least three types of change which are "passive or natural," "mandated," and "self-generated" that affect individuals throughout their lives.

1. *Passive or natural changes* are those changes that are not noticeable at the personal level but nonetheless do take place, i.e. growing, crawling, walking, etc.

2. *Mandated changes* come from top down to the individual level in the form of laws, demands and/or policies.

3. *Self-generated or proactive change* is usually initiated by an individual, a team or an organization. Its successful implementation needs research, support, reliability, reasons, credibility, and/or strong leadership.

People learn or adapt to the passive or natural changes by osmosis and usually there are not many things one can do to prevent or stop these changes. For example, parents and care-takers usually attempt to help or encourage children to walk or crawl but these will take place regardless of outside forces or influences. This passive change can be very dangerous at the organizational level because often top executives are caught by surprise when they are not prepared for it. Mandated changes are usually decided upon by the top people of the society or an organization to prevent chaotic situations from taking place. For example, having traffic rules saves many lives while not having such general rules can be very costly. These are usually based on the Golden Rule principle which states that one should do unto others as he or she would have them do unto him or her. Finally, the self-generated changes are the best types and usually the most difficult to deal with in the initial states. It is the self-generated changes that create the planned results in the long-term. Self-generated changes are proactive and value-driven. Therefore, they can be goal oriented and focused toward self-chosen ends and targets. This deals with Newton's principle of physics, which states that a body in motion moving to a certain path tends to stay in motion in that path until acted upon by outside forces. So, if you generate purposeful changes toward certain goals then you are likely to get those results unless you are confronted by resistance which cannot be overcome.

One of the most stressful situations throughout the world, especially in the Untied States, is balancing work and family lives because while people may value being connected to their families they often may be away from them in order to work and produce the basic necessities of life in order to have a family. This is why many professionals plan to work and go to school at the same time to get more advanced education. As the Proverb states, "Those who don't find time for exercise will have to find time for illness." Those who don't find time to gain the right skills and get the education needed will have to spend time dealing with much resistance when managing change. For example, education in general "pays" personally and financially, because, according to the Bureau of Labor Statistics, those with a Bachelor's Degree will earn about $2.1 million over their work life while those with a Master's Degree will earn 20% more to a total of $2.5 million. One of the majors changes since 1992 has been the 33% increase in the number of college graduates and the fact that more fields now require a Master's Degree for career advancement. Acquiring more education can afford one more respect from one's colleagues and employees, while equipping one to make better decisions in both the planning and execution stages of change. For example, those who are in human resources departments tend to get more formal certifications and advanced degrees in specialized fields for effective human development and change management. According to Pamela Babcock (September 2005), author of the article entitled "*A Calling for Change*," more company leaders are trying to make human resources a truly global function so the department's professionals can always be a strategic partner. She stated that experts want the HR function to be more transformational as it involves transitioning people through major changes. Babcock (2005) wrote that "CEOs often want HR to help shape organizational culture, or to place more emphasis on executive development and succession planning." Babcock advised HR professionals in charge of managing change to keep in mind that "Just because the CEO is ready for a change doesn't mean everyone else is ready to accept a transformation." Therefore, one must not assume that everyone wants change and welcomes it. As such, change agents must try to get others to "buy-in" to the new change before beginning the implementation process. It is also critical to remember, Babcock stated that, "Change can be stressful and disruptive for anyone." Effective change management through the human resources personnel and change agents requires the right skill sets and an approach that balances speed with inclusiveness and collaboration since engaging everyone impacted by the change in the system is critical if the change is to be sustained. The attributes require to bring about effective change include integrity, a proven track record, leadership skills, the ability to capture the respect of other business leaders, and a vision for what the future can be. Other important traits that change agents need to possess are financial acumen and great presentation skills in one-on-one format and to large audiences (Babcock, 2005). Overall, change agents need to initially learn the organization's culture and assess its problems by getting the company's pulse and developing a good relationship with leaders and their staff.

Managing Change

Managing change means managing human behavior - robots, machines, and computers are very easy to change and these machines do not resist change. It appears that the main reason change implementation is difficult is because people are resistant to it. According to Lewin (1947), there are three general steps that must be followed to successfully manage change; unfreeze, change, and refreeze. To unfreeze, the individual must *see* the need to change and be motivated to change. In an organization, it falls on management to provoke and inspire individuals to see the need for change. From an individual perspective, the ability to see the need for change is also critical. Seeing this need in a proactive manner instead of a reactive approach may mean have a huge positive financial impact. More than likely everyone has witnessed people who seem to always see what is coming on the horizon and are proactive in reacting to it while others wait and hope for the best. Often times they are just waiting for the inevitable. Continuing education can be a critical component to successfully seeing beyond the horizon. This also has the added benefit of not only helping the individual but of also helping the organization. One of the most noteworthy assets an organization has is the ability to adapt to the increasing pace of competition and organizational changes are employees who are eager to acquire new knowledge and skills (Maurer, 2001; Maurer, Pierce, & Shore, 2002). In learning organizations, individuals adopt lifelong learning attitudes, which are vital to competing in the postmodern marketplace. Learning organizations specialize in creating, acquiring, and transferring knowledge throughout the workforce (Garvin, 1998). Learning organizations, according to Senge (1990), are "organizations where people continually expand their capacity to create the results they truly desire, where new and expansive patterns of thinking are nurtured, where collective aspiration is set free, and where people are continually learning how to learn together" (p. 3). In fact, Bassi and McMurrer (2004) found that companies that spend aggressively on developmental activities outperform the S&P 500 by 4.6%.

Individuals in learning organizations take a "systems approach" to problem solving. One aspect of a systems approach is the ability to determine the end state and maintain the belief that the desired result will be accomplished. The ability to *see* the desired end state and believe it is achievable is well documented in the literature. This theory has been labeled the Pygmalion effect, self-fulfilling prophecy, or the Thomas theorem (Merton, 1948). As Thomas (1923) characterized it, "if men define situations as real, they are real in their consequences" (para. 1). The Pygmalion effect has been studied most often in educational environments where an educator believes that a student can achieve a certain goal or standard and consistently conveys that message to the student. The student will take this confidence and will ultimately behave and/or achieve what the educator expects (Murphy, Campbell, & Garavan, 1999; White & Locke, 2000). While this theory has been studied primarily in educational environments, it has also been discussed in religious (Tozer, 1961) and business situations (Reynolds, 2002). In business environments, Reynolds (2002) observed that the Pygmalion effect occurs in both positive and negative situations where a leader's expectations, either positive or negative, had a comparable effect on employee performance.

Another aspect of a learning organization is the ability to question the status quo. Questioning of an organization's espoused values or assumptions leads to an atmosphere conducive to learning, leading to developing a learning organization. Merton (1948) found that "only when the original assumption is questioned and a new definition of the situation introduced, does the consequent from of events give the lie to the assumption. Only then does the belief no longer father the reality" (p. 197). Senge (1990) stated that learning organizations were those organizations that were able to continually shape their own future. Two of Senge's (1990) five disciplines of a successful learning organization are directly related to continuous learning by an organization's employees: personal learning and team learning. Personal mastery is the ability, according to Senge (1990), to continually create what matters to that individual. Associated with personal mastery is team learning. Team learning is realized when individuals are learning and are not only free but encouraged to question organizational assumptions. In some situations this actually leads to additional conflict within an organization. "Contrary to popular myth, great teams are not characterized by an absence of conflict. On the contrary, in my experience, one of the most reliable indicators of a team that is continually learning is the visible conflict of ideas" (Senge, 1990, p. 249).

Therefore, change management is about helping people understand the need for change, accept change, implement change, and to become advocates of change. Change management takes more than knowing how to create function trees, models, Pareto or Gantt charts, dazzling presentations, activity lists, or making fishbone diagrams to determine how work should be performed. Change managers must be able to not only help and influence people at all levels to overcome their resistance to change but also to gain their consensus for implementing it quickly. Change is naturally difficult for everyone because it causes people to move away from their comfort zone into unfamiliar territory. For example, if people are asked to fold their arms the opposite of how they usually fold their arms then it might feel uncomfortable to them. This change can be awkward, and can cause people to think whether they are doing it right or wrong, whether they are doing it efficiently, whether this change has a purpose to it or not, and whether they are doing it for the right reasons. Change management means controlling the elements involved in the change process, knowing why change is needed, proactively planning for change, understanding the phases of change, understanding the roles of communication and involvement in the change process, learning how to appreciate and reduce resistance positively, and how to create a fire within each person through clear values and a meaningful mission statement in order to make change a successful reality.

As effective leaders and change managers, we need to listen intently to the concerns of all stakeholders, acknowledge them, and then act accordingly to "walk our talks." Those who are doing the job and those who are affected by the final products and/or services can provide helpful clues for identifying, interpreting, facilitating, and implementing change. Effective change management requires dealing with change in the long term by being patient, proactive and resilient. While some managers who focus on short-term results to provide quick pain relief medication to deal with the symptoms of change on temporary basis, it is not very effective in the long run.

Many organizations are suffering from the delay of adapting to change and from the delay of satisfying customers' expectations. Companies are losing market share and profit margins because they are unable to keep up with the increasing rate of customer expectations. The faster individuals and organizations change, the more they will minimize their losses in the industry. In order to stay competitive in any industry, employees need to create innovative ways of adapting faster than before. Corporate executives need to realize that a firm's success depends on its flexibility to quickly internalize, adapt and meet customer expectations better than its competitors. This realization has focused many corporate executives to become better change managers and to adapt as well as accept change as quickly as possible.

Change, however, can be positive or negative. It may affect one for the good or perhaps somewhat negatively, but that is not a good reason to view change as negative because one cannot be sure of the situation or its future results. Also, one should keep in mind what actually happens does not necessarily "make or break" a person but it is one's response to the situation that can make or break a person. So, there are changes that will affect one positively, and then there are changes that can affect one negatively. For example, getting married, promotions, moving to one's dream home, and going to high school or college are considered to be positive changes. While deaths, accidents, demotions, getting laid-off from a good position, and other unexpected or traumatic changes are considered to be negative changes that require patience and future oriented focus in order to overcome their negative side effects. Both positive as well as negative change can be very stressful and may cause an individual to respond negatively to it. Change, especially if it is unexpected, can be scary, difficult to deal with or accept, cumbersome, and at times very frustrating. Human beings are all expected to die sooner or later, but most people are not properly prepared to deal with such circumstances appropriately. Accidents, illness, violence, and mature age take the lives of people every day. This can be difficult emotionally and financially, especially if people are not prepared. According to the National Funeral Directors Association and based on personal experiences, the average cost of a funeral in the United States is running between $5,000 to $10,000 these days. From an organizational perspective, there are numerous companies that are using "reduction in force" strategies to become more competitive or just to survive, which causes much frustration to many people both emotionally and financially. However, human beings have dealt with change from the beginning of time, and the only difference is that now it comes much faster than it has ever come. Therefore, people need to learn to adapt to change as quickly as possible in order to minimize or eliminate the negative impact of change. Generally, there are two responses to change from a company or individual perspective: reactive and proactive.

Proactive and Reactive Responses

Reactive. Reactive responses are unplanned and their purpose is to catch-up with the industry or competition before the firm, or industry along with the people, are out of the "picture." Reactive responses are negative because they are often based on emotions, feelings, and circumstances without much consideration for or reflection on one's mission or purpose in life. Reactive companies and people are usually on the defensive and this can lead people to live lives that are based on urgency. In this situation, people are driven into many directions which creates a very stressful life because they cannot find time to plan.

Proactive. Proactive people and firms are opportunity-minded, they plan for the future as much as possible, and they plan for and expect change. Proactive people are visionaries and see things from a larger perspective. They see things from a bird's eye view as well as a worm's eye view or as Senge (1990) wrote, they see the forest *and* the trees. Proactive responses are anticipated, planned and aligned with the company or one's personal purpose, and mission in life. Proactive people do not resist or meet change through a head-on collision. Part of this proactive planning for employees in the current organizational atmosphere may be to gain additional training or advanced degrees. Handy (1995) introduced the concept of portfolio workers which he linked to artists or photographers who have a portfolio of past work they have completed. In this same way, he argued, other professional people need to look for jobs and opportunities to enhance their portfolio to better compete in today's ever changing marketplace. When proactive people encounter change, they move from having a point of view to a viewing point in order to see all the possibilities and perspectives of change. They use change to their advantage and thrive on it similar to martial artists who go along with change in the same direction and simultaneously gain more power and fluidity as they strike the target. Proactivity allows a person to turn a life of work into a work of art. Proactive people do what they love and consequently love what they do. Therefore, they never have to "go to work" because they choose to do things they love and things they want to accomplish for personal joy.

Change is one thing that employees of national and international firms can be certain about in today's environment. Highly effective individuals are prepared to constantly accommodate change. Highly effective individuals know that it is not change that hurts or makes one feel bad in the long-term; but it is one's response to change that really hurts the future. Change happens and then its negative affect can be over faster if, and only if, we allow ourselves to focus on the future and plan to make the best of it rather than moaning about the past. The leaders of today need to remain open and flexible in order to deal with *planned and unplanned changes* that will be affecting them and their organizations. Sometimes people know about a policy or technology which will be implemented and its prospective benefits are clear and known to everyone. Therefore, employees can purposely plan to deal with such changes appropriately and people will not be shocked because they were expecting change. However, individual employees face many unplanned changes which require them to adapt without much prior planning. Obviously, it would be helpful to forecast change and plan accordingly, but unfortunately that is not always possible. Therefore, employees need to be prepared and to adapt to the unplanned changes that affect them from all directions of life.

Stress Management Skills

The stress people experience today is much more intense than what was experienced by previous generations of the workforce. According to experts, stress is a reaction to change and the body's mental, emotional, and physiological response to anxiety-producing events and situations. According to *"Conquering Stress,"* a little book by KRS Edstrom (1993), less stress equals more success in whatever one does. Stress is basically what one thinks it is and what one perceives it to be. Stress is the epidemic of twenty-first century's hectic work life. While stress has been around since the days of Adam and Eve, the increased emphasis on stress is due to the fact that too much of it can cause major physical, psychological, and behavioral illnesses. One must learn to proactively fight stress, flee it, and "flow" with it, in order to effectively deal with the changes that cause stress. Nearly 75% of Americans describe their jobs as successful and 34% have considered quitting their jobs due to high levels of stress (Edstrom, 1993). Research shows that 90% of workers tend to experience high levels of stress at least once each week and over 75% of all visits to primary-care physicians are stress-related disorders (Edstrom, 1993). Over 112 million Americans take medications for stress-related illnesses and symptoms. Stress costs American employers over $200 billion each year in absenteeism, lost productivity, accidents, and medical insurance; and over 60% of industrial accidents are incurred by extreme levels of perceived stress (Edstrom, 1993). It is extremely important that change agents and global employees learn effective means of conquering stress and managing it, before it leads to any type of illness, absenteeism, loss of productivity, accidents, or mental problems.

Stress, an unavoidable consequence of life, occurs at all levels in organizations as a result of many factors including time pressures, personnel conflicts, and the quantity of work expected to be completed at a given time. According to Stephen Robbins (2001), *stress* is a dynamic condition where one is confronted with either an opportunity, constraint, or a demand for which the outcome is perceived to be uncertain and important. These dynamic conditions, when not managed effectively, can lead to physiological, psychological, and behavioral symptoms. Hans Selye, known as the Father of Stress Management, said that stress is the "wear and tear" on the body that occurs in daily life; more specifically, stress is "the nonspecific response of the body to any demand made upon it" (*The Stress of Life*, 1976). The word "nonspecific" implies that everyone responds differently to stress at different stages of his or her life. The body goes through many changes when under stress, including physical changes. Originally, these physical changes served to protect early humans against environmental stressors: "the fight or flight syndrome."

The Fight or Flight Syndrome. The "fight or flight syndrome" is credited to Walter Cannon who taught that when faced with an enemy in the environment, animals and early humans had to muster their strength to do one of two things: run away or stand and fight. Therefore, the body's physical reactions during stress help prepare people for fight or flight. Some of the most common physical changes are as follows: increased heart rate, increased respiration rate, increased skin perspiration, increased dilation of the pupils, increased blood pressure, increased muscle strength, decreased gastric functioning, decreased abdominal and surface blood flow, and increased secretion of adrenaline. Unfortunately, today, people cannot always fight or run away, so the chemical reactions of the body to stress make people sick instead.

The General Adaptation Syndrome (GAS). Hans Selye proposed that stress goes through three stages that together make up the General Adaptation Syndrome. *Stage one* is the alarm stage. At this point, the stressor has just been recognized and the body has become mobilized for fight or flight. The body's homeostasis (normal balance) is disrupted and internal organs become ready for action. *Stage two*, the resistance stage, is the longest stage of the GAS. It begins when the body is persistently exposed to the stressor. The body struggles to resist the alarm reactions and to return to a homeostatic stage. *Stage three,* the exhaustion stage, occurs if stress continues longer than the body can resist. At this stage, organ systems break down. The body can no longer adapt to the stress load placed on it; and the result of the exhaustion stage is a disease of adaptation such as ulcers or cardiovascular disease.

According to estimates, about 50-80 percent of all physical diseases tend to be stress-related. Stress is believed to be a principal cause of many cardiovascular diseases, perhaps the number one killer in "workaholic" cultures (for example, in the United States of America). It also may be a main contributing factor to the development of cancer, the number two killer in the United States. Also, stress can place one at higher risk for diabetes, ulcers, asthma, migraine headaches, skin disorders, epilepsy, and sexual dysfunction. Each of these diseases, and a host of others, can be psychosomatic in nature; that is, it is initially either caused or exacerbated by mental conditions such as stress.

Subjective effects of stress include feelings of anxiety, aggression, frustration, guilt, or shame. Individuals are also apt to feel irritable, moody, tired, tense, nervous, or lonely.

Behavioral effects of stress represent readily visible changes in a person's behavior. Among these effects are things such as increased accidents, use of illegal drugs or alcohol, outlandish or argumentative behavior, laughter out of context, very excitable moods, and/or eating to excess.

Cognitive effects refer to diminished mental ability, and may include such effects as impaired judgment, rash decisions, forgetfulness, and/or hypersensitivity to criticism.

Organizational effects take the form of absenteeism, diminished productivity, high turnover, poor relations with workers, and/or general job dissatisfaction. Stress wreaks havoc on organizational productivity. Highly stressed employees, based on personal experience, seem to have more frequent accidents, are often irritable, and are unable to cope with daily situations.

Another organizational consequence that has received much interest is corporate liability for employees whose illness is linked to job stress. Some people are suing and winning legal cases where work-related stressors cause burnout. Burnout is the work-related equivalent of a nervous breakdown. The burned-out employee has succumbed to long, continuous stress, and consequently is no longer able to function at a reasonable level of effectiveness. Where does all this stress come from? One can divide general causes of stress into at least three categories: environmental, personal, and sudden stressors. *Environmental* stressors include conditions in the environment that cause mental or physical stress. These conditions include noise, pollution, temperature, diet, toxins, and drugs. *Personal* stressors include factors, such as family or financial problems, as well as amounts of change with which a person has to cope. *Sudden* stressors refer to intense stimuli, such as narrowly averting an automobile accident, or the surge of nervous energy felt when someone startles or scares one unexpectedly.

As mentioned by Pritchett and Pound, as well as other experts, there are numerous forces driving major changes that impact people's day-to-day activities; and the major forces seem to be people, technology, information, innovation, and globalization. Instead of making the wrong assumptions in this new economy, it is perhaps more productive to surrender to upcoming changes by aligning one's behavior and expectations with it, while using the changes to one's advantage. Pritchett and Pound, in the survival guide, suggest to everyone that one not should expect others to come along and relieve one's stress. Instead, today's professionals should put themselves in charge of managing the dynamic pressure since they are probably the best persons in their lives who will be able to do much to lighten their psychological load. When you seem to be going against the tides or against the whole world, just think of what Robert Orben said: "Sometimes I get the feeling that the whole world is against me, but deep down I know that is not true as some of the smaller countries are neutral."

Stress Management Techniques

Like beginning anything new, starting a doctoral program or a new job brings with it additional stress. Choices of personal stress management techniques depend on the individual's personality. Four of the most popular techniques, are time management, physical exercise, biofeedback, and meditation. *Time management* helps one control stress by better organizing time and setting priorities. *Physical exercise* is an appropriate substitute for the fight or flight response of long ago. It provides a physical release for the chemical reactions caused by stress. Exercise not only "burns off" the physical effects of stress but also strengthens the body's organ systems to be better able to withstand stress. *Biofeedback* refers to a number of techniques that give concrete feedback to the individual regarding bodily functions such as pulse rate, blood pressure, body temperature, and muscle tension. By being cognizant of these physical phenomena, one can learn to control them, thus bringing the body to a more relaxed state. *Meditation* encompasses a variety of mental exercises that focus one's attention on something other than daily thoughts. Regardless of the type of meditation, it is remarkably useful in lessening one's sensory reactivity and in quieting the stress response. Best of all, when practiced with some regularity, meditation has a carryover effect; that is, it lowers one's normal reactivity even when not actively meditating.

There are at least three different organizational stress management strategies. Job redesign strategies start with an effort to determine what is causing job stress and then proceed to change the job so as to relieve this stress. Overload is often found to be a chief contributor. Overload may be a particular issue for non-traditional students who continue to work 8 hours, or more, a day and fit doctoral courses and family time in the remaining hours. While it may be difficult, fitting in some time off, even if it is only a few hours a week, where your mind can be off work, school, papers, or other homework is important. Another way to handle the additional stress school can bring is to set a ridged schedule of reading and writing and sticking to it. From an organizational perspective, supervisors may follow one of several strategies. Jobs can be redesigned in such a way that less coordination of effort is needed and thus less information processing is required. Alternately, supervisors could identify liaisons who are responsible for coordination efforts, and improve management information systems to provide what is needed at the appropriate time. In other cases jobs may be frustrating because of lack of decision-making authority. Traditional job enrichment approaches can work well because they give workers increased responsibility for decisions in their work area.

Environmental reengineering focuses on changing the physical environment by reducing stressors such as lighting, temperature, noise, vibration, and toxins. Supervisors might adopt one of two strategies for dealing with these stressors.

1. The first concentrates on protecting the workers from the negative consequences of the stressors: workers are required to wear goggles, earplugs, or masks. This strategy is often resisted by some workers due to habit patterns and must be firmly enforced by the supervisor.

2. The second strategy focuses on lessening the negative environmental stressors by reducing noise, improving lighting, and lessening the exposure to toxins. This latter choice is far more acceptable as a stress reducing alternative, but it rests largely on a company's economic analysis of costs

and benefits. Managers follow this alternative whenever possible instead of waiting for court settlements that force companies into compliance.

Of all corporate stress management efforts, wellness programs have been receiving the most attention in recent years. Corporate wellness is part of the trend to be concerned about the total human being. Programs vary from companies that shuttle employees back and forth to a local health spa during lunch hour, to those that install their own health spa facilities complete with nutritional experts and meditation rooms.

Type A Behavior

Friedman and Rosenman, cardiologists, provided the famous profile of a high stress individual known as a Type A Personality. This behavior pattern is highly correlated to coronary heart disease and is typified by such characteristics as:
1. Always moving, walking, and/or eating rapidly.
2. Feeling impatient with anyone who is moving "slowly," or not talking about something of interest to him / her.
3. Indulging in polyphasic activity--that is, doing two or three things at the same time.
4. Feeling unable to relax or abstain from working.
5. Trying to accomplish more and more things in less and less time.

The Type A person is in a constant race against time, the stereotypical "workaholic." People of this personality type can cause stress not only for themselves, but also for those around them. Friedman and Rosenman described the Type B personality as a low stress individual with varied interests, and a relaxed but active approach to life. Spera and Lanto (1997) provided the following description of Type A and Type B personalities.

TYPE A's	TYPE B's
Always in a hurry	Seldom in a hurry
Does several things at once	Does one thing at a time
Speaks, walks, and gestures rapidly and forcefully	Speaks, walks, and gestures slowly and calmly
Works late, brings work home	Works regular hours
Likes things clear-cut	Can tolerate ambiguity
Listens impatiently	Listens patiently
Easily angered	Slow to anger
Hard-driving, aggressive	Easygoing, nonassertive
Competitive, striving	Noncompetitive, satisfied
Expresses feelings easily	Tends to bottle feelings up
Restless, unable to relax	Enjoys relaxing, doing nothing

Should everyone strive to be a Type B? Not necessarily. Some Type A personalities seem to thrive on a hectic pace and actually feel invigorated by the pressure of time urgency. New evidence seems to indicate a difference between coronary-prone Type A's and their healthier cohorts. Those who combine their Type A tendencies with hostility and anger seem to be the most likely to suffer serious health problems. Overall, an individual's response to stress is not predetermined by his or her gender, personality type or body size. The reality is that most people are a blend of both types of personalities and respond differently to similar circumstance at different stages of their lives.

Summary

Change and stress are a normal part of life. This is as much true in higher education as it is in the workplace. Most achievement-oriented individuals are likely to be busy professionals who are never totally happy with their current status and continually set different goals and milestones for themselves. Such pressures can be very challenging and stressful. As such, project management, time management, stress management, and change management and conflict management skills, which were briefly discussed in this chapter, are essential for all doctoral scholars and professionals in the workplace. In any case, one should always remember to focus on what is important, and then work on other tasks that appear urgent.

CHAPTER SIX

6 – Passing the Comprehensive Exam

A ssessment is an important part of higher education. All graduate schools and colleges are likely to have various forms of assessments, such as comprehensive exams, oral defense, dissertation, and/or peer-reviewed publication requirements to show that they are achieving what they promise to deliver. Assessment is a form of a measurement to improve and hold oneself accountable to outcomes that were chosen for achievement.

Integrating a systematic testing and evaluation plan into the curriculum for student learning and learning assessment is a basic necessity in today's competitive world of education. Fortunately, many educators and administrators have successfully implemented effective testing and evaluation methods both on campus and in their distance education programs. However, much more may need to be done to make this an ongoing process of continually enhancing the programs holistically and accommodating for multiple intelligences when testing doctoral candidates. Consequently, administrators should focus on the development, assessment, and implementation of comprehensive testing and evaluation strategies in their curriculums (online, on-ground, and blended formats of distance as well as traditional offerings), while focusing on effectively achieving learning outcomes equally well in all modalities.

Multiple Intelligences[12]

The fact that a person completes a college program, earns a masters degree, and gets accepted into a doctoral program represents high levels of academic intelligence. It is not just "book smarts" that make a person successful in academia. One must also work on mastering and strengthening his or her ability to get along with others and influence them toward cooperation and teamwork. Social and interpersonal skills are important elements of every person's personal and

---

[12] Coauthored with Stefanie Wilson, University of Hawaii.

professional success. Everyone should understand emotional intelligence and work on increasing his or her emotional and social intelligence quotient (EQ/IQ). Emotional intelligence is basically the capacity to know one-self and others. Emotional intelligence is about being able to effectively work and get along with others. It has been said that IQ contributes about 10% to a person's success in life, wisdom and knowledge contributes about 25%, and emotional intelligence contributes about 65% to one's personal and professional accomplishments. Through internal reflections and values clarification, one can further understand one's academic goals. Also, by learning various social and interpersonal skills, one can become skilled at winning and influencing more friends in the academic environments.

A doctoral researcher can increase his or her emotional intelligence through self-awareness, managing emotions and having self-control, motivating others, showing empathy, and effectively handling relationships. *Self-awareness* means observing oneself, learning and gaining relevant values and behaviors. *Managing emotions* mean handling feelings correctly so that they are appropriate for the situation and people involved. *Motivating* oneself requires channeling emotions in the service of a goal; motivating oneself requires having emotional self control. *Empathy* requires showing sensitivity to other's feelings and concerns and their perspective; it also means appreciating the differences in how people feel about things. Finally, *handling relationships* effectively means managing emotions in others; as well as gaining social competence and social skills on a continuous basis. Emotional intelligence is basically a type of social intelligence that requires the ability to monitor one's own feelings as well other's emotions, while considering factual information and other situational variables to guide one's thinking and decisions. These characteristics associated with emotional intelligence are the essence of academic success, leadership, and continuous learning.

Some scientists believe that "people smarts" are wired into each person's brain system. Daniel Goleman, in his 2006 article entitled "*Can you raise your social IQ?*" states that "Ideas about intelligence are being frantically revised as science discovers brain systems that make us smart in ways that have little or nothing to do with traditional IQ." Goleman states that empathy and social skills are two of the main ingredients for social intelligence. Empathy and social skills are inclusive of being able to make an effective first impression and getting a good sense of people's feelings and intentions. According to Goleman (2006), the "Social brain" engages when people are interacting, thereby creating a back-and-forth communication that keeps encounters on track and makes emotions contagious. For example, the brain-to-brain connection between two individuals coordinate the timing of laughter among them as it does the speed of a romantic kiss between two people who are physically and emotionally attracted to each other.

While it is true that people are intrinsically born with certain predetermined social IQ, Goleman (2006) says, everyone is able to improve on it. For example, Goleman recommends the following essential elements for developing better listening skills which are important for having empathy:

- *Commit yourself to real change*. Think about how effective listening could enhance your relationship with others in the community, family and work environments.

- *Get feedback from people who know you well and those that you admire or respect.* How do they think you can listen more effectively is one question that you can ask them. Model after great performers and great listeners in your life.
- *Be watchful.* When you are most likely to trigger a habit that you are trying to change, consciously break the habit by responding as you have already changed the behavior.
- *Use failures as opportunities.* Each time you revert to an old habit, think about how you could handle that same situation differently the next time.
- *Keep practicing.* All of life can be a laboratory for practice and experience. Learning as much as you can with each experience and don't be afraid to try new approaches and new motivations.

To be successful, doctoral students need to commit themselves to real change, listen well, get feedback from people who know them well, model after great performers, be watchful of their ineffective habits, learn from their experiences by using failures as opportunities, and practicing their research results and findings. Doctoral students as well as doctoral graduates should regularly "sharpen their saw" and stay abreast of updated or new information in their areas of expertise by reading new research and articles on a regular basis.

Assessment and Education

Public and private colleges are viewed as public property; and this view reflects the centrality of the American institutions today, said Carol Christ who is the president of Smith College and a former provost of the University of California at Berkeley (Forum, 2004). She further stated that "If accountability is our end, then the means to that end lie in an ethic of greater transparency…we in colleges must be more open about our business practices and in our governance." To this end, the Chronicles of Higher Education published a forum on its September 3rd issue titled *"How Can Colleges Prove They're Doing Their Jobs?"* which focused on accountability and assessment. The forum published thoughts and views from experts on accountability and assessment which included the following general topics: we need an honest conversation, no less than a cultural shift, a more systematic approach, focus on a larger context, the word 'public' is the key, and strive for openness (Forum, 2004). Charles Reed and Edward Rust Jr. suggested that "colleges should define goals for student learning and provide evidence that they have met them" (Forum, 2004). Material in the forum pointed out that "Private colleges aren't immune to calls for greater accountability…with tuitions continually rising, students, parents, and other constituencies are demanding proof that students are getting what they are paying for and learning what they need to know." So, some strategic planning, changes for the better, and documentation of improvement are needed in order for business schools to successfully move forward.

Gary Hamel, visiting professor of strategic and international management at the London Business School, stated that "business schools can be notorious institutions of habit" which has served them well for over a century but it is not going to get them through the next decade if they do not bring about appropriate changes. Business strategists in academia offer many suggestions for modern business schools wishing to be successful in today's technology-driven environment including that they need to defy conventions, be innovative and try different strategies to get better results, not follow fads, create new competitive contexts, go beyond doing research by actually experimenting, globalize the curriculum and its focus, and form the future instead of just following it (Westerbeck, 2004). Change is occurring faster than it has during any time in our history. This is as true in business/organizational environments as it is in academic environments. Higher education institutions should be creating meaningful change if they are to survive and thrive in the world of demanding stakeholders. This change must be driven based on the assessment of what the school claimed to deliver per its mission and its progress or intended application. Such assessment should be systematic, progressive, formal, and institution-wide if the organization is to receive a benefit from it. The role of learning assessment and evaluation to a university's future success is important for its survival. For example, for a teaching institution, the primary measure of learning would be the degree to which students actually learn the intended material. Administrators could ask relevant questions to determine the effectiveness of each program. Do students know what they should know? Can students do what they should be able to do? Have students developed knowledge and skills appropriate to their professions? Was the achievement of students' personal and professional goals enhanced by their experience at the university? Furthermore, Faculty members should be asking such questions as: What did our students learn, and how well did they learn it? Do students simply acquire information, or do they learn to analyze, synthesize, and exercise critical judgment about the subject matter? Do they learn to write clear, grammatical, logical arguments? Do they learn tolerance for differing perspectives? Can they logically defend their own opinions in a rational way? Can they apply what they know to other areas of their work and life? Does their learning last beyond the end of the course and program? If a teaching university is able to demonstrate continuing accomplishment of such essential student-learning goals, the logical consequence will be the school's accomplishment of the other goals and purposes.

From an internal perspective, the integrity of the learning assessment and institutional evaluation processes are essential because the data generated provide the energy needed for continuous improvement of how things are processed. The data also provide the means through which the faculty and administration assess the degree to which goals related to student learning and achievement are being accomplished. In addition, they serve as a tool in identifying gaps and making improvements. Technology can greatly assist in teaching and learning when used effectively. However one could ask: Do cyberspace technologies make the teaching and learning processes more effective? Does technology help students learn the material more efficiently as shown by the results of a systematic assessment? Perhaps technology used in distance education can assist students to learn the intended outcomes differently and a different amount of it in a speedier manner. As proven by scientific management principles and Ford's assembly lines for producing Model-T cars in black color, machines can create efficiency. However, efficiency does not always translate into long-term stakeholder satisfaction, and research shows that people learn differently, but not always efficiently since each individual has his/her own learning style. While cyberspace technology can make learning efficient, educators must also focus on the student's need as well as the need for increased effectiveness. In other words, through systematic assessments, educators should determine if the technology is delivering the right results or the intended outcomes as effectively as available alternative methods. Of course, an effective assessment program requires a strategic plan for each curriculum and each program. The plans for assessing students' academic achievement in each program must then be put into action and evaluation for continuous improvement. The elements necessary for supporting such a strategic process include the functions of planning, assessment delivery, analysis of the result, reflection, recommendations, and eventually continuous improvement in order to close the loop for effective deployment and documentation of assessment for each program.

Corporate management development trainers know that they need to assess learning in terms of the course's stated objectives (exit competencies or learning outcomes) and be able to provide evidence that demonstrates the achievement of learning outcomes, in terms of application and better management, if they are to continue receiving funding for their workshops. The same principle of assessment also applies in the academic world regardless of whether one is teaching traditional adults students (full-time students) or non-traditional adult students (part-time students that are working professionals) completing their program through distance education modalities. Academicians know that taking the strategic plans for measuring and assessing student achievement, analyzing them for improvement purposes, and implementing the resulting analysis throughout the university can present opportunities and challenges for schools committed to a process improvement philosophy. Universities use a good variety of tools that support the model of planning, delivery, assessment, reflection, recommendation, and continuous improvement of student learning. However, none of the tools can take the place of a faculty member's key role in effective deployment, improvement, and documentation of student learning in each session of his/her course so the next session can be improved, if needed. For example, an experienced faculty member can adjust his/her lecture or facilitation, while assessing the audience to see how much they know and how fast they are able to process the information. Continuous improvement comes from keeping one's "finger on the pulse" of the "customer" (students) to get the right data and information in a timely manner so the appropriate actions can be taken after its assessment.

Assessment can be seen as the process of establishing and/or understanding the learning outcomes that meet the learners' needs, assessing students to determine whether or not they have achieved the learning outcomes through factual evidence, documenting those results, and reflecting on how to continually improve the process of teaching, learning and learner assessment. The purpose of the assessment process is to continually improve and document or credential learning. A structured review of the assessment model can enhance the assessment process by providing a framework that supports thoughtful planning and communication to relevant stakeholders before and during the learning process, deployment of valid and reliable assessment strategies, informed reflection on the results, as well as improvement of teaching, learning and assessment in order to close the loop. When it comes to personal reflections for improvement, faculty members tend to have three formats for facilitation of learning: 1) the facilitation they plan to do; 2) the facilitation they actually do; and 3) the facilitation they wish they had done. This type of reflection can certainly lead to improvement when the third format is put back into the loop thereby improving the next facilitation they plan to do. This closes the loop and improves the learning process for the students. It has been said that some universities have three curricula: The one that appears in the catalog, the one that professors teach, and one that students actually learn. Along with the administrators, it is also the faculty member's responsibility to find out the degree to which the curriculum asserted on paper or imagined by academic leaders accurately portrays what goes on in the minds of students. Making the curricula visible, so its usefulness in terms of demonstrated learning and results through students' performance can be documented as evidence, is the business of *assessment,* an activity practiced by each faculty member teaching the course.

While each faculty member should take responsibility for improving his/her teaching to enhance the outcomes achieved, it is the responsibility of program chairs, directors and other appropriate administrators to design assessment strategies for measuring learning across all courses at all locations for determining the effectiveness of distance education programs. The American Association of Higher Education (AAHE) offered the following "Principles of Good Practice for Assessing Student Learning" at the AAHE Assessment forum in December of 1992 for those who are involved in the assessment process:

1. The assessment of student learning begins with educational values. Assessment is not an end in itself but a vehicle for educational improvement.
2. Assessment is most effective when it reflects an understanding of learning as multidimensional, integrated, and revealed in performance over time.
3. Assessment works best when the programs it seeks to improve have clear, explicitly stated purposes. It entails comparing educational performance with educational purposes and expectations.
4. Assessment requires attention to outcomes but also and equally to the experiences that lead to those outcomes.
5. Assessment works best when it is ongoing, not episodic. This means tracking the performance of individual students or groups through various modalities.
6. Assessment fosters wider improvement when representatives from across the educational community are involved.
7. Assessment makes a difference when it begins with issues of use and illuminates questions that people really care about.
8. Assessment is most likely to lead to improvement when it is part of a larger set of conditions that promote change.
9. Through assessment, educators meet their responsibilities to students and to the public.

Educators have a responsibility to students and to the public that depend on them to provide accurate information on how students meet their goals and objectives.

Of course, this responsibility extends beyond reporting to actually improving and enhancing the program in a purposeful manner. In order to meet their responsibilities and document student learning, program directors and chairs along with their faculty members often strategically create an outcomes assessment plan for their programs. These plans are usually comprehensive, systematic, structured, and goal-oriented. The purpose of a comprehensive assessment process is to contribute to the pursuit of an institution's vision by assisting faculty, staff, and administrators in identifying the needs of stakeholders and adapting courses, curricula, delivery methods, and services according to these needs. The following characteristics are often found in the student outcomes assessment process: (a) evidence is produced that measures student achievement of learning outcomes; (b) evidence is produced to show where course changes and improvements are needed; (c) faculty, administrators, students, and other stakeholders are involved in the assessment and planning processes; and (d) assessment is linked to the planning and budgeting process. As an example, the remaining section of this chapter explores NSU's School of Business Entrepreneurship and how its doctoral students are doing in their comprehensive exams. The Comprehensive exams, besides the dissertation and publication requirements for a doctoral program, provide evidence of students' success as to how well the curriculum is achieving its intended outcomes.

What is a Comprehensive Examination and why do I Need to Take it?

From a student's perspective, the comprehensive exams are pressure packed and have a "do or die" feeling surrounding them. Added to the pressures of the exam itself, are the potential family pressures and monetary pressures that failing means tens of thousands of dollars wasted. While the pressure put on students to pass the comprehensive exam should not be minimized or marginalized, candidates should realize that the vast majority of students pass their comprehensive exams.

We recommend a more regimented study sequence to prepare for the comprehensive exams. In most cases, you should start preparing for the exam approximately six months prior to the exam date. You should also get as much information on the exam as possible. For example, what is the format, over how many days will the exam be given, what topics will be covered, and what happens (what is the appeals process) if you fail any section of the comprehensive exam. In addition to these topics, some schools may also have study guides or provide some type of examination study sessions. If any of these are available you should not miss them. Furthermore, study groups may prove to be invaluable to make sure there are no holes in your studying. Obtaining other students' papers may also be a valuable resource in consolidating and solidifying your learning. It is difficult to give exact advice since every school's exams, as well as every course of study, is different. For example, some schools give the exam in one day while others cover one topic per day and the exam is spread out over several days.

While the time leading up to the comprehensive examination is extremely stressful, in hindsight, the studying involved with preparing for them has a benefit for most students. Preparing for the comprehensive examination gives the opportunity to reflect on, consolidate, and integrate the learning throughout the entire program. While taking individual courses it is easy to get tunnel vision on the one topic being discussed in a particular course, and many faculty members may not be adept at integrating the information in their course with others. Whether this was done or not, the comprehensive examination provides the student with this opportunity, particularly for those courses taken early in the doctoral program.

Doctoral Programs and the Comprehensive Exam at the Huizenga School

Nova Southeastern University has been active by offering various undergraduate and graduate degree programs in many countries including the United States, the Grand Bahamas, Trinidad, China, Brazil, France, Germany, Dominican Republic, England, Greece, Panama, Venezuela, Jamaica, and many others. They offer degrees in business, law, education, pharmacy, nursing, dentistry, medicine, optometry, conflict resolution, psychology, humanities, and many others. NSU's Doctorate Programs in business (Doctorate of Business Administration, Doctorate of International Business Administration, Doctorate of Public Administration, and the available specialties) have been very successful and students continue to enjoy the flexibility of completing the classes on weekends through national clusters, and the practical application of their courses. In fact, the enrollment into the doctoral program mostly comes from "word-of-mouth" advertisement and testimonials of previous graduates and currently enrolled students.

The Doctor of Business Administration (DBA) program at the H. Wayne Huizenga School of Business and Entrepreneurship (Huizenga School) attempts to transform mature students into more effective global leaders. Doctoral candidates not only learn the most advanced decision-making techniques needed for success in the twenty-first century, but also develop the research and writing skills that accompany high-level responsibility in the academic and business environments. The program encourages executives, educators, and consultants to use their professional backgrounds to explore, design, and manage large systems within the complex organizations of the increasingly multifaceted and multisectored economy.

The primary target audience for the program is comprised of consultants, college professors, as well as mid-level managers and executives, with moderate to extensive business experience, who wish to enhance their understanding of business administration. These students typically have approximately five years experience and average approximately 35 years of age or older. The Doctor of Business Administration programs (DBA) at the Huizenga School attract students from around the nation and abroad. At present, the program is delivered through the cluster format in various states in the United States and in Jamaica. Since the program's inception, cluster programs have been offered in a weekend format. Courses are delivered one weekend per month, Saturday and Sunday. Classes meet from 8:00 a.m. –5:00 p.m. for six days during a semester. Students may utilize this format to complete all of their core courses in the program. Students typically take at least one course per term to complete the D.B.A. program in approximately four years. The start of the Doctoral Programs at the Huizenga School can be traced back to the late 1970s. The D.B.A.

program consists of four components: (1) the common core; (2) specialty courses in the fields of accounting, finance, health services administration, human resource management, information technology management, international management, management, and marketing; (3) competencies in the area of the student's major as demonstrated through the successful completion of the comprehensive exam; and (4) research (dissertation-related units).

The D.B.A. program operates on a year-round basis. All course work, seminars, workshops, and the comprehensive examination can be completed within four years. Each student progresses at his or her own pace in researching and writing the dissertation; the total length of time in the program is normally about four years. Cluster classes meet monthly in a convenient weekend format at over ten locations throughout the United States and Jamaica. Students generally attend cluster courses at one location, but the option to schedule at different locations is available for those who move, or who wish to attend a course during a term other than when it is available at the home cluster. This flexibility in scheduling is unique to the NSU program. Due to its flexibility and practical relevancy, the program has been particularly popular among corporate managers and consultants who wish to teach and conduct further research in their fields.

According to NSU's statistics on business doctorate students, the proportion of African Americans enrolled in the program nearly doubled from 13% in 1988 to 24% in 2002 over the 5-year period. The increase is due to the popularity of the program among students of diverse racial/ethnic backgrounds. According to the Black Issues in Higher Education (June 5ᵗʰ, 2003 – Volume 20(8)), NSU's Business School is ranked number 2 in the nation for the number of doctorate degrees in business awarded to all minorities. Additionally, although the marketing strategy for the program does not specifically target ethnic segments, a multicultural dimension is reflected in the promotional elements used in the recruitment process. Finally, about 29% of the students enrolled in the program are females. This number of female students entering the doctorate programs is expected to increase in the coming years, as more females pursue advanced business education at Nova Southeastern University's convenient formats.

According to NSU's e-Bulletin (electronic, university-wide newsletter) on August 8, 2004, NSU Leads the Nation in the number of doctorates awarded to African Americans and Hispanics: "NSU is once again the number one producer of African American doctorates among both traditionally white institutions and historically Black colleges and universities, as well as the number one producer of Hispanic doctorates based on survey results published in the July 29, 2004 edition of *Black Issues in Higher Education.*" The NSU e-Bulletin (2004) further stated that NSU also ranked as the number one producer of:

- African-American doctorates in the discipline of education,
- Hispanic doctorates in the discipline of education,
- Hispanic doctorates in the discipline of business, management, marketing and related support services,
- Total minority doctorates in the discipline of education, and

- Total minority doctorates in the discipline of business, management, marketing and related support services.

Assessment of Doctoral Programs

A survey was conducted of students who graduated in the 1999 - 2002 academic years. Surveys were sent to all recent graduates whose current addresses were available at the program's database. Questions on the survey addressed: the students' pre and post-graduation status with respect to employment or pursuit of graduate or professional studies; collection of information concerning student satisfaction with the program, and how well it prepared them for employment, promotion, or advanced study; determination of program completion and its effectiveness on students' career advancement, salary, and job performance; and alumni perceptions of strengths and weaknesses of the program, as well as their overall satisfaction level.

The survey was divided into four sections. Section I collected background and status information in a forced choice format with regard to program delivery and pursuit of doctoral study. Section II collected information related to professional development, employment status, and skills acquisition of the graduate. Section III collected information related to alumni satisfaction with quality indicators of the program. Section IV collected data related to overall satisfaction and job preparedness with the program in a forced choice format.

From the 190 surveys sent to recent graduates of the doctoral program, 90 were completed and returned, giving an overall return rate was 47%. The following are some of the general results of the responses:

1. About 41% of the respondents graduated with a Doctorate of Business Administration (with Management specialty) degree and 8% of the respondents were DIBA and DPA majors.
2. About 66% of the respondents started teaching at the college level after graduation and that their degree was a factor in receiving teaching opportunities at the college level.
3. Over 91% reported that their experience in the doctoral program enhanced their employment opportunities either extremely, considerably, moderately, or somewhat.
4. Approximately 53% of the respondents reported that they received a promotion and/or a raise and believed that their doctoral degree was a factor. However, only 33% of the respondents changed jobs a result of their education and 64% of them received more income as a result of the job change.
5. With regard to the quality indicators for the majority of the questions in the Doctoral Programs, over 90% of the students consistently reported that they were satisfied, quite satisfied or extremely satisfied.
6. Over 90% of the respondents reported being satisfied, quite satisfied, or extremely satisfied with their doctoral program. Over 69% were either quite

satisfied or extremely satisfied. Although it should be noted that only graduates were surveyed, not those who left the program prior to graduation.

As reflected in many of the responses, the primary reason for joining the doctoral program is for entering academia at a future date. Doctoral faculty members thus are heavily involved with students in the areas of research, publishing, and dissertation development. If a doctoral graduate is interested in entering academia, this is one area he or she should look into as not all traditional and non-traditional schools are focused on research and publication. Some schools are primarily teaching institutions. In addition, core and specialty classes are designed to lead to the successful completion of these areas.

Anticipating and reacting to market demand, the Huizenga School, for example, used various methods to further support their students to increase the probability of success with the dissertation. Students are encouraged to begin their research courses during their first year so they can begin working on their concept paper for the dissertation. Students are also provided training programs for effectively using technology and the library for their literature review in the dissertation and course work. As stated in the mission statement, Nova Southeastern University offers academic programs at times convenient to students, employing innovative delivery systems and rich learning resources on campus and at distant sites. Survey results indicate that 60% of the respondents used and preferred to complete the majority of the program in the weekend format with classes conducted at a cluster (field-based) location. Given NSU's mission and responses from doctoral alumni, the Huizenga School continues to develop cluster sites meeting the educational needs of doctoral candidates throughout the United States as well as outside of the country.

The result of the assessment and surveys clearly indicate that the Doctoral Program prepares its students and graduates for success in their academic and professional endeavors. The results of the faculty evaluations at the end of course surveys also indicate that the faculty members are performing satisfactorily. Another success of the doctoral faculty is demonstrated by the high passing rates on the Comprehensive exam which indicate that the doctoral students are adequately prepared to demonstrate mastery of the subject matter for their program.

Comprehensive Exam Assessment

As enrollment stayed consistent over the eight-year period studied, so did the number of students completing their Comprehensive exams. Prior to the year 2001, there were two sections to the comprehensive exam at Nova Southeastern University. Most doctoral students took the first comprehensive exam in their second year while taking the second comprehensive exam toward the end of their program. So, they registered for the Comps in two separate sections. Starting with 2001, students were required to take both parts of the exam during the same time (one full day). This is why there are a lower number of students taking the Comp exam during 2001 and subsequent years as can be seen on Table 6.1.

Of the 968 students taking the Comp exam in the eight-year period, 88.74% successfully passed it in their first attempt; and 73% were males while 27% were females. As can be seen from the data, in the latter years there is a trend toward a slightly higher percentage of students failing their comprehensive exams on their first attempt. For example in 1997, the passing rates for the three periods were 98%, 98% and 94% but in 2003 the percentages changed to 91%, 71% and 89% respectively. The statistics also show that more women are taking the comprehensive exams then in previous years.

Table 6.1 – Comp Passing Rate Statistics

Year	Number of Students Taking the Comp Exam	Pass		Men		Women	
		#	%	#	%	#	%
2004	38	30	79%	16	53%	14	47%
2003	27	24	89%	12	50%	12	50%
	21	15	71%	9	60%	5	40%
	23	21	91%	13	62%	8	38%
2002	46	38	83%	31	82%	7	18%
	22	20	91%	15	75%	5	25%
	24	21	87.50%	14	67%	7	33%
2001	22	17	77%	11	65%	6	35%
	12	10	83%	5	50%	5	50%
	4	4	100%	3	75%	1	25%
2000	71	60	85%	48	80%	12	20%
	38	32	84%	22	69%	10	31%
	51	43	84%	31	72%	12	28%
1999	50	39	78%	24	62%	15	38%
	71	60	85%	52	87%	8	13%
	73	69	95%	46	66.6%	23	33.3%
1998	49	44	90%	29	66%	15	34%
	50	41	82%	30	73%	11	27%
	58	58	100.00%	43	74%	15	26%
1997	50	47	94%	38	81%	9	19%
	53	52	98%	42	81%	10	19%
	53	52	98%	41	79%	11	21%
1996	62	62	100%	52	84%	10	16%
Total	968	859	88.74%	627	73%	232	27%

To see if there is a statistically significant difference in the average passing rates or percentages of students in the first four years and the later four years, a t-test of the average sample means of the passing rate percentages for the two populations was conducted. The two categories are 1996-1999 which covered ten Comp exam periods (population one) and 2000-2004 which covered thirteen Comp exam periods (population two). It is hypothesized that there is no statistically significant difference in the average passing rate percentages for the two populations.

The results were tabulated for the two categories of populations that include a total of 968 students who took the comprehensive examinations. Using a 0.05 level of significance, the null hypothesis (Ho) is rejected because t= 221.657 is larger than the critical value of +2.0796. Also, because the p-value of 0.0000 is less than alpha (α) = 0.05, there is sufficient evidence to reject the null hypothesis. Based on these results, the students in the first category (1996-1999) seem to have Comp scores (92% on the average) that are statistically different than the students' in the second category (2000-2004) Comp scores (84% on the average). As such, one can conclude that the first category (1996-1999) Comp scores' are significantly higher than the second category (2000-2004) Comp scores.

So, according to the statistical analysis, students seem to be doing worse in their comprehensive exams during the last four years. There are many possibilities for this downward trend and the following are some options:

1. The expectations have increased and therefore more students are not passing the comp exam on their first attempt.
2. The answers are being evaluated with stricter guidelines.
3. The questions and answers may have changed but the right content are not being comprehensively covered in each course.
4. The students in first category (1996-1999) completed only one part of the Comp exam during a given time. As such, they only had to prepare for one Comp exam which might be a factor in their higher success rates.
5. Most of the students in the last four years took both Comps I and II together as one Comp exam which takes all day and can be stressful. This might be a cause for their lower percentage of passing rates. Furthermore, these students had to read more material as a review to prepare for answering more questions since all the questions were in one Comp.
6. Students today are not doing their work in each course as well as they used to in previous decades. Maybe faculty members are not expecting the same level of learning as they used to in the previous decades.
7. Today's students are not preparing as well as they should for the comprehensive exams.
8. The quality of students entering the program has decreased in the last four years.

While there might be many other possibilities, besides the ones listed above, for the lower passing rates in the Comp exam in the last four years the most likely reason could be that Comp I and Comp II exams are now being taken at one time. So, there is more pressure and more questions to prepare for and complete all the questions on the same day. Perhaps another sample of students in the next fours years (2005-2008) can be compared with the last four years to see if the average percentages of scores are significantly different.

While there seems to be a downward trend in the success rates of students in the last four years on Comp exams with an average passing rate of 84% for the years 2000 through the first term of 2004, the average overall passing rates for the past eight years is still 88.74%, showing good evidence of student learning. So, a great majority of students are able to successfully complete their exams on the first attempt. However, in the spirit of continuous improvement, the school can and should provide more resources and suggestions on how more students can perform better in their first attempt in the comprehensive examinations. Some of the basic suggestions for students to do better in their individual comprehensive examinations are to take good notes in the individual classes, make sure they understand the objectives of each class and be able to meet them at the outset of the class, take the comp exams shortly after completing the relevant courses, review all course material and projects completed in the classes the month before the Comp exam, review relevant literature and textbooks prior to the exam, take some time off work the week before the exam to reduce the pressure, and get plenty of sleep the night before the exam.

As another option, consideration could be given to changing the Comp exam to test the students' ability to apply knowledge to specific real world problems and dilemmas. At present, many of the exam questions seem to be subject content exams that are similar to summative questions used when the subject is examined at the end of the each course. This may place at least some students at a disadvantage as they may have attended that particular course several years prior to taking the comps. What is needed is a set of questions that can test the students' ability to deal with current issues that influence modern business. Typical Comp questions could be: 1-What are the issues and consequences of privatizing social security? Specifically, discuss the social agency theory as well as the theory of privatization as discussed through an economic paradigm by two different researchers from the last two decades. 2-What are the deontological and teleological ethical components of advertising directed at children? Discuss legal, ethical and socially responsible concepts from the perspectives of two commonly-referenced ethicists. These types of questions will test the student's ability to debate issues of importance to business as well as society while integrating as well as referencing relevant theories and current literature. This will also test whether they understand how to apply the theory that is covered in the core and specialty courses. It is also suggested that students should be given a choice of questions so they can select those that are more relevant to their area of specialization or expertise.

Overall, the world of distance and higher education, using blended formats of distance learning delivery, has achieved a special market in the adult environment by offering quality educational programs both nationally and internationally at times convenient to working adults. Due to professional faculty members committed to student learning, possessing the ability to combine academic theory with successful practical tools as well as their ability to effectively adjust to the changing educational needs of working professionals, doctoral educators have and can offer great value to their students and the community at large.

Summary

Systems thinking is applicable to researchers for seeing the whole not just the parts, as we;; as to see interrelationships rather than things, for identifying patterns rather than taking a static picture of the events. "Systems thinking" is the cornerstone of a learning organization and is designed to integrate the various disparate parts of a problem or issue. While there is no *perfect* organization, higher education programs should have an infrastructure in place that ensures learning happens at a high-level consistently. There should be an emphasis on the development of high-level curricula that blends pragmatic and theoretical knowledge. The systems infrastructure and student support services should be in place for continued growth. These systemic processes enable students, who may not have had the opportunity to achieve a doctorate in the traditional system of education, the prospect to go to school and continue to work full-time. This innovative approach to advanced studies brings added value and a rich vision of education to the process of institutional learning.

Today, cyberspace technologies offer many possibilities in the twenty-first century, but such possibilities cannot be realized without breaking the outdated industry rules of the past. Breaking industry rules requires effective training of both faculty members and administrative staff so they can jointly be more flexible in hearing their students' learning needs and so they can be empowered to be innovative in integrating student "feedback" in the education process while trying new learning strategies. This chapter presented the results of alumni survey and their level of satisfaction as a result of completing their degrees. It further explored the success rates of doctoral students in their comprehensive exam. Trends were analyzed and suggestions were offered for administrators and researchers to further explore and examine. It is hoped that doctoral program administrators, faculty members and students can use the content of this material to help new students understand the dissertation completion process and thereby successfully achieve their doctoral "dream" in an expeditious and productive manner.

CHAPTER
SEVEN

7 – Selecting a Research Topic and Committee

S electing a topic for a dissertation is either extremely easy, or exceptionally difficult. Some students begin their doctoral studies with, or because of, a passion for a specific research topic, while others may have little or no knowledge of a topic or an awareness of what is involved in writing a dissertation. For those in the last category, a dissertation is a large research project that is required at the end of the doctoral coursework. In general, the research conducted for the dissertation must be new research (not just "rehashing" research that has already been completed), a new look or angle on existing research, and it must be significant and substantial. Once students complete all their coursework they are considered in "ABD" status. ABD stands for "All But Dissertation," meaning that the student has successfully completed the coursework and their comprehensive examination and only has the dissertation to complete before graduating. While it is exciting to get to ABD status, students should also be aware that this is where many people get discouraged and consequently do not ever finish their degree. Many students have reported additional stress, a loss of the camaraderie they felt while attending classes with others, a feeling of isolation, and loneliness. It is our hope that this book, and in particular the next two chapters, helps alleviate some of these feelings and increases the number of students moving through ABD status into graduation and becoming doctors. This chapter will review possible avenues for selecting a research topic, selecting a dissertation chair, and committee members.

Selecting a Research Topic

A minority of students will enter their doctoral program with a well thought-out dissertation topic; however, most students will not. You should not feel intimidated or behind if you start your doctoral coursework without a dissertation topic. In fact, many students will change topics multiple times throughout their coursework even if they started the doctoral program with an idea for a dissertation topic. While changing topics is not uncommon, the sooner you select a topic, the better off and further ahead you will be. If you have a topic early in your doctoral coursework, you can tailor your research and coursework studies toward that area of study. You may find that many professors are willing to adjust some of the specific course requirements to meet your research interests, if you ask. In this way you may be able to conduct a substantial portion of your background research while simultaneously completing your required coursework. If you have not selected a research topic, look for areas of personal interest in your coursework and begin narrowing down a research topic.

Now, if you do not have any great ideas for research, where should you go? The good news is that there are many options. The first option is to look at the research the professors at your institution are currently conducting. There may be other similar research that could be conducted. This may also be an opportunity for a professor to become a mentor and committee chair for your dissertation. Find out more information on selecting a committee chair in the next section. As mentioned in the previous paragraph, another option is to adapt a topic from research you are already conducting from your doctoral course requirements. The downside to this method is that the first few courses may not really be of great interest to you and waiting for later courses may not allow you to take full advantage of *double dipping* – conducting coursework research and papers around your dissertation topic. A student can also look through "top tier" journals for ideas. Most articles in these journals will have a section on potential areas of future research. This is a great avenue, because someone who has researched a specific topic has identified gaps or holes in the research on a topic which is exactly what you are looking for in dissertation research. We recommend you mostly look at the last year or so of articles and that you initially look through the most prestigious journals. For example, in the field of management, you may want to look through such publications as the Journal of Management, the Academy of Management Journal, and the Academy of Management Executive. The final recommendation, and one that you may want to utilize even if you already have a research topic, is to study some recent dissertations of interest to you from the school you are attending. This not only helps with potential topics, but will also provide invaluable insight into the proper format for your dissertation.

Selecting a Committee Chair

As highlighted previously, according to Nelson (2000), the single most important factor in a student's decision to continue or withdraw from a doctoral program relates to the student's relationship with the dissertation chair. Poor relationships between doctoral students and committee chairs may be one of the largest contributing factors to the abnormally high number of ABDs that never complete their degrees. This section reviews many of the responsibilities of a committee chair, how to select a committee chair, and what to do when things go bad.

The committee chair is primarily responsible for providing advice and guidance on both the dissertation process and the student's direction for their research. The committee chair may also act as a type of cheerleader/encourager throughout the dissertation process. In this way the committee chair is similar to a mentor. In fact, some schools have adopted the name mentor instead of committee chair. According to Smallwood (2004), doctoral programs in the sciences normally have lower attrition rates than the humanities. Some of this lower attrition rate may be attributed to the fact that programs in the sciences normally work, starting at the beginning of the program with one professor and therefore a relationship builds between the student and professor. Likewise, the typical mentoring relationship enables an individual to follow in the path of a more experienced colleague who can pass on knowledge, experience, and open doors to otherwise out-of-reach opportunities. Kram (1983, 1988) introduced the four phases of the mentor-protégé or mentee relationship. These stages include; initiation, cultivation, separation, and redefinition (see table 7.1). Like the committee chair/student relationship, mentoring relationships are "characterized by an evolutionary process" (Kram, 1988, p. 47) taking five to ten years to progress through the four stages. Unfortunately, for many doctoral students, they don't have 5 to 10 years from selecting a committee chair to fully develop the mentoring relationship. Mentors and protégés also bring different expectations into the relationship. Young and Perrewe (2000) found that for mentors, career-related activities, such as successful task completion, were closely related to what mentors considered a successful mentoring relationship. Protégés, alternatively, rated the social support obtained through mentors as being the most critical factor in a successful relationship. If these findings hold true for the doctoral student / committee / chair relationship, the different expectations may bring additional stress into the doctoral student – committee chair relationship as the chair may only be focused on task completion and the student interested in other factors like social support, friendship, acceptance, and counseling activities. Building an effective relationship may be even more problematic for non-traditional students who may not have the benefit substantial of face-to-face interaction with their committee chair. This may lead to additional frustration and misunderstandings between the chair and student. According to Pauleen and Yoong (2001), the difficulties found in building relationships are proportional to the distance the individuals are apart from each other.

Like the mentoring process, the authors have identified some major attributes for committee chairs. These attributes include knowledge of the political process, methodology and topical expertise, patience, the desire to publish, along with the ability to motivate and stay motivated. As one doctoral student remarked, "finding a chair with at least two of these strengths [knowledge of the political process surrounding the dissertation, methodology and/or topical knowledge, and the ability to motivate/act as a cheerleader] is key to successfully completing their dissertation in the standard timeframe. Although others seemed to complete their dissertation in spite of their committee chairs; it took longer, but they did complete their dissertations."

Table 7.1 – Phases of Mentoring Relationships (Kram, 1983; Scharff, 2005)

Phase of Mentoring Relationship	Duration	Characteristics
Initiation	First 6 to 12 months	Strong expectations on the future of the relationship by both mentor and protégé.
Cultivation	Next 2-5 years	Expectations developed during the initiation phase are tested. Protégé is self-confident and optimistic about career. Relationship can include both counseling and friendship.
Separation	Next 2-5 years	Marked by "turmoil, anxiety, and feelings of loss" (p. 618). Separation of mentor and protégé is both organizational and psychological as the protégé moves on and/or receives promotions outside the mentor's organization.
Redefinition	One to ten years	Does not occur in all mentor/protégé relationships. A friendship between mentor and protégé is formed where protégé has gratitude toward mentor for the guidance they provided early on. Many times this phase occurs when the mentor and protégé attain peer status.

So how can you ensure that you and your committee chair are set up for success? We offer the following advice:

1. First, understand your university's basic requirements for who may serve as a dissertation chair. Many universities require a chair to have served on a specific number of dissertation committees prior to serving as a dissertation chair, while other schools allow any full-time faculty member to chair a dissertation committee (Carlin & Perlmutter, 2006).

2. We highly recommend students interview a few potential dissertation chairs. This interview is really a two-way interview. You are looking for a chair that you can work well with, that will support you, knows the political climate within the university, and has a proven track record of success. Alternatively, the potential committee chair is looking for a well thought out problem statement, a student with excellent grades, and one that can communicate – orally and in writing – effectively. This may be an area where some international students have difficulty. Because English may be a second language, they may not always be able to effectively communicate their research topic in oral. As one international student remarked "I received three key words as advice for committee chair selection. 1. Respect, 2. Understanding, 3. Self-determination. On respect, I should look for a professor that is ready to respect me and accept me the way I was, not minding my nationality and my writing problems. On understanding, look for a professor that understood my topic, the dissertation process, and understand my educational and professional background. On the third point, look for a professor that believes in my self-determination to succeed and who is ready to assist me all the way, not minding all my shortcomings. At a minimum, your interview of committee chairs (and potentially all committee members should include):

a. *How many successful dissertations have you chaired?* We recommend that, if possible, you select a chair that has chaired at least two successful dissertations. If this is not possible, you should select a chair that has at least been a member of two successful dissertation committees. While the past is not an indication of future success, and we understand that people have to get started at some point, we would recommend that now is not the most opportune time for you to select an individual without a proven track record of success.

b. *Which methodology do you feel most comfortable with?* Optimally you would like to select a committee chair that is comfortable and has had success in the methodology your dissertation will be using, although a significant factor is your experience and confidence in the methodology for your research as well. For more information on the different methodologies, see Chapter 8.

c. *How many dissertations are you currently chairing (or on committees)?* This may give you an indication of the professor's workload and ultimately how much time they will have available to dedicate to your dissertation. If you are just beginning the dissertation process, and a potential chair has a number of other committees they are chairing, it may be less of an issue and you may want to ask where their current studies are in the process. Many of their current studies may be in the final stages of the dissertation process and not have an affect on you as you complete your dissertation.

d. *What do you feel are the most important attributes in students successfully completing their dissertation?* This will give you an idea of how the chair works and what he/she feels is important. Ultimately, you are looking for a chair that will work with you and respond to you in a timely fashion.

e. *What do you feel are your biggest strengths and weaknesses?* This is an important question because you want a committee chair that complements your strengths and does not have similar weaknesses. Personality and a connection with your ultimate committee chair is important.

f. *How familiar are you with the dissertation topic?* You should understand your committee members' and chair's interest in and current knowledge in your field of study. Will they be the experts in the topic, and if not, what strengths do they bring to your committee?

3. Choose an individual as chair that you get along with.

4. Choose a dissertation chair with a sense of humor. It is a long hard process. Selecting an individual that you can joke with, have fun with, and will laugh with you will help tremendously. As one doctoral student remarked, "a keen sense of humor and perspective are key in a chair. You'll need both during the darker moments of the dissertation process."

5.   Choose a mentor that has had past success in getting students through the dissertation process.
6.   This may be difficult to ascertain, but try to select a committee chair that has the time to dedicate to you and your study. One potential indication of the individual's promptness and responsiveness may be how quickly they responded to student's concerns or provided feedback on papers during your coursework. Promptness and responsiveness are key for all members of your committee.
7.   Choose a chair that is a subject matter expert in your field. Although depending on your study this may not be possible. Additionally, we believe that the first few recommendations are more important than having a subject matter expert as your committee chair. If your chair is not a subject matter expert, it is very beneficial to have one of your committee members as an expert in your area of study. At a minimum you should find a chair and committee members who are interested in your topic.

While all Chairs are different, once selected, the following is one example of a possible response that one can expect from a candidate that serves as a Chair and Committee Member on a dissertation:

Dear doctoral colleague,
As you know, I am interested on this topic and will be happy to assist if our expectations, plans and timetables match. As such, I must make my expectations and time limitations known to you for this process so you can make a decision on whether you are able to work with me with such limitations. Similarly, for me to serve as the Chair, the following are some expectation and conditions for effective teamwork and the completion of this research:

1.   Just so you know I travel frequently throughout the country and abroad. When traveling abroad, I might not have access to the internet for a period of three to four weeks. However, I do promise that I'll get to your submissions (especially when I am expecting something from you) within a four week arena (when traveling to foreign countries). When traveling nationally, I'll always try to give you a response or an acknowledgement within one week (if not sooner). Please keep in mind that complete dissertation proposals and drafts are often quite long and can take longer timeframes for review and feedback process; in such cases, a period of two to three weeks should be allotted for feedback and/or approval. That is my commitment to you and this research process. *Will this timeframe work with your plans?*
2.   The dissertation research process is a huge commitment and requires self-initiative to carry on without being "pushed" or constantly reminded by the Chair or one's committee members. Of course, the Chair and committee members are there to assist in reviewing your material and providing guidance when needed, but they cannot do

more. This teamwork process requires that you be the "driver" of this research since the Chair and committee members serve only as guides, advisors, and mentors. *Are you able and committed to be the "driver" of this research?*

3. The researcher or "driver" is expected to work very closely with the Methodologist and Committee member (who serves as a reader) to complete the document qualitatively. Some of their feedback may not always be to your liking, yet their suggestions may always need to be integrated into your research prior to approval. *Can you work closely with your committee members?*

4. Each researcher should be dedicated to work on a specific plan to get the dissertation finished in a timely manner (the next few years). This is important since in two years too many things and plans can change. *Do you have a plan in place with specific timeframes for completion and graduation?*

5. The researcher must commit to fully "proof-reading" each submission, or to get an editor to edit the written material prior to submission to the committee members and Chair. *Are you able to "proof-read or get an editor" for your written material so it does not have minor editing errors?*

6. The researcher must be fully familiarized with the school's dissertation process and guidelines. All submissions must be aligned with the expected and established norms. *Are you familiar with the university's dissertation process and can you align your submissions with the standards?*

7. Most students are able to get a conference publication once they have completed the research process for the literature review (or the first three chapters) to get one quick publication reference or citation on their Curriculum Vitae (CV). If you do not have a "blind peer-reviewed" publication yet, you can work with me once you have completed your literature review (Chapter II), or when you have a "publishable" quality paper (on any topic) for a conference or a journal. Speak with me when you are ready for this publication process so we can get you published as quickly as possible. The important point is that you do NOT have to wait until your dissertation research is finalized to get an academic publication at a conference or journal. Overall, each researcher is expected to publish at least one major journal publication with his/her Chair and/or committee members during, or upon, the completion of the research. In the cover letter as well as the journal publication, your name will appear first, followed by the Chair and then the committee members as appropriate. Some journal publications and review process takes a period of six months or two years. Assuming there is no rush on your part, this means that you may have to wait one or two years after your graduation to get your material published in a quality journal. *Are you committed to continue your work on editing or formatting the final paper with the guidance of*

the Chair to get a journal publication from your literature and research upon its completion?

Overall, do you have a plan on when you want to finish? And, can you submit "edited or proof-read" copies of your completed material to the Chair and committee members? If the answers are yes to these and the above questions, then I'll be happy to serve as your Chair. In such a case, you can send me your resume (or CV) for my record and we can continue the process as you see appropriate. Furthermore, I'll be happy to suggest other faculty members that you can contact for serving as your Methodologist and as a Reader (that is if you have not contacted anyone yet). Otherwise, I suggest that you contact other faculty members who have similar interests on this topic that can serve as your Chair and/or committee members. If you need possible names, call me and I'll be happy to suggest faculty members' names that are doing research in this area. I look forward to hearing from you.

Common Issues in Finding and Selecting a Committee Chair

Carlin and Perlmutter (2006) proposed that students often have the choice of selecting faculty that are renowned in their field, yet offer very little in the way of advice and support for the student. Alternatively, a student may select a younger faculty that shows extreme enthusiasm over the study, yet can also be so enthusiastic about the topic that they can almost take over the study. In the mentoring literature, this is described as theoretical abuse. "Theoretical abuse is defined as a mentor attempting to satisfy his or her own meaning-making needs at the expense of the protégé by imposing interpretations of events on the protégé" (O'Neill & Sankowsky, 2001, p. 208). In dealing with theoretical abuse the protégé can contest the mentors meaning; comply with the mentors meaning although disagreeing; or fully endorse the mentors meaning "abdicating any position of his or her own" (p. 210). Another political disadvantage of younger faculty members is that they may not be fully aware of the political climate within the university leading to additional time to get through the dissertation process.

A second issue raised by doctoral students is the limited availability of top quality committee chairs. One doctoral student remarked that, "the selection of a dissertation chair can feel like an exercise on the TV show *Survivor*. Whereby, if one doesn't select a chair quickly enough, the only chair available may not have the knowledge around the topic or the political skills to assist the student through the dissertation process." According to Johnson (2007), competition is a major factor in students finding qualified committee chairs. Faculty are looking for the best and brightest and may be very reluctant to establish a relationship with students until much later in their studies assuming that many will drop out. As Smallwood (2004) remarked, "it's about separating the wheat from the chaff, the good students get through" (para. 3). Normally, however, your school should be able to give you guidance on the right time to select a committee chair. We recommend that when you get to that point in your studies, you do not procrastinate in interviewing potential chairs, as most faculty members will only accept a small number of students. An associated issue is that students may not even have exposure to enough faculty members that are eligible to become committee members or chair, further limiting the choices.

Another common concern expressed by doctoral learners is their inability to contact their dissertation chair. After a student completes the comprehensive exams and course work, doctoral students may not see or hear from their classmates once they enter the *All But Dissertation* (ABD) status. Many report feelings of isolation and loneliness. A possible solution is for educational leaders to create a culture that requires the dissertation chair and the student to log in frequently – perhaps weekly, into an online class or communicate electronically relating to progress and/or problems. Such fostered communications might help avoid inertia during the ABD phase. This may be an area to approach your dissertation chair with.

Dissertation Committee Members

Once the committee chair has been selected, you should go about interviewing additional faculty members for possible inclusion on your dissertation committee. Most schools require two other professors, although each school may have specific guidelines on who can serve as members of a dissertation committee. For example, some schools may require at least two members to be faculty of the school, leaving the third member to be a terminally degreed individual from another school or area. Some students have used the third member to help set up future job opportunities or to ask a family member to sit on their committee (assuming they meet the school's requirements for membership on the dissertation committee).

The first step in interviewing and accepting others into your dissertation committee is to ask your newly appointed committee chair who they have worked well with in the past. If the answer comes back as "anybody, pick who you like," this may be a warning sign of potential conflicts on the horizon. We recommend you select a team, to the greatest extent possible, with a proven track record of success. Just like any sports team, success depends on both talent and team chemistry. Without team "chemistry" and an ability to work together, you may have to facilitate months of bickering back and forth between faculty that are not willing to concede a point or opinion. Due to busy schedules and diverse personalities, one should remember that not all faculty members are able to work well with each other at all times. It is probably a "shock" to think that not all faculty members are able to work well with each other as committee members, but it is a reality. Faculty members have their own preferred styles of working with doctoral students, and some of the preferred methods might be in conflict. For example, some Chairs prefer to read everything and approve it before it goes to the Committee members; while others prefer that the Committee members read each draft and approve it before the dissertation draft is being sent to him or her. It is best that everyone on the committee agree on the process recommended by the Chair. This is one of the reasons that it is suggested that one first work on getting a Chair for his/her dissertation, and then work on finding the Methodology person as well as the Reader for the committee as recommended by the Chair. Also like a sports team, you need to know people's strengths and make sure you have fielded a good team. For example a football team with all star quarterbacks will probably not win any games. A football team needs linemen, tight-ends, wide-receivers, and running backs to complement the quarterback. Assess your weaknesses and those of your committee chair and make sure that these weaknesses are filled with strengths by other members of your committee. With this in mind, we recommend that you study prospective dissertation committee candidates' backgrounds, areas of interest, their publication history and record, and their availability. You can find out more about the candidates by looking at the school's website for each candidate's biography and complete curriculum vita which are often publicly available. One can also check out the topics which the faculty regularly teaches as this might indicate his or her areas of interest. If the candidate's published work, such as journal articles or books, are readily available it is best to skim through them and take a notice of his or her writing and research style. Chances are that he or she will expect the same level of quality or research from his or her students as well. Once you have finalized reviewing several candidates to serve as the Chair or committee member for the dissertation project, then, prepare to have an interview with this person through a "conference call" discussion, or better yet, a face-to-face format.

After interviewing and selecting individuals to serve on your dissertation committee, we also offer the following general advice in relation to the dissertation process:

- Once you have your committee together, we recommend you develop a research timeline. If possible, get your committee together, either in person or via teleconference, and get feedback and finally buy-in to your research timetable. This way you can update your committee on where you are on the timetable that everyone agreed to.
- Don't take delays personally. Assume that you will have them, and plan for them. As one doctoral student remarked, "your dissertation may be the most important thing in your life, but it isn't in theirs. Shocking."
- Students should understand that there may be politics going on behind the scenes. As Carlin and Permutter (2006) highlighted, non-tenured faculty may agree with more senior faculty just to improve their chances for obtaining tenure at the university.
- Once you have selected your committee and started working on your dissertation, gracefully accept the input of your chair and committee members. None of these individuals are perfect, yet, in most cases, they are more knowledgeable than you are on the dissertation process.
- Try to see the process through your dissertation committee's eyes. The members of the committee do not have time to micro-manage your dissertation or to drop everything to answer your question immediately. If you have questions, accumulate them and send them periodically instead of a question every day.
- All of the members of your committee are busy people. So knowing what strengths each committee member brings is key. Focus your questions on their strengths. For example, if you have selected a committee member

because of his or her strength in methodology, avoid sending them questions not related to your methodology.

- Use your committee chair to sort out any discrepancies among your committee.
- Be involved with your Chair and Committee Members on publishing articles in journals and presenting papers in conferences. Ask them to co-author topics of interest with you through opportunities that might be available.

Specific Advice for Non-traditional Students

As previously noted, non-traditional students, many of whom take courses on-line, have some additional issues to consider. Studies have shown that distance and the lack of regular face-to-face interaction between mentor and protégé or mentee cause some specific issues you should be aware of. According to Scharff (2005), there is a lower quality exchange relationship between managers and virtual employees. Specifically, issues have been identified in the area of psychological support. Psychological support includes acting as a role model, counseling, acceptance, and friendship. Each of these may impact whether a non-traditional student stays with the program and completes his or her dissertation. As one doctoral student remarked, "the dilemma faced by many non-traditional students is not building a strong enough relationship with the faculty to understand their knowledge and passion for the dissertation topic."

The same study suggested that virtual employees needed to communicate more frequently than face-to-face employees to reach the same quality of relationship (Scharff, 2005). Therefore, we recommend that you setup routine telephone conversations with your committee chair to make sure you are heading in the same direction your chair thinks you are. This is also a time when you can ask your chair any questions you may have instead of bombarding them with daily emails. Because in many non-traditional schools the faculty may not know one another, you may be wise in initiating an initial teleconference so that the members of the committee get to know one another and so that you can highlight your research timeline. Finally, you should build in flexibility into your research timeline assuming that there will be delays.

What happens if I made a BIG Mistake?

Regardless of how well you plan and interview the members of your dissertation committee, you may find that you made some huge mistakes. There might be times when you find that one member of the committee is not working well with the other committee members or that one committee member can't agree on a direction for the research. While your school may tell you that it is your committee and that you can change committee members, you should make sure that you have explored all avenues prior to getting a new committee member. The first step in resolving a conflict may be to speak to the individual. If this does not work, your committee chair may be able to intervene on your behalf. There may be times, however, when your committee chair is either unable or unwilling to intercede on your behalf with another member of the faculty. Prior to eliminating a faculty member from your committee, you should make sure that you understand your school's rules regarding a change and also have the other two committee member's agreement. There are "political" aspects that may need to be taken into consideration, and one or both of your other committee members may not be willing to support the change. Prior to making a change, you should also realize that there may be a further delay in your study as a new member will need to get *up to speed* on your research topic. This delay may be unavoidable if you run into an individual that is completely unrealistic, and you do not believe you will get through the study with your current committee make up.

Summary

This chapter and most professionals tend to emphasize that doctoral students should begin their dissertation research as early as possible in the doctoral program. We acknowledge that while this is a good way to go about it when one is clear on the research question, this process is not for everyone or for those who are not fully familiar with their topic's recent literature. Therefore, it is perfectly okay to first complete one or two years of doctoral courses in order for one to become familiar with the literature in one's area of research as well as research methodologies, then find out what research is needed, and finally determine what might be an appropriate research avenue. Once a doctoral student is clear about the needed research and his or her motivation to investigate a specific topic, then he or she should begin immediately and ask a team of other interested individuals to serve as mentors in the process.

Having a common understanding of the process and each others' needs are important for effective teamwork. The dissertation committee is basically a team; and a high performing team requires certain commonalities and agreements in order to function well. The team leader is the Chair; but, of course, the committee members can take a leadership role in their respective areas of responsibility and expertise for the research process. While the Chair and committee members can lead and guide the learner, the student is always the driver and in control of his/her progress. Therefore, it is time well spent to interview several possible candidates, and eventually assemble the "right committee." As such, a doctoral student should be very careful in selecting the right individual for his or her dissertation Chair as the Chair can have many obligations and responsibilities. The H. Wayne Huizenga School of Business and Entrepreneurship (June 2006) provided a number of excellent recommendations and responsibilities that Chairs are responsible for and the following are some of them. First of all, one must understand that the dissertation Chair is the leader of the dissertation committee. Ideally, he or she leads the student and the committee in developing, conducting, and publishing quality research as per the requirements of the school and industry. As needed, the dissertation chair should maintain effective channels of communication between the student and the committee members. The chair also ensures that the student and all committee members respond appropriately and in a timely manner to students within two weeks of their receipt. Overall, the chair is the main subject matter expert on the topic of research. If and when appropriate, he or she can assist the student in the theoretical and conceptual foundation of the total design of the dissertation in the proposal and in the draft. Overall, the chair has the responsibility to review and "sign off" on the proposal and draft documents before they are sent to the school officials for approval. While the Chair can serve as the leader of the dissertation process, students must understand and be cognizant of the fact that they are the "driver" of this process; and consequently they must be proactive in moving the research forward. The student must constantly communicate his or her needs to the Chair and other committee members so they can guide and mentor as needed. The student must be the "driver," and drive carefully in the right direction; otherwise, the "automobile" and the research will not get too far.

Having an exceptional dissertation committee may help get you through the "political" process, yet it still takes a significant amount of personal time and effort. According to one doctoral student, "so the question remains, why are there students that don't finish? Ultimately, it appears the students were either not motivated, focused on a topic, or had the skills to complete the dissertation. A committee chair can help all three of these areas, but is not the sole reason for the person's success in completing the dissertation... there is only one person who is responsible for the lack of progress... and I look at him in the mirror every day." Similarly, Pittenger and Heimann (2000) suggested that self-efficacy, the belief that an individual can accomplish a given task, is a critical element for both the mentor and protégé and may be the critical element in successful completion of the dissertation research project. While self-efficacy and your committee members help, you should also remember other individuals, like family, friends, colleagues, and other doctoral students, can provide advice and guidance when things become difficult.

As stated by William Arthur Ward, "A true friend knows your weaknesses but shows you your strengths; feels your fears but fortifies your faith; sees your anxieties but frees your spirit; recognizes your disabilities but emphasizes your possibilities." One should always remember that the future of what is to come and what is to be belongs to people who see possibilities, encourage possibilities and take advantage of possibilities before they become obvious to others. To best take advantage of possibilities, one must be ready for them before they become obvious. Ralph Waldo Emerson encouraged us all to "Finish each day and be done with it. You have done what you could; some blunders and absurdities have crept in; forget them as soon as you can. Tomorrow is a new day; you shall begin it serenely and with too high a spirit to be encumbered with your old nonsense." The key for making the best of each new day is to replace "problems" with possibilities since one's measure of success is not whether he or she has a tough problem to deal with, but whether the problem is the same one that existed before. Despite obstacles and challenges, stay focused on being happy and the expression of a positive attitude because joyfulness keeps the heart and face young. Laugh often since a good laughter can make one a better friend both intrapersonally as well as interpersonally. Stay happy and positive despite the fact that there may never be a guarantee of a happy ending as emphasized in the following statement:

I wanted a perfect ending. Now I've learned, the hard way, that some poems don't rhyme, and some stories don't have a clear beginning, middle, and end. Life is about not knowing, having to change, taking the moment and making the best of it, without knowing what's going to happen next. Delicious Ambiguity! (Gilda Radner).

CHAPTER EIGHT

8 – The Dissertation Project

T he dissertation has always been a normal part of a doctoral program, and most schools are likely to have this requirement before a degree can be conferred. The dissertation is usually a very important and mission-critical aspect of understanding research, conducting research, and publishing new knowledge in academic conferences and journals. For additional information on exactly what a dissertation is, selecting a dissertation topic, and selecting a dissertation committee, review Chapter 7. As previously discussed, one of the most important elements of a doctoral program is the selection and determination of a succinct research question that excites the student to get it answered. This research question should be important, timely, provide the foundation for the building of existing literature in the field, and be of interest to existing journal editors. This research question forms the basis of the dissertation, which begins with chapter one. The first chapter of a dissertation is basically the longer and more developed version of what is often known as the prospectus or the concept paper; and thus at many schools the initial chapter will parallel the prospectus / concept paper.

As highlighted at the beginning of this book, an alarming number of students complete all their coursework yet never earn a doctorate degree. This unfortunate result is known as ABD or *All But Dissertation* status. Some have estimated that only 40-60% of those that achieve ABD status actually complete their degree. The focus of Chapters 7 and 8 are to provide the reader with information and recommendations which have proven to be successful to help increase that "passing" percentage.

Setting the Course

As studied in most academic and professional courses, leadership is basically the process of determining the vision toward a "brighter" destination and inspiring everyone involved, by direct and indirect influence, to reach the objective through the efficient use of available resources. Leadership is about being effective in selecting the right destination and choosing the correct direction and track for getting there. Management is about efficiency and making the best use of available resources to achieve one's goals with the lowest social, emotional, financial, and physical costs. While there are philosophical differences between leadership and management as defined here, they both overlap the functions of selecting the right means, track or vehicle for getting there. Our philosophy is that leadership must come first (determining the destination and perhaps directions to getting there), and management comes second to make sure the organization is able to achieve the goal of reaching the destination as efficiently as possible using available resources. Good leadership and management skills are especially important when one is the sole person responsible for a specific goal or outcome, such as the earning of a doctorate degree. Thus, doctoral students must be effective leaders and efficient managers of their time and available resources to successfully earn their higher education dream of achieving the terminal degree of their choice, while balancing its work with life's other important priorities (such as one's health, family, friends).

It is true that before climbing the "ladder of success" one must make sure his/her ladder is leaning against the right wall; otherwise, one might end up in the wrong place or location that is of no interest to one's overall life purpose. In this case, the "right wall" is about leadership, and "climbing" deals with management skills. Doctoral students must determine what topic and research question they would like to focus on during the course of their doctoral program before actually doing it. Selecting the right topic and research question is a very important process, and must not be rushed or jumped into too quickly. Appropriate planning, research, and studying must go into this process to make sure this is the topic one is willing to pursue over the next one, two or three years (depending on how fast one is willing to complete the program). The selection of the right topic and research question is important because choosing the "wrong" topic or question might create boredom and diminish a person's level of excitement as well as his/her motivation when minor "roadblocks" and "obstacles" come along the way. The selection of the topic and research question might make the difference in earning the doctorate degree or simply completing the courses and remaining ABD (all but dissertation). The point is that one must carefully and consciously choose the topic and research question as per his/her interest, motivation, knowledge, skill, time availability, research population connections, and other available resources that can help successfully complete the dissertation. One must spend enough time (and then a little more) in determining the right topic and research question for the dissertation project. As discussed in Chapter 7, once the right topic and research question(s) are selected, the rest is about managing the process or efficiently completing each needed task to achieve the outcome. In other words, a doctoral student must be a good leader and a very skilled manager to successfully achieve the terminal degree.

With regards to effective leadership on the dissertation project, doctoral students can begin their research by developing a prospectus or concept paper. This step may be helpful even if your school does not require that one be written. Once the topic and research question are selected and approved through a prospectus (or concept paper), then one can begin to manage the standardized steps of completing the dissertation process through its traditional five chapters. The selection of topic and the research question as well as the preparation of a prospectus or concept paper, preliminary literature, and Chapter I should be focused on answering such questions as the following:

1.   Why should this premise (idea) be researched?
2.   Why is this research topic important?
3.   Who would benefit from this research?
4.   What key research, prior to this dissertation, has addressed this premise?
5.   Which authors have done similar work on topics?
6.   Who are the key (important) researchers in this field?
7.   What is the contribution that these researchers have made?
8.   What are the conclusions of key researchers concerning the topic?
9.   How will the research follow or complement key researchers' work?
10.   How will the research expand or add to the "body of knowledge"?
11.   What are the potential "real world" applications of this research?
12.   What established theory, model, methodology, and survey instrument will be used to provide a sound analytical approach?
13.   Who is to be sampled, what is the sample size, and what is the expected return rate?

As a researcher, you must have a clear and focused research question or problem statement. A good research problem should deal with something that you have a genuine interest in; it should not be trivial; the area must be one that needs to be researched; and it should be amenable to either qualitative, quantitative, or a mixed method of research. Other questions to consider can include, but are not limited to: Can the student get the required data and the permission to get data? Can the student obtain specialist knowledge, especially statistical help? Is the student capable of doing the research, especially the statistical analysis? Can the student do the dissertation within a reasonable amount of time? Is the dissertation publishable through academic journals?

Almost all doctoral programs are concerned with the assessment of their students in the comprehensive exam and research areas. According to Beck-Dudley (2006), "we continually evaluate the effectiveness of the program, which has brought us to the following conclusions: producing terminally-degreed students for the academic market, as well as creating excellent scholars, teachers and members of the academy." Most doctoral programs require research activity the day the student enters into the university for the first course. Similarly, in most schools, producing sole-authored, peer-reviewed, research papers and journal paper submissions are expected. Of course, the dissertation process is established to help students become familiarized with primary research and the publication process.

Overall, it is important for doctoral students to begin their research on a topic of their interest during the initial stage in the program. Some faculty members or experts are likely to advise students to select a topic for their doctoral dissertation that will change their lives in a major way by making a huge contribution to academia or the practical world. Of course, this is one view and, although this is not the objective of a doctoral dissertation, it is an admirable goal. However, another practical and more realistic advice from experts is that a doctoral student should look at the dissertation project simply as a major task that must be completed to get used to the research process and to show that one can successfully do primary research. The latter view or advice is probably the best one for working adults who are trying to earn a terminal degree as part of their academic goal. There is no reason to try to change the world through a dissertation project, even if this were possible. Thus, stay focused on one specific (and doable) project, start early, and get it finished for the sake of doing primary research and completing one study as part of the doctoral program requirement.

Content and Format of the Dissertation[13]

In order to complete the dissertation in a reasonable period, we recommend that from the onset of your doctoral program you set a schedule for reading journal articles directed at your dissertation every week. This reading can be pursued even before an exact topic and problem are formulated (see Chapter 7 for more information on selecting a dissertation topic and conducting a reading schedule). While some schools may differ slightly on their dissertation format, the following is some general advice on writing and formatting your dissertation. For precise format questions, it is recommended that you review your school's dissertation guidelines.

Chapter One of the Dissertation

The first chapter should contain the following: purpose of the research, statement of problem and any sub-problem(s), background, justification for the study, definition of key terms, some relevant and recent literature, delimitations of the study, assumptions, expected contribution, and how the student intends to add to the body of knowledge. Delimitations should not be confused with the "Limitations," as the latter of which belongs in the last chapter of the dissertation. *Delimitations* of the study state what the student is not doing; for example, not surveying everyone everywhere, but only a class of participants at a selected geographic locale. Limitations, which are discussed in the dissertation Chapter V, are in essence the student's "confessions"; that is, now that the work is done, what should the student have done differently and why. The problem statement is the crucial element to the entire study. It will drive the methodology and the hypotheses. Many students make the mistake of selecting a methodology and then attempt to force the preferred methodology into a problem. For example, some students dislike statistics so much that they choose a qualitative methodology even when it does not fit with their problem statement. In most cases the committee chair will guide the student in another direction – either by changing the problem or methodology – but there have been cases when the student gets to the proposal stage prior to the issue being identified. The further along the process one is, the more difficult it is to change, and the more time is wasted going down the wrong path. The problem statement should drive the study's methodology – either quantitative, qualitative, or mixed methods. In other words, once you have solidified the problem the study wishes to address, the methodology to best study that problem

---

[13] Coauthored with Frank Cavico, Nova Southeastern University.

should be "second nature." One should remember that the research problem or premise is the general area to be investigated; the research propositions or research questions are more specific and state what one expects to find by means of the research; and the hypotheses are very specific statements, stated in the Null and then Alternative format, which the researcher will accept or reject based on his or her research findings. Each of these sections should flow, one into the next. For example, the problem statement should flow into one or more research questions. Each research question should lead to one or more hypotheses (assuming it is a quantitative study). Finally, each hypothesis should be tested using several questions on the survey instrument. Likewise, working in reverse, every question on a survey instrument should be tied to a specific hypothesis, which is tied to a research question, which is tied to the problem statement. The research problem/premise is typically stated in Chapter I of the dissertation; the research problem/premise, the need for the research, and the propositions are further justified and referenced in Chapter II; and the research problem/premise, propositions, and hypotheses in Null and Alternative forms are usually repeated again in Chapter III.

One must remember that the research problem is the purpose of the study, the student's statement of intent, which must be stated in a clear and concise manner, as it will be the premise to be tested. The problem statement should give a one or two sentence background, state the problem, and follow up with what is hoped to be accomplished. The student should be able to answer the following question: Can the research problem be concisely and precisely stated, ideally in one or two sentences? If so, create this sentence which will be the research question; then study it, memorize it, know it by heart, and stay focused on it until it is answered. The problem statement also supports the methodology expounded upon in chapter III of the dissertation. There are three general methods: quantitative, qualitative, and mixed methods. Each of these methodologies would have a very different problem statement. Even within each major type, the problem statement may differ slightly. An abbreviated example of each type of problem statement is given below:

Quantitative: "Sixty-four million Generation X workers made up about 29% of the U.S. population and approximately 39% of the labor force in 2000 (U.S. Census Bureau, 2004). A high percentage of Generation Xers do not stay with the same employer for more than five years, and most of them change jobs or contemplate quitting within the first three years (Rodriquez, et al., 2003)... A quantitative, descriptive, correlational research study of Generation X and Y professionals working in Baltimore, Maryland that assessed the relationship of leadership behaviors to their job satisfaction needs and job departure tendency was expected to yield new understandings of how knowledge professionals' needs and intent are influenced by their perceptions of their immediate supervisors' leadership behaviors" (Chan, 2005, pp. 7-8).

Qualitative: "While pressures on leaders mount, many lack the depth of leadership knowledge or awareness needed to improve performance. Despite the evolution of leadership thought, Americans receive modest exposure to successful leadership theories and qualities that one might glean from the past (Bolt, 1996). In this context, examination of an historical figure like Robert E. Lee might yield new understandings of leadership.

This case study, which will employ a hermeneutic mode of inquiry, will describe the circumstances, processes, relationships, and systems pertinent to Robert E. Lee's leadership behavior during the Battle of Gettysburg through the exploration of primary texts. This case study might suggest changes in the way theoreticians understand nineteenth century leadership and the possible implications of such new understandings for present leadership theory. A case study applied toward an historical individual may yield insights that enlighten existing academic literature and improve organizational leadership performance" (Schlesinger, 2006, p. 8)

Mixed methods: "Although virtual environments require the same basic management and leadership responsibilities, the limited ability to meet with virtual employees face-to-face may encumber managers when conducting individual performance feedback and employee developmental activities (Bell & Kozlowski, 2002). This mixed methods study will explore the relationship between the virtualness of the employee and the perceived level of performance feedback, developmental feedback, trust, and leader-member exchange. The study will also explore the patterns of perceived feedback effectiveness and best practices for communicating feedback to virtual employees. The results of this study may provide information how leaders might provide feedback and developmental activities that are more effective to virtual employees, leading to increased employee performance, motivation, and loyalty (McDermott, 2001)" (Scharff, 2005, p. 5). In a mixed methods study, there is both a quantitative and qualitative component. Both of these components should be easily identifiable within the problem statement.

Chapter I of the dissertation normally begins with a short introduction to the study. Significant effort should be given to writing a good introduction as it sets the tone for the study. Many have recommended that the introduction should include a "hook" in the first couple sentences. The *hook* is used to hook the reader on why the study is important and why they should continue reading the study. One way to create a hook is to highlight some alarming statistic within the first few sentences (i.e. unemployment is increasing by X%, funding is decreasing by X, medical expenses are increasing by X%, market share increases or decreases, etc.). The researcher should also know the difference between the problem statement and sub-problems, which too can be studied now and also in future projects. "Problem" is broader formulation; the sum of sub-problems, which are narrowly stated, and which add up to the problem; but which are mutually exclusive, and thus each can be researched independently. Overall, the student must research the background of the problem and provide justification on why one should spend such a major part of one's life in further studying it. One should fully provide justification for initiating this research by comprehensively answering the following questions:

1. Why should this premise (idea) be researched; why is the research topic important; and who would benefit from the research?
2. How will the student's work follow or complement others' work? How will the research add to or expand the body of knowledge?
3. What are the potential "real world" applications of this research?

Chapter I may also include a definition of specific or unusual terms used within the research and the assumptions of the study. With regards to the definition of specific terms, it is best to remember that specific and/or complex terminology must be clearly defined either in Chapter I or in the literature review section of Chapter II. Also, with regard to assumptions, one should clarify what facts are taken for granted in the study? For example, most qualitative studies assume that the random sample accurately reflects the characteristics of the entire population. Overall, with regard to the delimitations, the student must state explicitly what he or she is not doing (for example, certain sample size, geographic area, type and/or level of position sampled). To clarify once again, delimitations are "up front" constraints to the study, while limitations are shortcomings ('confessions") that have been revealed during the course of the study and which are addressed in Chapter V of the dissertation.

Many schools require the submission of a concept paper or prospectus for the approval of one's research question(s) and to demonstrate commitment to a focused problem statement. As stated before, the concept paper or prospectus should be in essence a short-form version of Chapter I of the dissertation. The Concept Paper or Prospectus is normally 5-10 pages (plus any other references and supplementary material). It should include a concise discussion of the core literature as well as a description of the literature the student intends to review. A preliminary literature review is not always required in the prospectus or concept paper. The research approach, that is, the dissertation's basic methodological design, should be stated, but succinctly in a paragraph or two. The Prospectus or Concept Paper also must have integrated relevant and current scholarly research to show that the student has done appropriate review of the literature. Full references must be included. Many schools use the American Psychological Association (APA) style for dissertations. While APA is used at the majority of schools, others may use a different format. Students should purchase a book on whatever format their school uses, and make sure that they are using the latest version. Nothing is more frustrating than to get close to completion only to find hundreds of formatting issues stopping your dissertation from being approved. Most of the time students have plenty of opportunity to assess their acumen at formal academic writing during their coursework. After the coursework, if you do not feel proficient in academic writing or APA, it may be well worth the time and money to hire a writing editor or an APA editor. Overall, one can summarize that the first chapter is basically the longer and more developed version of the Prospectus or Concept Paper, and thus it should parallel it. The first chapter should contain:

- *Introduction to the study.* This section should succinctly introduce the reader to the study. We also recommend the first paragraph have a "hook" to get the reader interested in the study. Additionally, the introduction should address the current gap within the existing literature.
- *Background.* This section briefly highlights some of the previous studies relating to the topic.
- *Purpose of the research.* This section is normally short and in only a couple sentences highlights what the study hopes to accomplish. This section normally includes words such as purpose, intent, objective, or goal of the study.
- *Statement of problems and sub-problems.* Problem statements are normally short (about a page) and broadly define the issue being studied. Many

schools require the words "the problem is…" within the problem statement to ensure the student has identified an issue.

- *Research Question(s).* Research questions are used as a guide for the entire study. According to Creswell (2003), research questions "shape and specifically focus the purpose of the study. Research questions are interrogative statements that the investigator seeks to answer" (p. 108).
- *Hypotheses (for quantitative studies).* Hypotheses are generally identified in quantitative studies. Hypotheses provide "a tentative explanation for the phenomenon under investigation (Leedy & Ormrod, 2005, p. 4). Most schools require both the alternative hypothesis (you will find a difference) and the null hypothesis (there will not be a difference) be listed in the dissertation.
- *Justification for study.* This section is normally short and identifies why the study is significant and worthy of doctoral research.
- *Definition of key terms.* Providing a list of definitions insures a shared meaning among readers (Scharff, 2005). Any unusual terms or terms used in different ways should be identified in this section. For example, the term *employee feedback* may be one that is in the definition of key terms if you are using that term to mean one specific type of feedback. You should not, however, define everyday terms.
- *Delimitations of the study.* Delimitations are used to narrow the scope of the study or to list what is not included or intended in the study (Creswell, 2003; Leedy & Ormrod, 2005). Limitations are in essence the student's "confessions" about what should or could have been done differently and why.
- *Assumptions.* This section lists all the areas assumed to be true within the scope of the research.
- *Summary.* Each chapter within the dissertation normally ends with a summary of the chapter and the study.

The research problem/premise is typically stated in Chapter I of the dissertation; the research problem/premise and the propositions are also stated at the end of Chapter II at many schools; and the research problem/premise, propositions, and hypotheses in Null and Alternative forms are stated again in Chapter III. As part of tradition and requirement, one should know that there will be much repetition of the research question and the hypothesis in a dissertation.

Chapter Two of the Dissertation

The major objective of Chapter II, which is the Literature Review or historical summary of what has been written thus far in regard to the specific variables being studied, is to review the pertinent literature, that is, the literature that applies the theory to the research problem. The idea is not to "write a book," but rather to focus on the literature that pertains directly to the research premise or problem, the research propositions, the hypotheses, and the variables therein. At the end of the Literature Review, the student should include a succinct paragraph or two demonstrating how the review of the literature has logically led the student to examine the research problem/premise, propositions (that is, what the student expects to find), and hypotheses. It is not necessary in Chapter II for the student to state the hypotheses in Null and Alternative form, as that component of the work belongs properly in Chapter III.

While providing a summary of general literature; focus should be on the literature that applies the theory. The researcher basically answers: What key research has addressed the research problem or premise? What authors have done similar work on the topic? Who are the important researchers in the field? What are their conclusions? What contributions have they made? This chapter needs literature that explains how the theory applies to the research problem. Emphasis should be on the application of the theory, especially literature that helps to identify potential solutions to the research problem. The chapter also needs literature that justifies the research question, problem statements, and hypotheses. Do not merely "regurgitate" the work of others, especially if they are not related to the current research problem. Be systematic and chronologically, recognize any hierarchy to literature sources. Overall, remember that the:

- The major objective of Chapter II, which is the Literature Review, is to review the pertinent literature, that is, the literature that applies the theory to the research problem.
- Focus on the literature that pertains directly to the research premise or problem, the research propositions, the hypotheses, and the variables therein.
- At the end of the Literature Review chapter, the student should include a succinct paragraph or two demonstrating how the review of the literature has logically led the student to examine the research problem/premise, propositions (that is, what the student expects to find), and hypotheses. Note that it is not necessary in Chapter II for the student to state the hypotheses in Null and Alternative form, as that component of the work belongs properly in Chapter III.

Dr. Albert Williams, a colleague and an educator of statistics and research methodology, along with other experienced doctoral faculty advisors, recommend that students do a thorough literature search for their topic if they are to successfully complete the first three chapters or proposal for the doctoral study. This can be best achieved by doing a thorough study of each article that has been published in the specific area dealing with the proposed research question. Each article has to be reviewed and summarized with regard to its relationship to the research questions proposed. Students must provide the highlights of each article as well as get the objective of the article, the methodology used, and the findings and recommendations. Oftentimes, the abstract of each published article is a good starting point and the introduction also tends to have a number of the main points studied. The conclusion must also be studied well as it points to the overall findings and future research possibilities. However, for more details of the methodology, students must go further into the body of each article, "dissect" it, understand it, and summarize the main points in one's literature review or the second chapter of the dissertation. As students complete this literature search, they will come across some key articles that pertain to their specific research question(s) and, as explained by Dr. Albert Williams, getting these main points into the second chapter are the "trump cards" for the dissertation's literature. The literature review, or this "leg" of the journey in the dissertation completion process, is extremely important and must be done extremely well. Some general questions regarding Chapter II may be:

How do I keep track of all the information required? Obviously, some degree of organization is required. Yet even for the most organized, the volume of information to complete Chapter 2 may be overwhelming. Some preplanning, prior to starting Chapter 2, should be considered. Nothing is more frustrating than printing or copying articles only to find out that you had already read them. Using a database to keep track of all the articles you have read (whether you find them useful or not) may prove extremely helpful. This database can keep track of the articles/books read as well as a summary of each article. For those that aren't familiar with database searches, similar functionality is available on most commercial software programs.

Where should I go to find literature on my topic? Most research institutions have substantial libraries. Regardless of the university, you should not limit yourself to on ground resources. Many universities also have access to large commercial electronic databases as well. Two of the larger are ProQuest and InfoTrac. There may also be topic specific databases. For example, there may be specific databases targeted at the medical or education fields. Because of the volume and nature of some publications, it is recommended that you limit your reading to only peer-reviewed (scholarly) journals/sources. Running multiple searches in these online databases should help students find a "gold mine" of relevant material.

How do I know when I'm done researching? This is a great question, and one that most students find difficult. This may be especially true with the number of electronic resources available. The volume of articles available electronically on any topic is staggering. One way to limit your research is to focus on peer-reviewed journals/articles. In your research, you are expected to read all the available literature on your topic and summarize relevant elements in Chapter II. You will know you are done when you have reached the saturation point. In other words, you are perhaps done when you are no longer identifying new articles while reading others. This is also *why* you want to select as narrow a topic as possible. Selecting very broad topics may not only be difficult to test, but also the volume of articles may be overwhelming.

I was told that I set the pace for my dissertation research, is this true? Yes, this is true to some extent. You can certainly delay the process, however, there is little you can do to speed up the process dramatically. There are a number of steps the dissertation has to go through and a committee of three professors that must agree that your research is ready to move to the next step. So the short answer is that you have significant control over slowing the process down, but perhaps very little impact in speeding the process up.

Chapter Three of the Dissertation

Chapter III is the methodology section of the Proposal and dissertation. As stated in the section on Chapter I, the methodology should be developed from the problem statement. In general, there are three different methods, quantitative, qualitative, and mixed methods. There are numerous books available on each of these methods. In general, quantitative studies include true experiments, quasi-experiments, and correlational studies. Quantitative studies are based on survey data and statistical analysis. Within the broad scope of qualitative methodology, many types exist including phenomenology, grounded theory, narrative research, case study, and ethnography. Phenomenology studies groups over time to identify patterns and interactions from the group's experiences. Grounded theory attempts to develop new theories based on the processes and actions of the research participants. Narrative research studies the oral traditions of the research participants. Case studies focus on identifying themes within the system and may be historical, process based, or activity based. Lastly, ethnography studies subsections of groups subdivided by various ethnic groups in relationship to society. Regardless of the type, qualitative studies are normally based on open-ended interview questions, observation, or document analysis (Creswell, 2003). A mixed methods approach includes elements of both quantitative and qualitative methodologies. Because a mixed methods design utilizes both quantitative and qualitative methods, mixed methods research tends to neutralize the drawbacks inherent in any one methodology (Morse, 2003).

The goal of Chapter III is to propose a methodological "recommended path" for the dissertation. It should, in detail, describe your research plan and what tests you will utilized to develop your recommendations. If you are completing a quantitative or mixed methods research, this detail should be based on a number of hypotheses that will be tested. Hypotheses should be limited to a manageable number based on time constraints as well as the student's statistical capabilities. The statement of five to six hypotheses, stated in the Null and Alternative format, is a good foundation for a dissertation research. If you are completing a qualitative study, Chapter III should include details of exactly what process and procedures will be utilized to obtain and analyze the data.

In the methodology chapter, one needs to restate research question and problem statement from the previous two chapters. One should understand that hypothesis testing means that one is to assess the likelihood that a premise is true. Accordingly, formulate hypotheses in Null and Alternative formats. If Null format is rejected, then the Alternative format is accepted. The result is that one narrows the range of falsity and thereby expands the body of knowledge. The researcher should keep in mind that there is a difference between a hypothesis and a proposition. Hypothesis is a narrow and specific assumption that can be tested and accepted or rejected; whereas a proposition is more of a general plan or agenda for research, which is not necessarily tested. It is best not to have any complex or "mixed" hypotheses; that is, there should be one hypothesis for each variable. Otherwise, one may get into trouble whereby some of the hypothesis is true and another part is false. Chapter III should really clarify every question about this research, and it should state the population, sample size, sampling method, and expected outcome. Be realistic about sample size, but attempt to secure a sample as large as practically possible (200 is recommended as a minimum for quantitative studies). The researcher also needs a random sample so as to generalize results; otherwise, one should state the limitations and possibilities of the research. State the survey instrument to be used to secure research data as well as the questionnaire to be used with the survey instrument. How will you get permission for using the instrument or survey? Identify exactly what is to be measured by using this instrument.

Chapter III of the dissertation, in addition to the aforementioned components, normally includes the following:

- *Population.* In all types of research, the population should include where you are getting the data. In quantitative research this would normally include the overall population and the sample size you will be using. In qualitative research the population could include the actual individuals being surveyed but could also include other means like books, movies, memoirs, etc. Mixed methods research would include elements of both.

- *Design.* This section would highlight the design of the study. In other words, exactly how the research will be carried out. This section normally highlights a step-by-step approach method of data analysis (that is, what is the student going to do with the data; and what statistical tools will be used to analyze the data).

- *Method of analysis* (that is, what is the student going to do with the data; and what statistical tools will be used to analyze the data). According to Goodman (2003), three major types of research errors have been identified that need to be addressed in any research: sampling, processing, and observational errors.
  - *Sampling Errors.* Major sampling errors are comprised of non-inclusion errors where individuals are included in the survey sample that should not be as well as non-response errors.
  - *Processing Errors.* Processing errors include computational errors and utilizing inappropriate measures. Computational errors are mistakes made during calculation of statistics while using inappropriate measures includes employing inappropriate analytical techniques. Although these types of errors can never be eradicated (Goodman, 2003), both types of processing errors can be minimized by utilizing proper statistical techniques and software packages.
  - *Observation Errors.* According to Goodman (2003), observation errors can include errors in the question, interviewer, recording, or coding. Question errors occur if a question is misleading or improperly worded. Interviewer errors include any errors the interviewer makes while asking the question. Recording errors occur when the interviewer records the participant's response incorrectly. Coding errors occur when taking written survey information and transferring the data to an electronic format (either a spreadsheet or database).

- *Source of data.* This section would normally include the survey instrument or questionnaire, or source of data. Chapter III will normally have the survey instrument (although in most dissertations it would be at an attachment) and highlight what each question hopes to achieve. Each question in the survey should be directly related to one of the study's hypothesis.

- *Validity.* The validity of a study indicates the probability that statistically significant data and conclusions can be drawn from the study. Validity of an instrument equates to the degree to which it measures what it is intended to measure. "Validity errors reflect biases in the instrument itself and are relatively constant sources of error" (Leedy & Ormrod, 2005, p. 29). If a survey instrument is somewhat "old" or "outdated," the student will have to address the "validity" issue. For example, is the instrument still valid? Has it been updated? Do the questions and scenarios therein comport with current practices, usages, customs, and ideas? If the instrument is still fundamentally valid, but old, the student should point this out in Chapter I in the Delimitations section. The methodologist on the committee should be consulted before the student initiates, and certainly before the student completely, writes Chapter III.

- *Reliability of the study.* Reliability indicates the dependability that the survey instrument will produce a consistent result (Leedy & Ormrod, 2005). Reliability errors "reflect use of the instrument and are apt to vary unpredictably from one occasion to the next" (Leedy & Ormrod, 2005, p. 29). Leedy and Ormrod (2005) suggest ensuring that the instrument is administered in an identical manner as a method to increase the instrument's reliability. For qualitative studies, ensuring that the individuals facilitating the questionnaires are well-trained would also increase an instrument's reliability.

In addition to the sections above, many schools require students to address research ethics within Chapter III of the dissertation. According to the Council of American Survey Research Organizations (2004), all individuals and organizations conducting research have ethical responsibilities. These ethical issues, at a minimum, could include anonymity of research participants, unbiased analysis, voluntary participation by survey participants, and Institutional Review Board approval. Chapter III may also include a research map, which highlights the general steps that will be taken in the research.

It is best to avoid sensitive and political topics in questionnaires; start with non-threatening questions, for example, demographic information. The questionnaire should flow smoothly from one question to the next; and proceed from broad, general questions to the more specific. Keep questions clear and short, applicable to all respondents; and make the instructions plain and distinct. Keep in mind that people's time is very valuable; so the survey should be short and respectful of their precious time. If the survey is too long and complicated, there will be a non-response problem. Keep in mind that there is an inverse relationship between the length of the questionnaire and the quality of the information obtained. Note that pre-existing surveys and questionnaires are permissible if demonstrated as valid and reliable; yet the student must use them in a unique way so as to expand the body of knowledge and make a contribution. If a "new" instrument or questionnaire is being used, how does it measure and compare to other instruments or measures (convergent validity); and is this "new" instrument with separate dimensions really separate and distinct? Where on the instrument and/or questionnaire will information come from to test the hypothesis? Demonstrate or establish the validity and reliability of the survey instrument. That is the key.

Be aware that the terms validity and reliability must be clarified for each instrument that is being used for the study. Validity refers to the extent an instrument measures what one wants it to measure; whereas reliability means the measurement procedure is accurate and precise. That is, what evidence is there of measurement (validity), and how precise and accurate is the measurement (reliability)? There is also a difference between external and internal validity. External validity refers to the ability of the research to be generalized across persons, settings, and times; key factors are sample choice, size, and method (random), as well as credibility for qualitative research. Internal validity refers to the extent the measuring instrument provides adequate coverage of the topic. That is, what are the dimensions of a topic, according to the literature, what questionnaires have been used, and what questions have been asked? If an existing survey instrument or questionnaire is being modified by the student, then the modified version must be demonstrated as valid and reliable. Thus, it is better to seek and to add the supplemental information separately when using an existing instrument. In order to increase a study's external validity,

Leedy and Ormrod (2005) recommend three solutions. Using real settings instead of laboratory environments, according to Leedy and Ormrod (2005), will increase external validity, although there may be issues with maintaining control over all variables. Secondly, ensuring the sample selected for the study is representative of the total population is critical to ensure external validity. Finally, replication of the study's conclusions in various contexts is an indication of external validity. State explicitly the method to be used to analyze the data. Overall, reliability is the extent to which the instrument is free from variable error (random error), or the degree of variable error in the instrument. Validity is the extent to which the instrument is free from systemic error (bias), or the degree of systemic error in the instrument. Accuracy is defined as the extent to which the instrument is free from systemic and variable errors.

The researcher must also understand correlation and regression. Correlation means there is a relationship or association between two variables; it does not imply that one causes the other; whereas regression assumes causation; that is, an independent variable causes a dependent one. For example, does advertising cause sales (regression), or is there a relationship between advertising and sales (correlation)? Overall, the data secured must relate to and be tied into the research question/problems, so as to "answer" them. The research methodology and design process in Chapter III of the dissertation should clarify many issues including defining the research problem, premise to be tested, required information and data, and appropriate variables for the study. Know that statistical hypothesis is basically a statement about one or more parameters of the population. Hypotheses testing assess the likelihood that an assumption about some characteristics of the population is true. Rejecting or not rejecting the hypothesis means proving or disproving the hypothesis. Null hypothesis, the H_0, is basically an assumption about the population that is tested, using sample evidence. Alternative hypothesis, the H_1, is a statement about the population that must be true if the null hypothesis is rejected. The researcher must avoid complex or "mixed" hypotheses; in other words, one should only have one hypothesis for each variable. The researcher must then decide on whether the study will use a qualitative approach or a quantitative process to gather the data.

The biggest challenge for a dissertation study is to keep it focused and simple. One should not attempt to change the world, as this project is only for the student to prove that he or she can conduct quality research and focus on one specific research question. So, keep the focus of the dissertation narrow, time-bounded, and, given one's limited available resources, make sure the survey implementation and data gathering processes are easily "do-able." Overall, with regard to the entire study, make sure that the dissertation is a "do-able" one. Be keenly aware of time constraints; accordingly, allocate sufficient time; make an appointment with oneself; do a little every day, even if just writing a paragraph or a few sentences. Avoid the "Royal We" writing style, as it is one person doing the research; instead use a neutral more modest approach, that is, "the author" or "this study" type of description. It is always good to be humble. While the researcher might be the "king" or "queen" in his/her department, industry, or profession, it is best to remember that one is probably a novice in the research process; therefore, get as much help as possible and thank each person for his/her assistance and guidance. Overall, with regard to the study, seek the best approximation of the "truth" based on current knowledge.

Before beginning the research process, the learner should be aware of the institution's Institutional Review Board (IRB) policies regarding research requirements and prerequisites with human subjects. Most institutions have a policy stating that no pretests, "pilots," or surveys that will be published can be distributed without IRB approval; similarly, no "field work" can be conducted without IRB approval. IRB approval is often needed for any questioning of human subjects. However, for surveys, IRB approval can be obtained at the "center" level by the IRB representative, and thus petitioning the university's IRB may not always be necessary. The student can state in his or her Proposal that IRB approval will be obtained for any pretest or pilot, and then either option can be implemented; however, the full survey should not be distributed until not only after IRB approval, but also the approval of the student's dissertation committee.

In summary, remember that the goal of Chapter III of the dissertation is to propose a methodological "recommended path" for the dissertation. Hypotheses should be limited to a manageable number based on time constraints as well as the student's statistical capabilities. The statement of five to six hypotheses, stated in the Null and Alternative formats, is a good foundation for dissertation research. Chapter III, in addition to the aforementioned components, should include the following: population (sample size and who is being surveyed), sample methodology or design (e.g., random sample), survey instrument or questionnaire, source of data, validity and reliability of survey instrument, and methods of data analysis. The methodologist on the committee should be consulted before the student writes Chapter III.

Chapter Four of the Dissertation

Chapter IV is the analysis of the results from the data gathered as a result of what was planned in the first three chapters. For most schools, the required statistical software seems to be the Numbers Crunchers Statistical Software (NCSS) (Student Version), or the other popular software like SPSS or Minitab. Of course, students who are advanced in statistical testing are not limited to using these packages, so long as they are able to use statistical testing effectively. Chapter IV presents data, including the initial categories explored, exactly how the data was obtained, the patterns of feedback found, and the statistical analyses conducted. The methodological procedures followed during the pilot test (if applicable) and the actual study are also provided in Chapter IV.

Chapter Five of the Dissertation

The last chapter simply summarizes the purpose of the study, the conclusions, provides a link about the benefits of the study, makes some recommendations for academics, practitioners, and managers, discusses the limitations of the study, and provides guidance and questions for future study. The real purpose of Chapter V is to bring all your research, statistics, and findings into one "neat" package. Suggestions for future scholarly work should be provided, and should be tied into the limitation "confessions" where appropriate. This is where a writer can insert his/her opinion, recommendations, observations, suggestions, models, and personal thoughts regarding the topic into the dissertation. Researchers are encouraged to put their personal thoughts regarding the implications of their findings in this section of their dissertation. If they want their research to be useful to practitioners, then this is where they can expand on it and discuss the how, why, and variables as appropriate.

References for the Dissertation

A good researcher gives credit where credit is due, and accordingly cites all of materials that come from other sources. Furthermore, a review of the major works, studies and authors in the area of a specific research question and various independent and dependent variables being studied can provide credibility to one's proposal by demonstrating that one has thoroughly reviewed the field. The references section of the dissertation must include all the works cited (if a work is cited within the document, then it must also appear in the references, and if a work is in the references it must appear in the body of the work as a citation). Some schools also require a bibliography section in addition to the reference section. The bibliography, which appears after the reference section, includes all the references as well as all the works that the student used for the dissertation, for example, background books and articles, but which were not specifically cited. Some schools may also require a certain percent of research and references to have been conducted or published in the last five years. This policy ensures that students have found the most recent literature and research on the topic.

Appendices Section of the Dissertation

The appendix section can include copies of survey instrument, additional questionnaires, and "permissions" for using any copyright material. This section can also include any other data, figures, tables, or visuals that readers might to review to further understand a concept that is discussed within the dissertation.

Overall, the researcher must be aware of his or her writing format and the overall consistency or "flow." There should be, in the dissertation, a logical consistency "flow" proceeding downwards from the general to the specific, to wit: the title of the work stated, to the problem, to the sub-problems, to the research questions, to the propositions, to the hypotheses, to the instrument design, to the sample plan, to the method of data analysis, to the presentation of the data, to the explanation of the data, and finally to the acceptance or rejection of the hypotheses. Then there should be a consistency "flow" upwards from the acceptance or rejection of the hypotheses to the answering of the propositions and the solving of the research problem.

In the review process of your dissertation by the Chair and Committee Members, always submit clear and edited material for their review. Never submit draft copies "just get to their opinion" as this might give them a negative first impression about the quality of your work. As you may know, first impressions are very difficult to overcome. So, be cautious and always submit your best work to them. This way they realize that you have done comprehensive work and are serious about the quality of your submissions. Furthermore, with quality submissions you don't waste their time or yours. Also, with quality submissions for their review you are likely to receive good "feedback" as well. Although an editor is not required, an editor, or a colleague who can serve as one, is strongly recommended so that the student can concentrate on approach, substance, logic, and the writing of the work, and not be overly involved with editing and formatting. The editor must be very familiar not only with the latest version of the American Psychological Association (APA) but also the university's dissertation format requirements. Typically, the student's dissertation committee chair, colleagues at school, or a committee member might be able to recommend an editor. Note that there is an APA "crib sheet," (at www.docstyles.com) that has a pop-up box on the screen, for quick reference, but not as a substitute for an editor. Once the problem, research question, and concept paper or prospectus have been developed, the student should immediately work on securing a Chair (or advisor) and committee members for his or her dissertation process. See Chapter 7 of this book for more detail on setting up a dissertation committee.

Advisors and Expectations

Having a specific topic as a research question for the dissertation project can make one's doctoral life much easier, as one can begin reading the right journals, speak with the "right" authors in this field, attend relevant sessions in such conferences as the Society for Human Resource Management (SHRM) or the Academy of Management as appropriate, network with the academicians and practitioners, and secure a source or population for data gathering. Once the research question and dissertation topic is clarified, then it is one's responsibility to stay the course and complete the project as soon as possible, while continuing to successfully finish the required doctoral courses and the comprehensive exam in a balanced manner. At this stage, it is recommended that the student collect and review as many recently published dissertations in this area as possible. These dissertations can be gathered from the best schools from around the globe. However, another important aspect of the dissertation process is to secure and assemble the right committee for one's research. See Chapter 7 for more information on selecting a dissertation chair and committee members.

The Dissertation Defense

The final step in the dissertation process is the dissertation defense. This step is normally conducted once all three committee members agree that your research is ready. In most schools, this meeting is open to the public as well as other faculty members, although it is rare any one beyond your committee members and a few members from the faculty or administration attends. In general, you will be introducing your study, including the background, problem, findings, and recommendations of your study. Although you should seek guidance from your committee chair, your section of the dissertation defense normally lasts about one hour. In most cases, your presentation includes handouts of your research complemented with oral presentation and other visuals such as PowerPoint slides. At most traditional schools, your defense will be face-to-face, although this is not always an option at most non-traditional institutions where the student, the Chair, and committee members might be living across the country or even in different counties. At non-traditional schools, the student is normally responsible for coordinating, paying for, and setting up a conference call to conduct the defense.

Once you have presented your findings, you are then responsible for answering questions that the attendees have. While the question and answer period can be the most nerve-racking for the student, you should remember that it is your study and you are the most knowledgeable person on the topic and your research. Additionally, your committee members are also there to support you in the successful dissertation defense. If things go very wrong, they can "reel" the conversation back to more familiar grounds. While this is a possibility, it is rarely needed, as most students are over-prepared for their dissertation defense, and thus are almost disappointed at how easy it was compared to how well they prepared for every potential question that could be asked. However, as a general rule, it is far better to be prepared for the question that is never asked than to be unprepared for one that is.

Summary

As stated in NSU Huizenga School's 2006 Dissertation Guidelines, "A dissertation is an unpredictable process," as it can "involve uncertainty, ambiguity, and unexpected events." It is an uncertain process because the researcher is exploring unknown questions and topics. Therefore, one must be patient and persevere in achieving the dream of successfully completing the comprehensive exam and the dissertation projects in order to earn a doctorate degree.

While there is no *perfect* institution, higher education and doctoral programs should have an infrastructure in place that ensures learning happens at a high-level consistently, so their students can successfully achieve their academic dreams. There should be an emphasis on the development of high-level curricula that blends pragmatic and theoretical knowledge, so doctoral students can pass their comprehensive exams and successfully complete their doctoral dissertations in the allotted time.

Today, cyberspace technologies offer many possibilities in the twenty-first century, but such possibilities cannot be realized without breaking the outdated industry rules of the past. Breaking industry rules requires effective training of both faculty members and administrative staff, so they can jointly be more flexible in hearing their students' learning needs and so they can be empowered to be innovative in integrating student "feedback" in the education process, while trying new learning strategies in helping doctoral students become "doctors."

Most importantly, to become a "doctor" and in order to efficiently complete the doctoral dissertation process, you should be a self-motivator, and make sure to surround yourself with one or more respected friends who have expertise in your area of interest. Bernard Berkowitz is quoted as having said that "It is up to us to give ourselves recognition. If we wait for it to come from others, we feel resentful when it doesn't, and when it does, we may well reject it." So, be a self-motivator and make sure to "befriend" several great and caring individuals that can serve as coaches, guides, advisors, and confidants to you in this process.

A friend is like father who scolds you,
like mother who hugs you,
like sister who teases you,
like brother who fights you,
in short combine all worldly relations
you will have a friend, and that is what makes a friend above all relations.

By: Dr. Amanullah

9 – Conference Networking and Publishing

P ublishing is an important aspect of a doctoral program and the best way to do this is to develop a good network of colleagues and peers in one's profession through academic conferences and journals. Most doctoral programs that require students to publish will also encourage them to attend professional and academic conferences in their areas of specialization. Some of the professional and academic conferences in business and management include the Society for Human Resource Management (SHRM), the Academy of Management (AoM), Southern Management Association (SMA), Western Academy of Management, the Association for International Business, the Society for Advancement of Management (SAM), and other specialized events that take place annually so students and researchers can become familiarized with the authors in their fields. By attending these conferences, doctoral students can network with authors who are the primary and secondary researchers in their areas of study.

This chapter includes some of the specific professional events that have been attended by various doctoral students who also wrote about their experiences and benefits gained from each event. Furthermore, students also become aware of various journal publishers and editors who are looking for authors and co-authors to conduct research and write papers on various topics. One can also find consulting and speaking opportunities by attending these professional conferences and networking with experts in one's industry.

It should be clarified that it is the responsibility and obligation of each doctoral graduate to publish the findings of his or her dissertation research as quickly as possible. Furthermore, it is an obligation for the doctoral graduate to "honor" his or her committee members and dissertation chair for their time, guidance and mentorship through the publication of a quality journal article with them as coauthors. While honoring one's dissertation chair and committee members as coauthor of the research findings, a doctoral graduate is also promoting his or her name as well as the dissertation research. If the dissertation chair and committee members are coauthors of the published work, then they are more likely to reference it in their future articles and studies, and recommend the dissertation to others. Otherwise, without a great promotional program, the dissertation is likely to collect dust in the school's library with few individuals ever reading or referencing it. So, it is the responsibility of the doctoral graduate to get the dissertation results published, promoted and made available for others to read.

Getting Published

Publishing can separate the "boys" from the "men" or the serious graduates (researchers) from those who just want to earn the degree for the sake of having the title or diploma. Publishing can also further enhance teaching and consulting opportunities.

One of the best ways to publish is to transfer your personal experiences and learning in a written format so it can be used by others on a just-in-time basis. The learning that takes place in the classroom and when one is attending various professional conferences or seminars can be a great source for the writing of practical and unique narratives, case studies, and article publications. For example, one can take any of the following presentation summaries gleaned from the 2006 SHRM conference, research it, survey experts about it, and further develop it into a full paper for immediate use by one's industry, organization, department, or colleagues. Once the paper is fully developed and the various sources are acknowledged, the paper can be submitted for a review and constructive criticism by one's colleagues. Then, it can be officially submitted to a proper outlet for actual publication consideration through a conference, trade journal, or an academic journal that is seeking this type of content.

A great way to begin publishing in academic journals is by starting with one's dissertation research. Before one's dissertation is complete, students can do other papers and propositional papers that make good use of secondary research and sources to get one or two publications. Once the dissertation project is completed, one should prepare the entire study into one or two 25-30 page papers for submission to appropriate journal(s) for peer-review and possible publication. The student or graduate should prepare the draft of the paper and submit to the chair and committee members for their review and feedback prior to submission to the journal editor. Once everyone's input is integrated into the final paper, then it should be sent for review and acceptance consideration to the journal editor. The journal should be seeking papers on this topic, otherwise sending it to them will be a waste of time (for you and them) as they will not consider it for publication. So, find and gear the paper toward an appropriate journal. One way to find an appropriate journal is to look at the references within the paper you wish to have published. Are there any trends? Are there any specific journals referenced or cited many times? Every quality paper has a "home" and finding the right "home" is usually sixty percent of the processes. The other forty percent is the review, development, and final preparation process. In any case, the student should be able to get at least one good publication from the completed research and by publishing with the Chair and Committee Members as co-authors, the student is honoring them for their guidance, time and mentorship in the dissertation process. While the Chair or Committee Members may not encourage or push the student to publish the findings, it is an obligation for the student to get the material published and mention those who helped him/her as co-authors. Keep in mind that most schools do not compensate faculty members very well for guiding students through their dissertation process. So, it is often a voluntary process where the Chair and Committee Members agree to be a member of the team in hopes of learning something new from the student's findings and, hopefully, being acknowledged once the data are published. So, it is best to get the material published as quickly as possible before the data becomes outdated in the field. Keep in mind that getting your material published can also increase your credibility in the academic world and, depending on where it is published, it can also lead to possible consulting jobs.

The following presentation summaries are some of the specific benefits mentioned by doctoral students when they attended an academic conference and when they focused on getting the most out of each session and speaker for their practice and/or dissertation. Some of the speakers have even served as informal advisors in guiding students toward a sample population for the dissertation research and studies.

Presentations Summaries from the 2006 SHRM Conference

How to Do Your Job without Losing Your Mind or Your Sense of Humor[14]

The purpose of the Monday session *"How to Do Your Job without Losing Your Mind or Your Sense of Humor"* was to provide strategies to reduce stress and refocus your energy to create balance in your career and life with humor.

Jean Gatz communicated with the Human Resource practitioners through selected music that related to their everyday life of stress at work, such as "You had a bad day." She then went on to describe how she was born into a stressful situation at a funeral home in Virginia and then moved to a cemetery in New Orleans as her father was in the death business. The humorous portion of her story was centered on her childhood friends in both locations.

The presentation, however, was geared toward forgetting your job, title and concentrating more on self, personal time and the session. Her belief is that new ideas and strategies will make most people more effective and better employees while gaining a sense of humor. Gatz then asked the audience to think about how stressful it is to plan a car trip and then list three things that would be done to plan the perfect trip. If filling your gas tank was on the list then "What are you doing to full yourself?" Other points relating to a planned car trip or driving included: (1) Take your drivers license – Earn the right skills, education and credentials, (2) Don't rely on auto-pilot and cruise control – Are you doing your job on auto, if so then it is boring due to lack of passion for the job, (3) Be prepared for detours – Get off the well trodden path and overcome fears, (4) Choose passengers carefully – That trip called life and job, (5) Don't be afraid to stop and ask for directions – What skills will you use? and (6) Drive defensively to avoid accidents – Are you frozen in a job without passion? Gatz then goes on to discuss the four categories of how most employees feel about dealing with change that ranged from excited to not ready but maybe later. The major

---

[14] Prepared by Joann Adeogun, Nova Southeastern University.

questions that employees must ask themselves are "What is stopping me from moving forward and how much longer can I wait?"

Personal analysis. Splendid! Jean Gatz presented an easy to follow model of taking a road trip in a car to analyzing where someone is headed in their professional and personal life. She then added humor to her presentation as a way of demonstrating how to get through life's day-to-day obstacles. What struck me most are her questions to the audience about creating a defining statement. What is your brand? Who are you? How do you deliver results? What do you do? Are you living life by default? Are you taking risks that bring excitement? Are you thinking more with your head than your heart? These questions all lead me to believe that a revolutionary change is needed in how we view our day-to-day life at work. The work environment should be enjoyable both for employees and management. The challenge for Human Resource practitioners is how to incorporate a productive, enjoyable and satisfying workplace. Gatz's approach is to incorporate more pride and joy in the departments, teams and individual jobs with humor. Yet, getting top management to see the benefit of a well rounded workforce will take some time. Maybe, just a small dose of humor each day is what is need to keep the competitors away and the employees happy.

Laughter is said to be the best medicine. So, incorporation of humor into my future career will be at the forefront of my next assignment. Creativity and appreciation for the relationships that are built amongst my peers will encourage open, honest and direct communication. This information from Jean Gatz's presentation can be added as an additional bonus to my dissertation when distinguishing between intrinsic and extrinsic motivators.

Summary. Wow, imagine a workplace where humor is encouraged. What Gatz taught me is to not sweat the small stuff. Recognize stress signals in yourself and others, then find a way to laugh. Most importantly I must take care of myself emotionally, mentally and physically by finding a balance of joy in everything I do. Human Resource professionals have the ability to create programs that are geared towards employee wellness and wholeness. With a little research, finding the right company that can meet these needs is plausible. However, Human Resource professionals should not stop with just wellness and wholeness programs but encouragement of open and honest communication throughout their prospective companies. Lead the way HR....to attitudes and behaviors that help create pride and joy at work.

CARE Packages for the Workplace: Regenerate the Spirit at Work[15]

This session provided participants a clear understanding in a caring and humorous fashion of how a new spirit in the workplace can increase employee and organizational performance during times of change. This session was action-based with numerous ideas from the presenter's twenty years of experience in the human resource field.

---

[15] Prepared by Eleanor Marschke, Nova Southeastern University.

Personal analysis: Barbara Glanz works with organizations that want to improve morale, employee retention, and service, by helping them infuse joy into the work and in their lives. This presentation was the most interesting educational hour the author has spent in the last ten years. It was an emotional event that produced positive tears and laughter, and brought about an understanding of how important it is to care about the individuals around you and with whom you work. In today's culture and unreliable business climate, human resource professionals are striving to revitalize their workplace through an infusion of spirituality. Spirituality in the workplace is about experiencing one's real purpose and meaning at work beyond paychecks and performance reviews. The presenter is known as the business speaker who speaks to your heart as well as to your head, and she has presented to organizations and associations worldwide. She is the author of numerous books that are related to her topics of expertise:

- The Simple Truths of Service-Inspired by Johnny the Bagger.
- Balancing Acts: More than 250 Guilt-free, Creative Ideas to Blend your Work and Your Life.
- Handle with CARE: Motivating and Retaining your Employees.
- CARE Packages for the Workplace –Dozens of Little Things You Can DO to Regenerate Spirit at Work.
- CARE Packages for the Home: Dozens of Ways to Regenerate Spirit Where You Live.
- The Creative Communicator – 399 Ways to Make Your Business Communications Meaningful and Inspiring.
- Building Customer Loyalty: How YOU can Help Keep Customers Returning.

The speaker used parts of these books to arrange a seminar that was challenging and motivating. She presented the material in such a manner that the audience could take away exciting concepts applicable to each person's career, family or life. As this attendee was speaking to Barbara before the seminar started, she wrote an inspiring note in a book the attendee had purchased, and encouraged this writer on her dissertation topic and work.

Information presented in this session could be used as motivation for corporate America, but there was little value from a scientific stand point of view. However, there were some valuable points such as:

- Morale: State of the relationship between an individual and an organization. Morale reflects and reveals the heart of an organization.
- Management's ability to create a sense of pride and spirit in an organization is the most effective way to recruit, retain, and motivate a high-performance workforce.
- The length of an employee's stay in an organization is largely determined by his/her relationship with his/her immediate supervisor.
- Companies can optimize the performance of employees by engaging in an ongoing organized program of promotion, motivation, communication, recognition.

Barabara Glanz' company trademark is the CARE logo:
- *C* for Creative Communication
- *A* for Atmosphere & Appreciation for All
- *R* for Respect
- *E* for Enthusiasm.

In the context of CARE, she used many real life examples, and, in the bibliography section of her presentation, she included quotes and references from 61 experts in the field of motivation, retention, human resource, and spirituality at work. In summary, I recommend this speaker to any group, corporation, and audience. She truly has a spirit of excellence and wants to see each individual achieve his or her best. Hers is a genuine spirit.

CARE Packages for the Workplace[16] - A Second Perspective

The purpose of the Tuesday Session *"CARE Packages for the Workplace: Dozens of Little Things You Can Do to Regenerate Spirit at Work"* was to better understand how new spirit at work can create a more caring, creative and joyful employee, as well as increase organizational performance, productivity and profit.

Barbara Glanz started this presentation with three questions "What percentage of employees are slot fillers – not my job or not the policy?" The 75-80 percent stats reveal that employees are just doing enough to get by. "What percentage of workers today is giving their very best?" Only 12-15 percent gives their best. "What percentage of employees said they got no appreciation for work last year? An unbelievable 65% were not appreciated by the employer. These statistics prove that most employees are just trying to survive.

Barbara's presentation centered on respecting the employee as a whole life being. Basically this means knowing the passion of each employee and what brings them alive. Understanding and embracing the balance between the human and business level of interaction should be the main focus of the each organization. There are four areas where organizations can meet this challenge of balance: First, provide Creative Communication – surprise the employee with attention getters. Second, create an Atmosphere and Appreciation for All – encourage fun in the workplace and get to know employees as individuals. Third, foster Respect and Reason for Being – treat employees fairly and emphasize a deeper, broader purpose of work. Finally, develop Empathy and Enthusiasm – support work/life programs and celebrate frequently. Barbara Glanz states "If you take personal responsibility at the human and business level and CARE you CAN make a difference in your organization!"

Personal analysis. Phenomenal! Barbara Glanz's presentation from the start drew the audience into wondering how to make a difference in every employee's life today and tomorrow. I remembered how it felt to receive a CARE package in the mail from family members as a child, so applying that same feeling to employees would need to be conveyed in the workplace. Barbara provided examples of how HR can

---

[16] Prepared by Joann Adeogun, Nova Southeastern University.

make a huge difference in developing a workplace that is more caring, creative and joyful. The idea that registered with me most is starting each meeting with three minutes of "good news" instead of going straight to what needs to be done and changed in the department. What should have surprised each HR professional in the room is a survey that asked 12,000 employees why they left their last job. Seven percent left because the supervisor never said "good morning." Shocking! Remember people leave bosses not organizations. The cost associated with replacing employees can be up to $50K. HR can be the focal point for spreading contagious enthusiasm and training supervisors about the work the organization is doing. Does the employee understand the mission and purpose of the organization? If not, help them understand how valuable they are to the success of the organization with a passion about the job they do each and everyday. Ask often how your employees are serving your customers.

Spreading contagious enthusiasm has become my new motto for success in my personal and work life. My goal is to take these simplistic steps given by Barbara Glanz and elaborate even further within my next career. Engagement, recognition and celebration of each employee are the only ways that organizations will be able to survive in the competitive market. I plan on being a huge part of that competitive environment.

Summary. Barbara Glanz is simply amazing in her approach to spreading enthusiasm that makes the workplace more caring, creative and joyful. We should all periodically ask the question "How is what I do everyday making someone's life better?" The CARE package method from this presentation will help answer and define the difference we all can make at our workplaces. The Human Resource profession is at the forefront of recognizing the contributions each employee can make on productivity and profit. Training of management will be necessary to pull this off, but I am optimistic that it can become a reality.

New Models of Work[17]

The purpose of the Masters Series *"New Models of Work: Avoiding the Coming Crisis of the Changing Workforce"* was to inform the audience of the trends in critical talent shortages in the labor market and how organization can prepare for this deficiency.

Tamara Erickson's presentation was timely for the audience of Human Resource professionals that are faced with the increasing problem of finding the right incumbent to fill the job. Erickson spoke about the supply and demand of 2006 in the workforce as dependent on where you live in the United States. In the United States as compared to other countries there will be little change and slow growth in the working-age population between the years 2010-2050. The changing decomposition of the workforce will have dramatically different patterns of growth by age from 2000-2010: 1). Declining number of mid-career workers age 35-44, 2). Few younger workers entering, and 3). Rapid growth in the over age 55 workforce. The United States will not be alone in the slowing pattern as European countries will also see a

---

[17] Prepared by Joann Adeogun, Nova Southeastern University.

decline. Several reasons exist for this change in the labor market: 1). The sudden boom in life expectancy, 2). Dramatic drop in birth rates, 4). A serious skill mismatch, 5). Emigration back to home countries, 6). An increasingly global workforce, 7). New countries in the global labor pool, and 7). A highly diverse population.

Personal analysis. Interesting and thought provoking! Tamara Erickson's presentation made you question if there will be enough labor to support the ever booming demands of businesses in the future. What interested me most about the presentation was the generational diversity of the emerging workforce that are being forced to coexist and the increased ethnic and racial diversity. The emerging workforce includes the Traditionalist, Leading-Edge Boomer, Trailing-Edge Boomer, Generation X, and Generation Y. Technology for the different generations range from a treat to an expression of self.

Targeting the right group of the emerging workforce is going to be the challenge for HR. Policies and procedures must be written that attract and retain those who require work/life balance and flexibility as the workforce ages. The recruitment efforts of the twentieth century will not work for those of the future. Prepare today as if there were no tomorrow. Know what is important and bring value to employees then adapt for optimized engagement.

If in the future, I am in a HR position that requires using my knowledge to forecast future shortages and overages in the labor market then this presentation will be my first source of inspiration. However, if my position is a subset of HR then knowing the information presented by Tamara Erickson can prepare me to attain and retain critical talent that will be so scarce in the near future. This new found knowledge will not be included in my dissertation but hopefully in future publications. Nevertheless, my eyes will focus on watching how organizations handle this changing and shrinking population of future workers.

Summary. Human Resource is definitely going to have to figure out how to handle the changing demographics of the workforce. Waiting until we are in the middle of a storm to get an umbrella will not work. Marketing efforts will need to focus on the generational diversity of the emerging workforce. Telecommuting and flextime will be at the forefront of the retired workforce and so will satellite offices located within neighbors close to employees. Technology will continue to play a key role in the toolbox of the future worker. Organizations will need to prepare now for what is inevitable; more job openings than workers

A Carrot A Day[18]

The purpose of the Super Sunday Session *"A Carrot A Day"* was to reveal how superior organizations are using strategic recognition as a way of building retention, reducing turnover and improving overall employee commitment with an emphasis on creating a stronger workforce by way of a steady diet of carrots as apposed to the stick.

---

[18] Prepared by Joann Adeogun, Nova Southeastern University.

Chester Elton presented this session as an interactive audience engagement that educated and entertained. He provided stuffed carrots to audience members that answered music trivia questions correctly describing some managers, such as "What a Wonderful World" (Louie Armstrong) and "Hards Days Night" (Beatles).

The main point Chester Elton tried to convey is that finding the right people is hard but recognition of those people increases your impact on business goals. There are fours ways that any business can keep employees pumped: (1) Pay employees fairly, (2) Celebration, (3) Benefits, and (4) Recognition. Winners celebrate at work on an ongoing basis and recognition is the most powerful thing that can be done for the organization. A prime example brought out in the presentation was the linkage of recognition to the operating margin (ROE, ROI and ROA). Have the goals of the organization been communicated to the employees? If your lowest person in the organization gets it then everyone else will (bottom-up not top-down communication)?

It just makes good business sense to engage employees. Find out what's important to the employee (money, time-off, etc.). Keep in mind however, that most supervisors have 100 percent control over the workplace environment but none over compensation and benefits. Elton provided statistics of why employees leave most organizations and the number one reason given was the supervisor. The second reason given for leaving the organization was a 3 – 5 percent increase in salary. Therefore, employees or managers needing back up to support these statistics can supply the Jackson Organization's remarkable research on the bottom-line benefits of effective recognition.

Personal analysis. Engaging and electrifying! Chester Elton's presentation provided additional insight into how the bottom-line or business objectives can be met by simply feeding employees a steady supply of carrots (recognition). Even more appealing is how everything he said was just plain common sense. How can any Human Resource professional expect to retain the best and brightest without recognizing their contribution to the organization? Something as simple as saying "Thank you" more frequently can make a difference in turnover rates. Human Resource professionals are at the forefront of building a culture of engagement and recognition with direct link to organizational value. The key deliverable that must be asked is "What is important to the organization and employee?" Once this question is answered then the strategic goals of the organization can be aligned, measured and owned by all. How appropriate the subject of recognition with a large group of Human Resource professionals that are the key decision makers at their prospective organizations. The follow-up to this presentation should be with CEOs and Presidents of organizations that have not quite gotten the full message of "Spend a little money now on recognition or lose a lot more later to your competitor."

My future career will be spent making employees feel valued and appreciated with praise that is specific and timely after attending this presentation. This will be accomplished by continually participating in seminars that stress this area of heightened awareness and reading books and articles. In addition, this information will be incorporated into my dissertation regarding monetary motivation as a linkage to increased job performance and satisfaction.

Summary. Limiting myself to one thing that was learned from this presentation is challenging. However, I believe the most important lesson is that people will not remember what you said but they will remember how you made them feel. If a steady diet of carrots is what is needed to make the organization a success and also engage employees to do their best then that is the key message that every Human Resource practitioner attending this session must take back to their prospective organizations. Just imagine an organization where employees actually believe that "When I work hard I can do anything." In order to reach this utopia, everyone in a management position would need to be trained not just on leadership skills but on how to recognize and celebrate the accomplishments of those employees that make us all successful.

> I see trees of green, red roses too
> I see them bloom for me and you
> And I think to myself what a wonderful world.
> ~ Louis Armstrong (What a Wonderful World)

A Carrot A Day by Chester Elton[19] - A Second Perspective

A session illustrated how companies can and should use recognition programs to motivate their employees and use strategic financial and non-financial rewards to build an employee base. Chester Elton, the presenter, is the author of *The 24-Carrot Manager,* and is known in the Human Resource field as the "Apostle of Appreciation." He is employed at the O.C. Tanner Company, which purports to provide powerful recognition tools to companies which want to tie employee achievement to organizational goals.

Not surprisingly, the presenter excelled in eliciting audience participation. The concept of "A Carrot a Day" — that managers should reward employees, every day, with honest recognition—can be summed up in the adage, "you catch more flies with honey than with vinegar." The premise is simply that positive reinforcement produces more productivity from employees, and that it is one of the most important messages that can be sent to an employee. It's also how management achieves excellent marks in communication from employees. The purpose of this seminar was to instill in human resource professionals the importance of creating a recognition strategy, and that while compensation and benefits get employees in the door; it is recognition that keeps them productive in the long term.

Personal analysis: As a highly productive salesperson and manager, this writer has experienced the glow that comes from recognition many times; however, the session provided motivation to view recognition from a different perspective. The term "employment engagement" is no longer just a "catchy" phrase. Human resource management must recognize that people truly are the most important financial asset to the corporation. Companies with higher employee engagement deliver:

- Higher returns on length of employee tenure than their competitors.

---

[19] Prepared by Eleanor Marschke, Nova Southeastern University.

- Higher return on Return on Investment, Return of Equity.
- Six times higher return on operating margins.

Overall, recognition increases the ability of a corporation to achieve its business goals. For example, Elton believes that employees who receive proper recognition will spot new business opportunities quicker, take initiative in their jobs and be more loyal. Numerous companies have some form of recognition programs; but, in order to reach a more effective level, companies have to implement them into their core values, mission and vision statement. These core values have to be strategic, simple, measured and owned by the employees. In the author's personal experience, Thomas & Betts has recognition programs in place but they are there to satisfy top management. For example, after attending this seminar, this writer had to contact the human resource department of the Fortune 200 Company to obtain her twenty year service award. Obviously, having her direct supervisor make the award would have made it much more meaningful. It was stated numerous times in this seminar that people do not leave organizations they leave their supervisors, and that 79% leave their current position due to lack of appreciation, however, in exit interviews those leaving claim they are leaving for monetary reasons. The overall objective in recognition is to enhance the communication process. The human resource professional has an opportunity to contribute to this process by doing the following:

- Thank employees frequently.
- Direct praise to the appropriate individual.
- Remember the best and forget the rest.
- Make employees feel valuable.
- Create a strategy of recognition.
- Reward results that are measurable.

This information will be useful in the author's research into the relationship of job satisfaction to organizational commitment; e.g., does a solid recognition program provide more or less job satisfaction? Numerous journal articles document that employee's stay in organizations because they believe in the goals of the organizations, and some stay because of the benefits, recognition, and financial gains. Others stay because they have no available alternative for employment. Since commitment is a behavior or attitude, it is critical for the corporation to have successful motivators in place to reward all employees.

In summary, this was a very engaging seminar, and the audience participation created an excitement that will be a lasting memento of the conference. There were 111 out of 800 exhibitors that had an association with recognition, awards, and incentives. These numbers speak volumes to the human resource professional that this is a strategic area that will continue to be recognized in the employee retention field.

General Colin L. Powell on Leadership: Opening General Session[20]

Colin Powell was the kickoff speaker, and he took no prisoners Sunday afternoon with his charm and wit in evidence to an audience of more than 13,000 human resource professionals. Powell's leadership style was first class and his resume is one the most impressive in America today. He encouraged the audience in many different topics but he was particularly inspirational in the areas of purpose and vision. His basic philosophy is that to lead people, leaders need to focus on those individuals who actually get the work done.

Personal analysis: General Colin Powell has been in the forefront of the United States Army for over 35 years. After rising to the rank of four-star general Colin Powell served two years as the National Security Advisor from 1987-1989, and then served as chairman of the Joint Chiefs of Staff from 1989 to 1993. This decorated veteran oversaw numerous crises in America and abroad and also was the key commander in Operation Desert Storm in the Persian Gulf War. Colin Powell became the 65th Secretary of State under President George W. Bush, and served in from January 2001 till January 2005. After retirement from 44 years of armed services, Colin Powell wrote a best-selling memoir, *My American Journey*, and has pursued a career as a public speaker, addressing audiences across the country and abroad. In 1997 Powell founded American's Promise with the objective of helping children from all socioeconomic backgrounds. Powell is the recipient of the Silver Buffalo Award, the highest adult award given by the Boy Scouts of America. In 2000, Powell was serving on the board at AOL/Time Warner and became a wealthy man through stock options. He used this wealth as a platform for his future career objective to provide to the less fortunate people in America. In July 2005 Powell joined Kleiner, Perkins, Caufield & Byers, a Silicon Valley venture capital firm that will speed into the future and investigate the alternatives to:

- Google (What is the next step in the Information Age?).
- Rising Fuel Costs (Alternative Material).
- Rising Energy Costs.
- Health Care and Bio Medicines (to keep Americans healthy so they do not need health care).

Colin Powell is also very engaged in non-profit work in America. He is consulting on a documentary of the Martin Luther King Project in Washington to insure that every citizen in the United States understands the importance of the life of Martin Luther King. Powell was instrumental in creating the Vietnam Wall Education Center that provides veterans' families a place to educate the generations who have followed.

Colin Powell visibly motivated each audience member. His four decades of leadership can be reduced to the statement that leadership is all about the followers, and if you truly have a sense of purpose that purpose will become contagious. His belief is that you need to nurture and take care of the troops or the people who work in your organization so that their performance is recognized and their contribution is

---

[20] Prepared by Eleanor Marschke, Nova Southeastern University.

valued on a daily basis. Good leaders set high standards and are always stretching the organization to meet and exceed the corporate goals and objectives. Powell's approach to honesty and integrity is to look reality in the eye and face the facts, either positive or negative, and have a strategic plan to address the needs.

This was the most dynamic seminar at the conference. Rather than a performance this was truly a personal perspective from a very public icon that left an indelible impression on this writer. One statement in particular struck a chord: "How do you know you are a good leader?" The answer is that your employees trust you!

Top Trends in HR Technology in 2006[21]

A session was designed to instruct and educate the HR professional in the current technological trends in human resource information systems. Numerous technology trends are shaping human resources, as well as other key components of the organization--management, sales, finance and operations. SHRM has identified technology skills as a key competency for the HR professionals due to the importance of technology to the delivery of HR services.

Personal analysis: John Ryder, who is clearly an expert in this field, presented an informative session regarding technology's uses to the HR function. His overview posed challenges to the audience in the form of questions:

- How do we keep up with technology?
- What are the emerging trends, issues and implications of not having an HR system?
- How would we serve our function, if we lost our technology?
- What is your company's drive for process standardization?
- Why do most companies fail to implement a complete strategy?

The answer to the above questions is that HR is dependent on technology, and since that dependence is gaining complexity as is the technology, there has to be a top management decision to support new trends in technology. This seminar addressed the Top Ten Trends in HR Technology in 2006:

- Proliferation of web-based employee services and products.
- Increased need for HRIS disaster recovery planning and testing.
- Emergence of the talent management suite.
- Software as a service.
- 24/7 wired world – mobile devices.
- HR professionals must have technology skills.
- The evolution of outsourcing.
- HR system rationale moves from cost reduction to providing value.
- Heightened need for HR data privacy and security.
- Growth in the use of e-Learning.

---

[21] Prepared by Eleanor Marschke, Nova Southeastern University.

Each one of these trends has issues and implications attached to them; however, the most common denominator was the training that was involved in each trend. Training has to have the commitment of top management due to the time frame and the expense involved in developing new technology. HR management has to be able to determine the strategy/value proposition to present to management on each one of these trends. Ever-changing software poses one of the main concerns that face HR professionals today. It is an increasing requirement for HR leaders to have strategic command of technology so that they are able to influence selections/decisions. Without technology skills, an HR professional cannot be a strategic business partner. SHRM has recognized the need for HR technology and places a high demand on the members of SHRM to understand and implement these technologies in their own corporations.

In summary, the HR professional has to commit to technology in order to deliver value to top management. This information challenging from an intellectual stand-point, and SHRM recognizes the importance of technology. Other companies also obviously believe the same in that there were more than 72 HR information and systems vendors exhibiting.

Vendors and Suppliers at SHRM 2006

SoundView Executive Book Summaries[22]

Meeting today's rapid business challenges requires executives and key personnel to have access to current resources. In the late 1970's the founders of SoundView pioneered the concept of outlining the key points and ideas of full-length business books into short, easy-to-read print summaries. According to its literature, SoundView's summaries are "not reviews, or excerpts, but skillful concepts that preserve the content and spirit of the entire book." Each year publishers and authors submit more than 1,500 books for summary consideration, and the editorial staff goes through a rigorous selection process to include only well-written books with cutting-edge ideas and immediate value for readers. Out of that selection and careful review, they choose the best thirty books. SoundView has the knowledge and experience to bring the reader the best books, summarized accurately, clearly and concisely in a form that is simple for the reader to absorb. Depending on the reader's preferences, SoundView can provide eight-page print versions or 20 minute audio summaries in a variety of delivery methods such as CD, online, or adapted to PC's, PDA's and MP3 players. Some benefits of this type of book summaries are:

- No travel hassles or expenses.
- No additional time out of the office.
- Have staff listen and discuss the books after an audio conference.
- Use these concepts as a seminar for other employees

---

[22] Prepared by Eleanor Marschke, Nova Southeastern University.

Application response: Successful executives worldwide purchase business books everyday. The question is do they really read them or are they corporate office window dressing? This concept can be a time-saving value to the corporation and to the human resource department as it allows employees to grasp the latest business thinking. It allows the executive to retain more content by reducing reading time and eliminates costly business seminars. It would be beneficial to a company to purchase a Corporate Site License for development of a set of key people. These key people would be more valuable to the corporation as they continue to review topics on management, leadership, finance, economics, sales, marketing, and career success techniques as they relate to human resources. The price on this subscription for a year of the top business books in summaries would be $169.00 in CD format, which is a minimal cost to keep key managers up to date on the latest business ideas. Nothing creates more self-esteem and true self-confidence than knowledge.

This time-challenged writer has subscribed to the program, and is looking forward to turning her car into a mobile learning.

Beyond This Day Bereavement Package[23]

Beyond This Day is a unique corporate memorial program incorporating a special bereavement book. It is non-religious, but inspirational, comforting and cost effective (about half the cost of sending flowers, with varied options for providing consolation to an employee).

One of the responsibilities of Human Resource Professionals is to console employees on the death of a spouse or family member. One of the most traumatic events that will happen in an employee's life, the death of someone close to an employee will likely affect the productivity over the course of a year. "Beyond This Day Bereavement Package" is a concept that is not new to the market; however, it may provide quality answers to a difficult situation. The product contains the following components:

- The Beyond This Day book is written in a way that provides comfort and practical advice to the family without endorsing any specific faith or belief. From a Human Resource perspective, this is crucial considering today's corporate culture.
- The product is a quality-bound book with a padded, gold stamped cover and beautifully edged pages. This book has numerous professionally written texts dealing openly and honestly with loss and grief.
- Presented in an engravable cedar box, the book has a keepsake compartment to store mementos of special significance.

Beyond This Day is cost effective, and is designed to have a lasting effect on the recipient. It is appropriate as a bereavement gift to employees, employee families, friends, coworkers or anyone who has suffered a loss in their family or circle of friends.

---

[23] Prepared by Eleanor Marschke, Nova Southeastern University.

Application response: After reviewing product offerings at more than 800 booths, this reviewer believes this product is a perfect acknowledgement of bereavement. The Beyond This Day program is a wonderful way to let a bereaved person know that people are sincerely concerned about them. It provides a lasting, proven, appropriate and dignified method to improve corporate/employee relationships and to offer condolence in a difficult time.

The closing point for this reviewer was that one simply selects a preferred package, determine the quantity to have on hand, and decide on the personalized inscription. There are no legal issues involved as it is appropriate for any faith or belief. It does not endorse any specific religion. The product has the ability for the corporation to be recognized as a partner to the person suffering the loss. It is appropriately designed to be displayed at funerals or memorial services, sent by mail, or presented directly to an employee or family member. In summary, the cost of the deluxe version is $43.00 and the author was so impressed that she placed an order for four Beyond This Day packages, and referred it to her employer's Human Resource Department with the belief that it will enhance the corporation's bereavement program.

American Management Association[24]

American Management Association (AMA) enhances individual and organizational performance to meet the business bottom-line through training, seminars, executive forums, customized learning solutions, books, and online resources at every phase. The company is globally located in Asia, Australia, Europe, Middle East, Central Asia, Turkey, and North America. The Executive Conference Centers are located in Atlanta, Chicago, New York, San Francisco, and Washington. AMA is a membership based organization of more than 400,000. Membership into AMA is either at a corporate cost of $1800, individual cost of $225-$45 or student cost of $95 per year.

AMA started in 1913 as the National Association of Corporation Schools then merged with the Industrial Relations Association of America in 1922. In 1923 the name was changed to American Management Association to more reflect where the association was headed with their mission and vision.

Upcoming conferences and special events include the complimentary Blended Learning Briefing scheduled for July 26, 2006 in New York City, as well as the World Business Forum scheduled for September 12-13, 2006 in New York City that will include such well-known speakers as Jack Welch, Bill Clinton, Colin Powell, Rudy Giuliani, and Renee Mauborge. AMA didn't stop with just conferences and special events. AMACOM is a book publishing division of AMA that publishes business and leadership topics that contribute to improving job skills and performance.

Critical application. AMA would contribute both to my personal and organizational mission/goals. AMA offers a complete course list of self-study certificate programs, college and university continuing education programs, as well

---

[24] Prepared by Joann Adeogun, Nova Southeastern University.

as, programs designed for businesses that must keep employees trained. Self-study courses afford most busy professionals the time to complete programs that they may not otherwise have completed. Additional certificates and continuing education can only add to my professional development. Organizations would benefit from the dedication of employees taking self-study classes that would add value to their skill-set at work. The time spent by employees completing the course is money well spent by the employer.

Cost associated with using the services of AMA is minimal. However, employees would need to devote the time necessary for completion of an online course with the understanding that there are no additional students or faculty contact. A certain percent of employees are allowed at no extra charge to attend conferences and events sponsored by AMA, so the employer would save.

AMA does expect a certain level of literacy in the context of what would be used in most workplaces to complete self-study courses, such as reading, writing and comprehension of the material.

Legally, AMA has in place a board of trustees, partnerships, sponsorships, councils, and the management team to govern over various decisions that are made by the association. Currently, I see no legal or unethical issue that would affect the performance of AMA.

Vantage Solutions LLC[25]

Vantage Solutions LLC is a full-service workplace consulting firm founded by Vanessa L. Smith in 1998 that provides cost-effective legal strategies for employers to cut lawsuits in a proactive manner. The company is based in Chicago and is managed by consultants who partner with human resource and key operations personnel to train, educate, advice, and counsel regarding organizational goals. Services offered by Vantage Solutions LLC include: 1). Law Firm Consulting, 2). Ongoing Advice and Counsel, 3). Employment Audit, 4). Employment Policies and Procedures, 5). Education and Training, 6). In-House Solutions, 7). Internal Investigations, 8). Diversity Management, 9). Dispute Resolution and 10). Immigration.

To demonstrate the need exists for legal services, Vantage Solutions LLC offers workplace statistics on General Matters, Benefits, EEOC Activity, Mediation, Sexual Harassment and Workplace Violence. Additionally, employment related questions can be sent to eSolutions at no charge to the requester. Another approach used by Vantage Solutions LLC to get the word out is "The Vantage Pointe," a quarterly published newsletter on topics having an affect on the workplace.

Vanessa Smith McTier, National Managing Counsel spoke at the 58th National Society for Human Resource Management Conference (SHRM) in Washington, DC on Monday, June, 26 2006. The topic she covered was "The Seven "Ps" – Auditing Your Path to High Performance.

Critical application. Vantage Solutions, LLC would contribute to any organization's mission and goals as the business caters to the workplace environment

---

[25] Prepared by Joann Adeogun, Nova Southeastern University.

by providing legal and practical advise. The services provided by Vantage Solutions, LLC would prepare the organization to address any employment law or Human Resource issue that may arise. Training can be provided by Vantage Solutions, LLC on site or at one of their many seminars. Also, if an organization is just getting started, Vantage Solutions, LLC can provide HR "In- House Solutions" for basic employment and law related day-to-day interaction.

The cost associated with using Vantage Solutions, LLC was not addressed at the SHRM Conference or on the company's website. This may be an area where Vantage Solutions, LLC can improve. The basic rate for services offered can be added to the website, along with additional items, such as the cost of the quarterly newsletter, etc.

Vantage Solutions, LLC primary usage is that of organizations where literacy level to use the service would not be an issue. The combined experience of the lawyers at Vantage Solution, LLC is 40 years, so legal issues would be minimum for organizations requesting their services.

In my opinion, Vantage Solutions, LLC appears to be just the right type of full-service employment and workplace firm that can be of service to organizations that are new to employment issues or need a refresher. The small legal team would bring a wealth of information and experience that can guide an organization to service its employees ethically and fairly.

Summary

A doctorate program can open many new doors and opportunities. Whether one takes full or partial advantage of these opportunities depends on one's goals, objectives, and time availability. Nonetheless, one thing is for certain that the doctoral program will make one think, reflect and become a more disciplined writer (not necessarily a better writer, just a more disciplined one). As can be seen from the preceding writings, reflections and personal applications of content gleaned from various professional sessions or conferences, reflections about these topics and attendance at such annual events can be very fruitful for academicians and graduate scholars. Besides gleaning practical material for immediate application, one can also become familiarized with the authors and presenters who can be of great assistance with one's research. So, attendance at professional conferences can be helpful to glean new material and to network.

Furthermore, a student should try to publish his or her term projects that are completed in each doctoral course. Finally, one should try to get at least one or more journal article publications from the dissertation research. It is the student's obligation to finalize the dissertation research, prepare a 25-40 page paper geared toward the requirements of a specific journal, and get it published with the Chair and Committee members as coauthors. The student should lead this process, put his/her name first on this journal article followed by the Chair and Committee Members as coauthors, and then work on getting it published. If the student does not have time to follow-up on the publication of the journal article, then he or she should ask the Chair or one of the Committee Members to take a leadership role and get the research published through a journal as they see appropriate. Getting the dissertation research published through conferences and journals will increase its chances of being referenced and cited by other researchers in the coming decades. In other words, getting it published is an excellent marketing strategy for the study, the results of the study, and the student's hard work. Begin the publication as soon as the dissertation research is completed and approved, in hopes of seeing it in the final published journal format within the next few years.

10 – Life After School: Living the Academic Life

D octorate program graduates will have plenty of choices with regard to teaching, working in public institutions, continuing projects and management tasks in the corporate arena, and/or transitioning into an administrator's position in the education industry. People who transition from the corporate environment into academia tend to easily and comfortably fit into administrator positions in higher education. However, one must cautiously think about his or her desires and goals before taking administrative responsibilities. Taking an administrative position means less time spent teaching, researching, and publishing. In any case, you need to decide what role best suits you and your lifestyle. As an academician, one is likely to be teaching as well as assessing and validating knowledge and/or creating or exposing new knowledge through primary research. The good news is that there are many great opportunities in academia for doctoral graduates in the area of business.

According to a research study by Robert M. Wolk[26] (2007), the decline in getting more business doctorate faculty members (AACSB, 2003) presents an unusual problem for accreditation standards at U.S. business schools. Wolk states that while at the same time that accreditation requirements demand faculty members with business doctorates, the U.S. production of new doctorates declined by 1,327 from 1994 to 2000. A report by the Doctoral Faculty Commission to the AACSB's board of directors in 2003 predicted a shortage of 2,119 business terminal degrees by 2013. The supply and demand difference presents a threat to the survival of business education. The commission (AACSB, 2003) found two reasons for the shortfall (Wolk, 2007). The first reason emanates from the discovery that most producers of business doctorates are public universities that have been experiencing budget shortfalls and have restrained growth in their programs. The second reason rests on

---

[26] See the dissertation research by Robert M. Wolk at Nova Southeastern University.

the discovery that more than half of the business doctoral students are in the U.S. on temporary visas. In 2003, the AACSB released a task force report to address the pending faculty shortage utilizing a four point program of recommended actions. The first recommendation is for the development of alternative sources for qualified doctorates by establishing programs to attract candidates from other fields (Wolk, 2007). The second action advocates a marketing approach for attracting candidates for business doctorates. The third recommendation advocates investment in institutions for increasing the number of doctoral students in business concentrations. The fourth action involves the use of online education allowing for easier transitions for busy executives to achieve doctoral status. Together, as emphasized by Robert Wolk, these four alternatives highlight the seriousness of the pending problem of business schools competing for a scarce resource. As higher education institutions continue to enhance their success rate in the recruitment, retention and graduation rates of doctoral students, it is also hoped that more master's level graduates will proactively initiate their journey toward becoming protectors and keepers of knowledge by earning a terminal degree at one of their neighboring schools.

Be a Keeper and Protector of Wisdom: Amaguk

Doctoral graduates, whether they are teaching or are serving as administrators will have the responsibility of keeping knowledge, validating knowledge, passing it on, and enabling others to continue the tradition.

At the atrium of Nova Southeastern University's H. Wayne Huizenga School of Business and Entrepreneurship building, there is a statue of a Native American (Indian) man that is a symbol demonstrating that workers, faculty members and students are responsible not only for the generation of knowledge but also the protection of wisdom and the route to it. This statue is also represented on the cover of this book. The Amaguk statue, according to the information provided at the Huizenga School, is supposedly a symbolic gesture. For example, to wear the "Robe of the Wolf" a member of the Nez Perce tribe had to demonstrate the "Wisdom of the Elders." Their belief is and has been that people live on through their teachings. This is very important for creating an identity, especially for those doctoral students who want to become educators and "formal" teachers at the colleges and universities.

The statue also symbolizes that to be worthy of respect, one must acquire knowledge, use it wisely, and be able to impart his or her understanding to others in an appropriate manner. This is the way of the Hagihana – the Wolf Family of the Arapaho. Legend has it that the Bella Coola, Pawnee, Hidatsa, Lakota, and the Ahtena Indians all shared the Wolf Robe as a distinguished honor to persons best at the acquisition and passing of wisdom. Of course, doctoral graduates who teach and pass on their knowledge to others have the honor of such rewards, at least intrinsically. Legend also has it that in cultures that lived in great harmony with their environment, the wolf has been revered as a brave and caring leader. On the other side, cultures that are in discord with their environment seem to have shared at least the following two traits: first, knowledge was used to control others, and, second, mentoring to all willing to learn was viewed as evil. Holders of a terminal degree are asked to use their wisdom and knowledge to help and mentor others so they too can contribute to the wellbeing of our society and future generations. Overall, besides validating and creating new knowledge, holders of terminal degrees are also expected to be protectors and growers of wisdom.

Continue Researching, Writing, and Publishing

By earning a doctorate degree, one has certainly proven beyond a reasonable doubt that one can conduct research, write, and publish when needed. One must also realize that very few people in the world are capable of doing scientific research at such a high level in one's specific profession. Therefore, in a way, having earned the terminal degree becomes an obligation to research, write, and publish at least one or two articles every few years in order to advance and validate knowledge. The late Peter Drucker, management expert and author, said that "The problem in my life and other people's lives is not the absence of knowing what to do, but the absence of doing it." Or as the Roman philosopher Seneca (3 B. C. – 65 A. D.) wrote, "it is not because things are difficult that we do not dare; it is because we do not dare that things are difficult." As a terminally-degreed educator and researcher, you know what to do and can easily discover what needs to be done in almost all situations; then it is only a matter of simply beginning, and doing it one task and one step at a time. Many people have successfully done it before; you and I can do it as well.

Continuous learning is an important part of being in academia. Dr. Robert Sellani, professor at Nova Southeastern University, often says that the job of a faculty member is to validate and create knowledge. In institutions that are labeled as teaching schools, the former tends to be more of their nature and characteristic, and in institutions that are primarily research-oriented, the latter tends to carry more weight. However, all schools would love and prefer to have faculty members that can teach and validate knowledge while continuously publishing in their fields of expertise. While validating knowledge and creating knowledge are two great responsibilities, faculty members and educators are often required to serve on academic committees and provide community service during a certain percentage of their time each year. Community service might include serving on a board for a non-profit organization, doing a free seminar on a topic of interest to the community, helping with a conference where professional volunteers are needed, and serving as chairs, reviewers, and discussants for journals and conferences in one's field.

Teaching Responsibilities and Expectations

The profession of teaching goes back hundreds and thousands of years. People like Plato, Socrates, Jesus, Mohammad, Confucius, Buddha, and modern day educators have been teaching us life philosophies and science so we can become better and live more productive lives. You and I can be a part of today's group of educators by continuously learning and educating others. As it has been said before, "The person who dares to teach must never cease to learn," and "The person who can make hard things easy is the educator," said Ralph Waldo Emerson.

Joyce A. Myers said that "Teachers can change lives with just the right mix of chalk and challenges." So, educators have many responsibilities and obligations. One must remember the words of William Butler Yeats that "Education is not the filling of a pail, but the lighting of a fire." As an educator, you can excite, delight, and ignite a fire in the hearts and bellies of students who volunteer to learn something new and make society a little better through their calculated contributions. Help them become more and do more; that is the true job of an educator.

One can perhaps highlight the responsibilities of an educator with the acronym "T.E.A.C.H.", which stands for *T*eaching, *E*ducating, *A*ssessing learning achievement, *C*reating knowledge, and *H*oning one's facilitation skills. Overall, faculty members are likely to, and should, be involved in doing the following:

- **T**eaching the lessons of each course as outlined and planned.
- **E**ducating students about the reasons and application of the lessons.
- **A**ssessing the gained knowledge of students in the class and curriculum.
- **C**reating new knowledge through continuous research, reflections, and writing.
- **H**oning one's own skills on the above tasks to make sure one is learning from experience, reflections, and scientific inquiries.

Of course, each school's faculty manual should highlight the responsibilities and obligations of teachers. These responsibilities are usually aligned with the vision, mission, and curricular outcomes of the university. While the vision and mission of schools vary in terms of working and core competencies, each curriculum is likely to be focused on enabling the students to think critically and become knowledgeable professionals in their fields. In one of his messages at the Huizenga School's faculty training manual, Dr. Preston Jones in 2003 emphasized the words of Dr. James Moore by saying that "For most businesses today, the only true sustainable advantage comes from out-innovating the competition. It matters not which particular organization stays alive, rather, it's only essential that competition among them is fierce and fair – and that the fittest survive" (James F. Moore, 1993 - Harvard Business Review). Dr. Preston Jones, Associate Dean, continues to state that "One Huizenga School goal is to create managers and leaders with the skills to compete effectively in global markets. Senge, Drucker, and other well-known management scholars consider competition as necessary to bring out the best in all of us. Business students seek to learn from faculty the skills required to compete with the very best. We, as faculty members, have the most important job in the world!" Dr. Jones explains that working adult students would say to their faculty members the following thoughts and expectations: "Teach me how to compete! Teach me to learn! Teach me to *innovate*! Teach me to *create value* for my organization and myself. But above all, please teach me to *think*!" While many young business students may not always articulate these thoughts as clearly they can, educators must continue to focus on achieving the learning outcomes and delivering an excellent educational experience for all of their students. Dr. Jones explains that "excellence" is the great differentiator. He goes on to state that the first step towards excellence is achieving the goals of each course in the curriculum. Each class session and each contact with the student is an opportunity for educators to become better prepared to meet the competitive challenge for their students and themselves. Overall, remember that as educators and protectors of wisdom, you are the key in teaching students to effectively and efficiently *compete, innovate, create value,* and *think critically*! You are their vehicle for achieving *excellence* (the great differentiator) and they are yours.

Teaching Essentials

Mahatma Gandhi once said that you should "*Learn as if you will live forever, live as if you will die tomorrow.*" Extraordinary teachers continuously learn and pass on relevant (and updated) information to their students. There is an interesting book titled "*Extraordinary Teachers: The Essence of Excellent Teaching,*" by Dr. Frederick Stephenson, Associate Professor of Marketing and Distribution at the University of Georgia's Terry College of Business. The book is basically a compilation of about thirty six papers written by teachers that are considered to be extraordinary and have also received the Josiah Meigs Award for Excellence in Teaching (the highest teaching honor given by the University of Georgia). Throughout the book, six characteristics of extraordinary teachers are discussed. Extraordinary teachers:

1. Have great passion for their work.
2. Know what to teach, how to teach, and how to improve.
3. Excel at creating exciting classroom environments.
4. Connect exceptionally well with students.
5. Challenge students to reach their full potential.
6. Get extraordinary results using variety of skills.

Dr. Stephenson goes on to mention the applicability of the six characteristics no matter at what level one is teaching. To become an extraordinary facilitator of learning, you may want to get this book as it makes for excellent reading. The papers are all extremely inspiring; or you can always pick up another book related to extraordinary and exiting teaching and facilitation skills in higher education.

Of course, the goal for faculty members is to be and keep on becoming extraordinary teachers. As educators, we all want our students to say that "my professor had great passion for the subject area, knows how to teach, created an exciting environment where I wanted to learn and participate, connected my experience to the learning objectives of the session/course, challenged me to stretch and learn beyond my known abilities, and assisted me in achieving extraordinary outcomes." Good luck in being and/or becoming an extraordinary educators and mentor.

Mentor Others to Earn a Doctoral Degree

Learning organizations utilize double-loop learning to maintain momentum and a competitive advantage. Argyris (1994) introduced the concept of single and double-loop learning. Single loop learning is one dimensional, similar to a light that senses when it is too dark and turns on. Double-loop learning is multi-dimensional. In the case of the light sensor, double-loop learning would question if the current setting was the most effective, if the current wattage in the bulb was sufficient, if the beam needed to be more concentrated or broad, and why the current settings were selected. Argyris (1994) posited that most learning and changes in organizations are single-loop and do not ask why the existing process or procedure was originally put in place or if the new process is the best process.

Collins (2001) agreed with the double-loop learning approach. He believed that the iterative process of developing, testing, and revising ideas then seeing them break under the weight of the evidence and rebuilding them yet again, was a key to an organization's overall success.

> Because double-loop learning depends on questioning one's own assumptions and behavior, this apparently benevolent strategy is actually *anti*learning. Admittedly, being considerate and positive can contribute to the solution of single-loop problems like cutting costs. But it will never help people figure out why they lived with problems for years on end, why they covered up the cover-up, why they were so good at pointing to the responsibility of others and slow to focus on their own (Argyris, 1994, p. 79).

This brings up an interesting dilemma for those working in non-traditional environments. Is it possible to have double-loop learning via email, conference calls, or any of the other communication methods virtual educators and students have at their discretion?

Regardless of format, we believe that mentoring is an important part of successfully getting students through a doctoral program. Mentoring becomes even more important for off-campus, virtual, and international students who may also have to deal with distance and cultural issues. Advanced degrees are now becoming the norm in various professions as well as in different cultures and countries in order to be able to teach college courses and to effectively conduct research in one's field, industry and country. Besides becoming aware of the common reasons for why people earn a doctoral degree, mentors can, and should, gain the skills of effectively dealing with diversity, change, stress, conflict, and time management so they can pass on such skills to new doctoral students. Such awareness and skills can be used to mentor new national and international students in successfully achieving their academic dreams.

Certainly, everything has a price and mentoring doctoral students is a privilege rather than a price. As we know, there is a price to pay for any form of success, fulfillment, accomplishment, and joy. It is true that there are no free lunches, at least not for long. If one does not pay the price of hard work, commitment and dedication that is needed for success in a doctoral program, one is likely to pay the price of failure for not completing it. So, it is best to prepare for success and get doctoral students through the program successfully, so they too can achieve and find more satisfaction by creating and sharing their advanced knowledge with others. Earning a doctorate is an accomplishment that is worth the time and effort needed to bring success in both one's career and personal dreams. The best thing one can do for a national or international student is to help them intrinsically understand their true reasons for pursuing a doctoral degree. Once they know their main reasons for earning a doctoral degree, their passion is likely to help them keep moving forward regardless of the roadblocks. This section repeats what has been alluded to or mentioned before and focuses on some of the reasons why students earn a doctoral degree, why existing faculty members need to mentor doctoral students so they can successfully graduate, and the benefits of having more terminally-degreed national and international colleagues.

Reasons for earning a doctorate degree. There may be number of great reasons for each person to pursue a graduate degree and specialize in a specific field of his or her interest. One of the most popular reasons is that when job hunting, finding other applicants with undergraduate degrees is now very common in the United States and most other developed countries. In order to distinguish oneself, possessing a master's degree or doctorate degree is sure to play an important role in the determining factor on whether to interview or hire someone. A doctorate degree can open doors that are not otherwise accessible to a person in today's competitive work environment. These opportunities can include research positions at corporations and government laboratories, as well as teaching and research opportunities in higher education. Furthermore, continually learning through a graduate degree further allows one to expand his/her knowledge. Most management and upper level leadership positions require a high level of education. Even in the government, whether it is in the United States or other countries, the higher the degree, the higher the grade level will be for applicants who seek employment in government. With a graduate degree in business or management, companies know that you have been developed to lead people and to understand business practices at a higher level. Hence, graduates are afforded more responsibility and career challenges leading to fulfilling and senior management opportunities.

Some people love to learn and take classes throughout their lifetime. For those types, a graduate degree is part of the natural cycle of learning as personal fulfillment may be found in educational pursuits. The wonderful thing about seeking knowledge is that it never ends. One may spend a lifetime seeking knowledge and in the end discover that it was in the seeking that one found joy.

There is a great need for more terminally-degreed educators. In general, people are likely to pursue a doctorate degree in order to obtain certain intrinsic and extrinsic benefits and advantages associated with completing and achieving it. Intrinsic benefits are the tangible, concrete, and readily apparent results of obtaining and having a graduate degree. One can earn a doctorate degree for hundreds of different reasons and each may be unique to him or her. While there might be patterns in general categories, most people enroll into a doctorate program because of an intrinsic motivation that is unique to them. Others might enroll into a doctorate program simply because it is expected of them by family members, governments, or their own organization. An important reason for national and international students to obtain a doctoral degree is that there is a huge need for faculty members in the fields of business across universities around the world. Studies show that the attrition of most doctoral programs average about 40% to 60%, which means that the nation is losing an important resource of highly trained personnel just as the demand is actually rising. Research also shows that the attrition is much more severe for women and minorities, since they tend to leave doctoral programs at a greater rate than the majority and international students.

Income possibilities with advanced degrees. Some possible reasons for earning a doctorate degree can be summed up as follows: personal / intellectual development, recognition, to enter into academia (research, professorship, lecturing), better employment opportunities and social mobilization or networking. Of course, there can be hundreds of different reasons and each person should do it for his/her own reasons. However, one must never underestimate the motivational value of other factors such as the capacity to earn more income and become financially wealthier. Of course, an important motivational factor in going to graduate school is the income ratio between bachelor's level and graduate level employees. People who continue their education are the ones who will probably end up with higher positions and bigger salaries in their organizations. Earning a doctorate degree is not necessarily going to make a person rich or a millionaire, but it can provide one with more opportunities with regard to research, consulting and teaching. According to the statistics reported by the U.S. Department of the Census (1995), mean annual income of persons who are 18 years of age and older are expected to be $82,749 for those with professional degrees, $67,785 for those with doctorate degrees, $46,332 for people who have earned a masters degree, and about $37,724 for those with bachelor's degrees. The Chronicle of Higher Education, in their August 25, 2006 issue reported that the average faculty salaries for a 4-year institution in the 2005-2006 year in the United States was $102,702 for a professor rank, $84,095 for an associate professor rank, $78,151 for an assistant professor rank, and $49,271 for an instructor in business, management and marketing related courses. In these 4-year institutions, the professionals that were paid a little higher than business faculty were those of engineering and legal studies faculty members. Of course, those with doctorate degrees are expected to be getting paid at the highest level of each rank as many 4-year institutions do have ranked faculty members who do not have terminal degrees.

Finally, it is the job of the existing faculty members and terminally-degreed professionals to serve as effective mentors to newly-entering doctoral students so they can successfully complete the program. Students can be encouraged to enter into the program by emphasizing the reasons that might be attractive to the individual and by helping them see how a doctorate degree can further enable them to assist others in their communities and cultures. The key is to help students reflect on the reasons for pursuing the doctoral degree, thus, making their passion a bit more clear. Being passionate about one's course of study will help overcome the challenges and obstacles that one is likely to face in the journey toward achieving this prestigious and honored degree.

Due to physical and mental differences regarding interest and ability, everybody is likely to have his/her own pace for growth, development and achievements. There is no reason to rush into anything or to push others into deadlines that are not realistic for them as per their perceptions. As the statement goes, "Anyone who imagines that all fruits ripen at the same time as the strawberries knows nothing about grapes" (Paracelsus). Understanding that each person is different and every individual should determine his or her own pace is a critical component of effective leadership and coaching. Since there are many things in life that one can control, it is best to avoid the pressures of unexpected events and unrealistic expectations that are beyond one's control or circle of influence; the key is to remain calm, wear a smile instead of a frown, and let life go on in a relaxed way; for tomorrow is another new day and one should stay focused on doing what is possible rather than stressing over the impossible. According to John Quincy Adams, "Patience and perseverance have a magical effect before which difficulties disappear and obstacles vanish." Besides being patient, one must also understand that, as stated by Carl Zuckmeyer, about "One-half of life is luck; the other half is discipline - and that's the important half, for without discipline you wouldn't know what to do with luck." Besides making one's own luck, it is best to also help others capitalize on their good fortunes by being a friend and a coach to them. As a friend and coach, keep in mind how good you feel when you have encouraged and supported someone else. No other argument is necessary to suggest that one should never miss the opportunity to give encouragement to others. This is the essence of being a good coach, a good friend, and a good leader all at once.

Teaching Philosophy – Thomas Box[27]

My teaching philosophy has four components - relevance, rigor, mentoring, and community service. Each of these components probably reflects experiences I've had with good and not so good instructors in the past. Trying to give equal importance and weight to each of the components has been a challenge. But, as a framework for organizing teaching innovations, it has been measurably useful.

Relevance. The issue of relevance is important in undergraduate and graduate education. In addition to learning theories and business philosophies, students must be exposed to current practices and issues that dominate the "real world" environment. I believe an instructor should conduct a periodic "reality check" to ensure that he/she is teaching the skills and knowledge that students will actually use in practice and that are deemed to be of importance by potential future employers. Some of the techniques I use are:

- Membership and active involvement with local Chambers of Commerce
- A careful, on-going study of business practitioner literature
- Maintaining personal relationships with the business community
- Maintaining currency in my professional fields – strategy, entrepreneurship and quality management.

Rigor. I teach at a regional university. As a result, we probably have a few students who are not well equipped for college-level work. Some would argue that we should respond to that lack of preparation by "watering down" the curriculum - making it less rigorous than the curriculum at more prestigious institutions. I take very strong exception to that notion for two fundamental reasons. First, the marketplace is unforgiving. Students who are not well prepared academically will

---

[27] Contributed by Thomas M. Box, Pittsburg State University.

likely have greater difficulties adapting and succeeding after graduation. Second, it has been my experience that students "rise to the level of expectations." By that I mean that most students respond positively to challenging and difficult work. Students from rural America have well-developed work ethics and abilities well above what it takes to succeed in most instances. Techniques that I employ to build rigor into any course are:

- Requiring written and verbal presentations from each student - the ability to communicate being an essential skill that must be developed.
- Requiring critical thinking and teaching students how to do that.
- Structuring courses so that success requires a fair amount of work each week.
- Utilizing testing procedures that tap the students' ability to integrate material that they have learned.

Mentoring. All faculty members, I suppose, are involved in student advising. I think mentoring should go well beyond that. In my view, mentoring means providing students with information about careers, classes, behaviors, and the realities of the workplace. It means being actively involved with employers and Career Services. Granted that some students don't need as much mentoring as others, it's probably true that most students (in varying degrees) can benefit from some mentoring. Techniques that I employ in the mentoring area are:

- Staying as well informed as possible on course and curriculum matters – including General Education and courses outside College of Business.
- Trying to keep up to date with the market place by maintaining close contacts with former students and employers.
- Functioning as a guide or coach for students.

Community service. College of Business instructors have a remarkable opportunity to contribute to the outside community - particularly in areas like economic development, entrepreneurship and business operations. Beyond having an opportunity to contribute, it is my very strong belief that they have a responsibility to contribute in this area - particularly at state funded institutions. Over the years I have had the opportunity to run our Small Business Institute and also to direct our Kauffman Entrepreneur Internship program. These programs have returned to the community (and students) much more than they have cost. They have been, by most estimates, positive contributions. Recently, I adopted a program developed by Gene Woolsey at Colorado School of Mines. Undergraduate students in my Quality Management class were assigned client small businesses that had quality problems. Utilizing Six Sigma, students developed a consulting report for their clients that described solution for the problems - including detailed cost/benefit analyses. Over the last three years student teams have generated annual cost savings for the clients in excess of $1,400,000. Techniques that can provide community service include:

- Helping real businesses solve real business problem on a pro bono basis.
- Combining the programs of the College of Technology and Business to develop new entrepreneurial business opportunities.

- Being willing to help - whenever needed!

Finally, I believe that training is the acquisition of skills. Education is instilling new hungers for learning. I work hard to be an educator.

Exercise Your Mind, Body and Spirit

Effective leaders, educators, and researchers must always keep their minds, physical bodies, and spirits in good shape if they are to effectively deal with stress and be a good role model for others in society. Keep your mind sharp by learning something new each day and each week. Keep your body in good shape by exercising three to four days every week for about thirty minutes each day. Keep your spirits high by reading motivational books, enjoying the present through appreciation and living in the moment, and by having a good sense of humor. Regardless of how hectic your research and reading schedules become, to improve your overall health and fitness, try to integrate the following activities into your daily routine:

- *Stretching* is an important component of fitness often neglected, especially by men. In addition to helping prevent injury and relieving muscle tension and stiffness, stretching maintains the mobility and flexibility of your muscles and joints. This maintenance becomes especially important as you age. Try to do some stretching every day.
- *Aerobic exercises* such as walking, jogging, tennis and basketball elevate your heart rate, and are best for cardiovascular health. Aim for 30 minutes of continuous activity at least three to four times a week.
- *Strength training* subjects your muscles to greater resistance than you would normally encounter in everyday life, which makes them stronger and firmer when done on a regular basis. Examples of strength training activities include lifting weights (bicep curls, leg presses, etc.), as well as squats, push-ups and sit-ups. Do strength-training exercises that work each muscle group two to three times a week.

Regular and routine exercise should help with stress management in the doctoral journey and beyond. If you get too stressed, you can always add some humor to your life by repeating and reflecting upon the "Serenity Prayer for the Stressed" that I heard from Anisa Qadir a few days ago:

Grant me the serenity to accept the things I can not change. And the courage to change the things I cannot accept; and the wisdom to hide the bodies of those who "ticked" me off. And when I earn a doctorate degree and become a big shot, help me to be careful of the toes I step on each day as they may be attached to the "BEHIND" I may have to kiss at a later day. Help me to give 100% at work: 12% Mondays, 23% Tuesday, 40% Wednesday, 20% Thursday, and 5% Fridays. And help me to remember that when I am having a really bad day at work and it seems that people are trying to "tick" me off that it takes 42 muscles to frown and only 4 muscles to extend the middle finger and tell them to BITE ME.

When the stress is way too high, just remember Hank Aaron's, the baseball star, motto: "My motto was always to keep swinging. Whether I was in a slump or feeling badly or having trouble off the field, the only thing to do was keep swinging." Keep on exploring new ideas, new avenues of research, and new goals. When it comes to earning such prestigious goals as getting a doctorate status, you do not need to always be such "*A Cautious Man.*" If you have the slightest opportunity or an interest in becoming a doctor or doing research in another specific area, then jump in with both feet.

The Cautious Man:
Once there was a very cautious man
Who never loved, laughed or cried.
     He never risked, he never lost
     He never won nor ever tried.
And one day when he passed away
His insurance was denied.
     For since he never really lived
     They claimed he never really died.
          (Unknown)

The decision of earning a doctorate degree and continuing one's research on a specific topic should be calculated decisions toward continuous learning and means of contributing more to society. Author and Minister Robert H. Schuller stated that one should "Never cut a tree down in the wintertime; never make a negative decision in the low time; never make your most important decisions when you are in your worst moods. Wait. Be patient. The storm will pass. The spring will come." Earning a doctorate degree is a good idea, and remember that "Good ideas are not adopted automatically. They must be driven into practice with courageous patience," said Hyman Rickover, Naval Admiral and father of the nuclear submarine.

While taking calculated chances, one must also exercise proper discipline. Julie Andrews, actress, said that "Some people regard discipline as a chore. For me, it is a kind of order that sets me free to fly." Dr. William James, psychologist, states that "Most people never run far enough on their first wind to find out if they've got a second. Give your dreams all you've got and you'll be amazed at the energy that comes out of you." Author Dorothea Brande writes that "Man's mind is not a container to be filled but rather a fire to be kindled." Always keep in mind that it is perfectly okay to become confused when learning new concepts and philosophies: "Until you are willing to become confused about what you already know, what you know will never grow bigger, better, or more useful," says Milton Erickson, psychiatrist and hypnotherapist. As a leader of your life, you must make decisions and lead it. Thomas Jefferson said that "A leader's job is to look into the future and see things not as they are, but what they can become." See yourself as you can be in the near and distant future on a continuous basis. Be courageous and remember that "Courage is not the absence of fear, but rather the judgment that something else is more important than one's fear" as stated by Ambrose Redmoon, writer. Also, keep in mind that "You are not here merely to make a living. You are here to enable the world to live more amply, with greater vision, with a finer vision of hope and achievement. You are here to enrich the world, and you impoverish yourself if you forget the errand," said the Woodrow Wilson, President of the United States. The road to true happiness must be intrinsically sought and traveled upon. John D. Rockefeller III, philanthropist, stated that "The road to happiness lies in two simple principles: find what it is that interests you and that you can do well, and when you find it, put your whole soul into it -- every bit of energy and ambition and natural ability you have."

Summary

Working on and obtaining a doctorate degree can afford one plenty of choices with regard to teaching, working in the corporate arena, or transitioning into an administrator's position in the education industry. Educational administrators must juggle many tasks at one time and deal with the politics of academia in an effective manner. Having a doctorate degree provides one the credentials to take administrative positions and effectively deal with continual challenges that may surface. The best choice for new doctorates might be to get some experience as a faculty member first, while volunteering to serve on various committees so they can become familiarized with what goes on in the background or in the operational aspects of higher education. The more one knows about what operational directors, associate deans, assistance deans, and program managers do for the university, the more one is going to respect their level of patience and commitment to education. Furthermore, this knowledge will equip one to be a better team player in assisting administrators to more effectively serve their main audience, which are an institution's students.

In regard to data, the following are pertinent facts about undergraduate graduation rates in the United States (Personal Communication with Dr. Vincent Tinto on February 27, 2007 - presentation at Nova Southeastern University): Only 42% of incoming freshman undergraduate students tend to graduate from some private universities after six years. However, National graduation rates in the United States for private institutions tend to average about 63%. Research consistently shows that student-faculty interaction is a key factor in student persistence. While the data for doctoral students, as presented in this book are not much better, student-faculty interactions, as well as having a clear understanding of the program level expectations seem to be the key factors in a student's success in completing the terminal degree within a six-year period.

Of course, a doctoral program can provide learners with the skills to work in any capacity other than academia. Most doctoral programs in the fields of business are designed for those professionals who are interested in developing the capacity to effectively influence and lead in their industries. Such programs are also very useful for those in management capacities, project managers and public administrators as well as individual performers who want to get credit for their hard work and leadership initiatives in the workplace. In doctoral programs, besides specific topical knowledge in one's area of concentration, learners often understand how to empower themselves and their associates, continually develop their leadership skills, how to influence others, how to work with core and peripheral team members to accomplish personal and organizational goals, embrace change in the twenty-first century workplace, become effective in managing chaos, and get the recognition that they deserve as a leader.

While a terminal degree may not necessarily guarantee financial success, the journey itself can certainly be one way to happiness in becoming more. As they say, happiness is the way. So, while in the doctoral program and beyond, treasure every moment that you have and treasure it more because you shared it with someone special, your friends and family members who are special enough to spend your time with...and remember that time waits for no one. If you have an earned doctorate now, enjoy it and share its value with your students, friends and colleagues. If you have thought about starting a doctoral program, then go for it and get started. As someone once said, be happy now and stop waiting until:

1. You get a new job or promotion.
2. You win the lottery.
3. Your financial burdens are totally in order or paid off.
4. You get a new car or home.
5. Your kids leave the house.
6. You go back to school.
7. You finish school.
8. You lose 20 lbs.
9. You can run five miles.
10. You get married or a divorce.
11. You have kids.
12. Summer, spring, winter or next fall.
13. You are ready to die.
14. You earn a doctorate degree.

Do what you want to do to achieve your academic goals and enjoy the process. There is no better time than right now to be happy and get started with your next goal in life. Happiness is a journey, not a destination. Happiness is the progressive realization of worthwhile and predetermined goals. So, set your goals and, as someone said, then "work like you don't need money; study like you are a noble prize winner; love like you've never been hurt; and dance like no one's watching." Have a positive attitude and, when possible, make a difference in at least one person's life. Remember, if you can perceive and believe a better state of being, then you are very likely to achieve it as well. Overall, learn as much as you can; stretch yourself as far as possible, but not beyond; never settle for less than your capabilities; aim for total integrity; and be the best that you can be!

May you have the:
- Hindsight to know where you have been;
- Foresight to know where you are going, and
- Insight to know when you are about to go too far.

"I Did It My Way!"
(*In the spirit of Frank Sinatra*)

I applied and I got in. I came to class, I followed directions.
I researched; I learned new skills and made friends who had connections.

    I worked hard, got evaluated and may I say "not in a fair way,"
    But, I have a mission to be a good student, so I did it their way.

I learned so many things although I know I'll never use them,
The courses I attended were all required, I didn't choose them.

    You'll find that to survive it's best to play the doctor their way,
    And so I knuckled down and spent my time doing things their way.

Well yes there were times when I wondered why I had to cringe when I could fly,
I had my doubts, but after all I clipped my wings and learned to crawl.
I learned to bend, and in the end I did it their way.

    Today with a terminal degree I find that I am now the good professor,
    Where once I was oppressed and I am now the cruel oppressor.

So, start today, live your life and have some fun. And may I say "not in a shy way,"
So when it ends you can say without regret "*I did it my way.*"

                               (*Adapted from Anonymous*)

BIBLIOGRAPHY

References

AACSB, (2006). *AACSB Bridge Program Fast Tracks PQ Faculty*. AACSB Communication: *eNEWSLINE*, Vol 5, No. 7.

American Association of Higher Education (AAHE), (December 1992). *Principles of Good Practice for Assessing Student Learning*. AAHE Assessment Forum.

Anonymous. Retrieved November 14, 2006 from: Http://en.wikipedia.org/wik/Wikipedia

Argyris, C. (1994, July-August). Good communication that blocks learning. *Harvard Business Review, 72*(4), 77-85.

Bassi, L., & McMurrer, D. (2004, March). How's your return on people? *Harvard Business Review, 82*(3), 18.

Beck-Dudley, C. L. (July 2006). Why We Haven't Done Away with Our School's PhD Program. AACSB Communication: *eNEWSLINE*, Vol 5, No. 7.

Bennis, W.G. & O'Toole, J. (2005). How business schools lost their way. *Harvard Business Review. 83*(5), 96-104.

Bindixen, M. (2004). *Supervising Doctoral Research*. NSU-Sponsored Seminar at the Huizenga School, April 29-30; Fort Lauderdale, Florida.

Bisoux, T. (2006). *Flex-Time For the MBA*. BizEd, July/August issue. Pages 22-27.

Bisoux, T. (2003). *Is There a Doctorate in the House*. BizEd, March/April issue.

BizEd, 2003. *Is There a Doctorate in the House*. BizEd, March/April issue. By T. Bisoux.

Business Week, 2004. *Is There a Doctor in the B-School? Universities are searching for ways to generate more business PhDs*. March 1st Issue.

Carlin, D.B. & Perlmutter, D.D. (2006, September 8). *Advising the new advisor*. Chronicle of Higher Education. C1-C4.

Carr, N.; Meyerson, D.; Rafarrete, R.; Saunders, J.; & Scharff, M. (2004). *A Systems Analysis of the UofP Doctor of Management Program*. Unpublished Manuscript. ORG701-Systems Thinking: The Web of Life.

Castenell, L., (1984). A Cross-Cultural Look at Achievement Motivation Research. *The Journal of Negro Education. 53*(4), 435-436

Cavico, F. & Mujtaba, B. G. (2007). *Legal Challenges for the Global Manager and Entrepreneur.* Kendal Hunt Publishing Company. United States. ISBN: 978-0-7575-4037-0.

Chan, D. S. (2005). Relationship between generation-responsive leadership behaviors and job satisfaction of generations X and Y professionals. UMI #3194291

Checkland, P. B. (1999). *Systems Thinking, Systems: A 30 year retrospective* Practice, John Wiley and Sons, Chichester.

Cole, J. S., & Denzine, G. M. (Spring 2004). "I'm not doing as well in this class as I'd like to": exploring achievement motivation and personality. In *Journal of College Reading and Learning,* 34, p. 29(16). Retrieved August 27, 2006, from *InfoTrac OneFile* via Thomson Gale.

Collins, J. (2001). Good to great: Why some companies make the leap... and others don't. NY: HarperBusiness.

Creswell, J. W. (2003). *Research design: Qualitative, quantitative, and mixed methods approaches* (2ⁿᵈ Ed.). Thousand Oaks, CA: Sage

Deci, E.L.,& Ryan, R.M. (1985). Intrinsic motivation and self-determination in human behavior. New York and London: Plenum Press.

Delamont, S., Atkinson P., & Parry O. (1997). Supervising the PhD: A guide to success. Philadelphia: Open University Press.

Denecke, D. (2005, November). Ph.D., Completion Project: Preliminary results from baseline data. Retrieved June 10, 2006, from www.cgsnet.org/

Douglass, M.E., & Douglass D.N. (1980). Manage your time, manage your work, manage yourself (5 ᵗʰ ed.) New York: AMACOM.

Duckworth, A. L. & Seligman, M. E. P., (2005). Self-Discipline Outdoes IQ in Predicting Academic Performance of Adolescents. *Journal of Experimental Psychology,* 16(12), 941

Eastmond, D. (1998). *Adult learners and Internet-based distance education.* New Directions for Adult and Continuing Education, 78, 33-41.

Electronic Journal. Retrieved from: http://www.youngmoney.com/print.asp/272

Faiwell, S. (2003). Graduate Degrees Pay Off In Higher Salaries.

Faust, J. E. (2003). The Devils Throat. Electronic Journal of 173ʳᵈ Annual General Conference. Retrieved June 16, 2003, from: http://www.lds.org/conference/talk/display/0,5232,23-1-353-19,00.html

Forum, 2004. *How Can Colleges Prove They're Doing Their Jobs?* Chronicles of Higher Education, September 3ʳᵈ 2004.

Garvin, D. A. (1998). Building a learning organization. *Harvard business review on knowledge management* (pp. 47-80). Boston, MA: Harvard Business School.

Goleman, Daniel (2006). Can you raise your social IQ? *The Gainesville Sun: Parade.* Sunday, September 3, 2006. Pages 10-13.

Goleman, D. (1995, October). Know Thyself. *Emotional Intelligence* (1st, pp. 46-55). New York: Bantam Books.

Goodman, A. (2003). *Introduction to data collection and analysis.* Retrieved November 17, 2006, from http://www.deakin.edu.au/~agoodman/sci101/mainlinks.php

Gradview.com (2003). Why Go to Graduate School? *Electronic Journal.* Retrieved July 28, 2005 from: http://www.gradview.com/articles/whygradschool.html

Graves, N., & Varma V. (1997). Working for a doctorate: A guide for the humanities and social sciences. New York: Routledge.

Gravois, J., (2005). Number of doctorates edges up slightly. *The Chronicle of Higher Education, 51,* A24-25.

Handy, C. (1995). Beyond certainty: The changing worlds of organizations. Boston, Massachusetts: Harvard Business School.

Hawley, P. (1993). Being bright is not enough: the unwritten rules of doctoral study. Illinois: CHARLES C THOMAS PUBLUSHER.

Hayes, Jill M. (1997). *Coordinated Systems of Community-Based Health Care Delivery: A Vehicle for Health Care Reform.* Journal of Pediatric Nursing, 12(5), 288-291.

Heathcott, J. (2005). Trained for nothing. *Academe, 91,* 14-17.

Henke, H. & Russum, J. (2000). *Factors influencing attrition rates in a corporate distance education program.* Education at a distance, 14 (11), Article 03. Retrieved July 25, 2001 from http://www.usdla.org/ED_magazine/illuminactive/ NOV00_Issue/story03.htm

Hesselbein, F. Goldsmith, M. & Beckhard, R. (1996). *The leader of the future.* San Francisco: Jossey-Bass.

Huizenga School Doctoral Program Retreat (May 2006). *Doctoral Program Updates, Changes and Dissertation Research Processes.* NSU-Sponsored two-day workshop. Fort Lauderdale, Florida.

Huizenga School, 2004. Website visited on September 2004 at: http://www.sbe.nova.edu/ and http://www.sbe.nova.edu/about/faculty.cfm

Jacobson, J., (2001). Why do so many people leave graduate school without a Ph.D.? *The Chronicle of Higher Education, 47,* A10.

Jacques, R. (1996). *Manufacturing the employee: Management knowledge from the 19th to 21st centuries.* Thousand Oaks, CA: Sage.

Jain, S. C. (1997). *Marketing Planning & Strategy.* 5th Edition, Cincinnati, OH: Southwestern Publishing, pp. 348-349.

Johnson, W. B. (2007). *On being a mentor. A guide for higher education faculty.* Mahwah, NJ: Lawrence Erlbaum.

Kaplan Test Prep (2002). Graduate School. Why Graduate School? *Electronic Journal.* Retrieved September 20, 2005 from: http://education.yahoo.com/college/essentials/articles/grad/graduate-why.html

King, D. A., (2006). What is your Expectation? Retrieved September 10, 2006, from: http://EzineArticles.com/?expert=David_Allan_KingKram, K. E. (1983, December). Phases of the mentor relationship. *Academy of Management Journal, 26*(4), 608-625.

Kram, K. E. (1988). *Mentoring at work: Developmental relationships in organizational life.* Lanham, MD: University Press of America.

Leedy, P.D. & Ormrod, J.E. (2005*). Practical research: Planning and design* (8th ed.). Upper Saddle River, NJ: Pearson Merrill Prentice Hall.

Leonard, D. (2001). A woman's guide to doctoral studies. Philadelphia: Open University Press.

Lavelle, L. (2006). The best B-schools of 2006. *Business Week.* 4006, 54.

Levine, D. I. (1995). *Reinventing the workplace: How business and employees can both win.* Washington, DC: The Brookings Institution.

Lewin, K. (1947). Frontiers in group dynamics: Concepts, methods and reality in social science, social equilibria and social change. *Human Relations, 1,* 5-41.

Linnenbrink, E. A., & Pintrich, P. R. (Summer 2002). Motivation as an enabler for academic success. *School Psychology Review*, 31, p. 313(15). Retrieved August 27, 2006, from InfoTrac OneFile via Thomson Gale.

Locke, E.A., & Latham G.P. (1990). A theory of goal setting & task performance: New Jersey: Prentice-Hall, Inc.

Lovitts, B. (2000). *Leaving the Ivory Tower: The Causes and Consequences of Departure from Doctoral Study.* Retrieved on June 3, 2006, from: http://www.findarticles.com/p/articles/mi_qa3860/is_200011/ai_n8922845/pg_11

Malberg, E. (2000). Retention and attrition of doctoral candidates in higher education. Ed.D. dissertation, University of North Texas. *Dissertation Abstracts International 63*(02A) (2002); AAT 3041915.

Mangan, K. S., (2006). Career track to tenure track. *The Chronicle of Higher Education, 52,* A10-11.

Maurer, T. J. (2001). Career-relevant learning and development, worker age, and beliefs about self-efficacy for development. *Journal of Management, 27*(2), 123-140.

Maurer, T. J., Pierce, H. R., & Shore, L. M. (2002b, July). Perceived beneficiary of employee development activity: A three dimensional social exchange model. *Academy of Management Review, 27*(3), 432-444.

Merton, R. K. (1948). The self-fulfilling prophecy. *The Antioch Review, 8,* 193-210.

McKay, D. R. (2003). Graduate School or Not? *Electronic Journal.* Retrieved July 20, 2005, from: http://careerplanning.about.com/csgraduateschool/a/grad_school_p.htm

Miller, R.B., & Brickman, S.J. (March 2004). A model of future –oriented motivation and self- regulation (1). (Effects of Time Perspective on Student Motivation). *Educational Psychology Review,* 16, p. 9(25). Retrieved August 27, 2006, from InfoTrac OneFlieThom on Gale.

Morgan, C. L., & Morgan, L. V. (1935, September). Effects of immediate awareness of success and failure upon objective examination scores. *Journal of Experimental Education, 4*(1), 63-66.

Morse, J. M. (2003). Principles of mixed methods and multimethod research design. In A. Tashakkori, & C. Teddlie (Eds.), *Handbook of mixed methods in social & behavioral research* (pp. 189-208). Thousand Oaks, CA: Sage.

Mounce, P. H., Mauldin, D. S., and Braun, R. L., (2004). The importance of relevant practical experience among accounting faculty: An empirical analysis of students' perceptions. *Issues in Accounting Education, 19,* 399-411.

Mujtaba, B. G. (2007). *Cross Cultural Management and Negotiation Practices.* ILEAD Academy Publications; Florida, United States. ISBN: 978-0-9774211-2-1.

Mujtaba, B. G. (2007). *Workpalce Diversity Management: Challenges, Competencies and Strategies.* ISBN: 1-59526-548-1. Llumina Press; website: www.llumina.com - (phone: 866-229-9244 or: 954-726-0902).

Mujtaba, B. G. and McCartney, T. (2007). *Managing Workplace Stress and Conflict amid Change.* Llumina Press, Coral Springs, Florida, USA. ISBN: 1-59526-414-0. Phone: (866)229-9244 or (954)726-0902.

Mujtaba, B. G. (2007). *Mentoring Diverse Professionals (2nd edition).* Llumina Press. ISBN: 1-59526-444-2.

Mujtaba, B. G. and Preziosi, R. C. (2006). *Adult Education in Academia: Recruiting and Retaining Extraordinary Facilitators of learning.* 2nd Edition. ISBN: 1593114753. Information Age Publishing. Greenwich, Connecticut. Phone: (203) 661-7602.

Mujtaba, B. G. (2006). *Cross Cultural Change Management.* ISBN: 1-59526-568-6. Llumina Press, Tamarac, Florida. Website: www.Llumina.com.

Mujtaba, B. G., McAtavey, J. (2006). Performance Assessment and Comparison of Learning in International Education: American versus Jamaican Students' Learning Outcomes. *The College Teaching Methods & Styles Journal*, Vol. 2, Num. 3. Pages 33-43.

Mujtaba, B. G. & Abratt, R. (2005). *Quality Assurance and Assessment of Doctoral Programs: The Comprehensive Exams.* Applied Business Research Conference Proceedings. January 3-7.

Mujtaba, B., (April 2005a). Comparing Jamaican Students' Performance with Students in the United States, the Grand Bahamas and the Online Program. *The International College Teaching Methods and Styles Journal*, Volume 1, Number 2.

Mujtaba, B., (April 2005b). Faculty Development Practices in Distance Education for Success with Culturally Diverse Students. *International Business and Economics Research Journal*, Volume 4, Number 4. Pages 1-13.

Mujtaba, B. & Mujtaba, L. (February 2004). Creating a Healthy Learning Environment for Student Success in the Classroom. *The Internet TESL Journal.* Vol. X, No. 2. Available at the following URL: http://iteslj.org/ or: http://iteslj.org/Articles/Mujtaba-Environment.html.

Mujtaba, B. G. (January 2004). Comparison of Learning Effectiveness Based on Teaching Modality Using Objective Examination for On-ground and Online Students in Managing Workforce Diversity. *Huizenga School Assessment Journal*, Report No. HS01-20-04.

Murphy, D., Campbell, C., & Garavan, T. N. (1999). The Pygmalion effect reconsidered: Its implications for education, training, and workplace learning. *Journal of European Industrial Training, 23*(4/5), 238-250.

Murray, B. (2000). Graduate Degrees. Helpful, but no silver bullet. *Achieve Magazine.* Retrieved September 29, 2005, from: http://www.usatoday.com/careers/resource/colach3.htm

Neely, L., Niemi, J. & Ehrhard, B. (1998). *Classes going the distance so people don't have to: Instructional opportunities for adult learners.* T.H.E. Journal, 26(4), 72.

Nelson, C. (2000, Nov/Dec). Attrition from Ph.D. Programs. *Academe, 86*(6), 44-51.

Nova Southeastern University, 2004. Website visited on October 2004 at: http://www.nova.edu/

NSU e-Bulletin, 2004. NSU Leads the Nation in the Number of Doctorate Degrees Awarded to Minorities. August 8. Retrieved on August 8th 2004 from: http://www.nova.edu/cwis/ia/pubaffairs/news/july-sept2004/doctorates.html

O'Neill, R. M., & Sankowsky, D. (2001, September). The Caligula phenomenon: Mentoring relationships and theoretical abuse. *Journal of Management Inquiry, 10*(3), 206-216.

Pauleen, D. J., & Yoong, P. (2001, December). Relationship building and the use of ICT in boundary-crossing virtual teams: A facilitator's perspective. *Journal of Information Technology, 16*(4), 205-220.

Perry, J. L., Mesch, D., & Paarlberg, L. (2006). Motivating Employees in a Governance Era: The Performance Paradigm Revisited. *Public Administration Review*. 66(4), 505-514

Petri, H.L. (1991). Motivation: theory, research, and applications (3 ʳᵈ ed.). Belmont: Wadsworth Publishing Company.

Phillips,E.M., & Pugh D.S. (2000). How to get a PhD: A handbook for students and their supervisors (3 ʳᵈ ed.).Philadelphia: Open University Press.

Pittenger, K. K., & Heimann, B. A. (2000, Summer). Building effective mentoring relationships. *Review of Business, 21*(1/2), 38-42.

Plumlee, R. D., Kachelmeier, S. J., Madeo, S. A., Pratt, J. H., & Krull, G., (2006). Assessing the shortage of accounting faculty. *Issues in Accounting Education, 21,* 113-125.

Pohlman, R. & Gardiner, G. (2000). *Value Driven Management: How to Create and Maximize Value Over Time for Organizational Success.* New York: AMACOM.

Pohlman, R. (2001). *Dean's Message.* Foresight publication by Wayne Huizenga School of Business and Entrepreneurship. Nova Southeastern University. Summer Edition.

Reinhard, D. (2002). Why Should You Consider Graduate School? *Electronic Journal.* Retrieved September 28, 2005 from: http://www.egr.msu.edu/ece/students/whygrad.php

Richards, C. & Ridley, D. (1997). *Factors affecting college students' persistence in online computer-managed instruction.* College Student Journal, 31, 490-495.

Reynolds, D. (2002, Summer). The good, the bad, and the ugly of incorporating "My Fair Lady" in the workplace. *SAM Advanced Management Journal, 67*(3), 4-9.

Roblyer, M. (1999). *Is choice important in distance learning? A study of student motives for taking Internet-based courses at the high school and community college levels.* Journal of Research on Computing in Education, 32 (1), 157-71.

Rossman, M. (2000). *Andragogy and distance education: Together in the new millennium.* New Horizons in Adult Education, 14(1), 3-9. Retrieved on October 20th 2004 from http://www.nova.edu/~aed/horizons/vol14n1.htm

Roth, J. A., (1955). A Faculty Conception of Success in Graduate Study. *The Journal of Higher Education, 26*(7), 3.

Scharff, M. (2005). A study of the dyadic relationships between managers and virtual employees. UMI # 3196635

Schlesinger, J. E. (2006). Lessons for leadership theory and practice: A case study of Robert E. Lee at Gettysburg using hermeneutic inquiry. UMI #3220679

Seifert, T. (June 2004). Understanding student motivation. *Education Research*, 46, p.137 (13). Retrieved August 27, 2006, from InfoTrac OneFile via Thomson Gale.

Senge, P. M. (1990). *The fifth discipline: The art & practice of the learning organization*. NY: Currency Doubleday.

Simpson, L., Owens, P.L., Zodet, M.R., Chevarley, F.M., Dougherty, D., Elixhayser, A., et al. (2005). *Healthcare for Children and Youth in the United States: Annual Report on Patterns of Coverage, Utilization, Quality and Expenditures by Income.* Ambulatory Pediatrics 5(1),6.

Smallwood, S., (2006). Driven by foreign students, doctoral degrees are up 2.9% in 2005. *The Chronicle of Higher Education, 53,* A12.

Smith, R. L., Maroney, K., Nelson, K. W., Abel, A. L., & Abel, H. S., (2006). Doctoral programs: Changing high rates of attrition. *Journal of Humanistic Counseling, Education and Development, 45,* 17-31.

Smith, P. (2004). *The quiet crisis*. Bolton, MA: Anker Publishing Company, Inc.

Smallwood, S (2004, January 16). *Doctor dropout*. Chronicle of Higher Education, (50)19.

Spitzer, D.R. (1995). Supermotivation: A blueprint for energizing your organization from top to bottom. New York: AMACOM.

Strauss, V. (2006, April 18). As many dropouts as degrees. Retrieved from *The Washington Post Company*, p. A06.

The Communicator: Council of Graduate Schools (January/February, 2004). *Addressing attrition in Ph.D. Programs.* Volume XXXVII, Number 1.

The US Education Information Center (2004). *Doctoral programs in business.* Visited on October 23rd 2004 on URL: http://www.useic.ru/ and their website on: http://www.useic.ru/study/apply/business.htm.

The Washington Post (2006). As many dropouts as degrees. Retrieved on June 2, 2006, From: http://www.washingtonpost.com/wp-dyn/content/article/2006/04/17/AR2006041701123.html

Thomas, W. I. (1923). *The unadjusted girl.* Retrieved July 6, 2005, from http://www2.fmg.uva.nl/sociosite/topics/text/thomas.html

Tozer, A. W. (1961). Knowledge of the Holy. San Francisco, CA: HarperCollins.

Tuckman, B.W. (1999). A Tripartite model of motivation for achievement: attitude/drive/strategy. Retrieved August 27, 2006, from: http://dennislearningcenter.osu.edu/all-tour/apa99paper.htm

U.S. News & World Report. (2002). Does Grad School Make Sense for You? *Electronic Journal.* Retrieved September 29, 2005 from: http://education.yahoo.com/college/essentials/articles/grad_makesense.html

Wolk, R. M. (2007). *Survival matters: business schools, ubiquitous technology and accreditation.* Dissertation at Nova Southeastern University.

Young, A. M., & Perrewe, P. L. (2000). What did you expect? An examination of career related support and social support among mentors and protégés. *Journal of Management, 26*(4), 611-632.

Author Biography:

Dr. Bahaudin G. Mujtaba is an Associate Professor of Management with Nova Southeastern University (NSU). Academically, Bahaudin has serviced as department chair, college chair, program director, and director of institutional relations for accreditation and planning. Bahaudin has worked as an internal consultant, trainer, and teacher in the corporate arena. He also dealt with retail management training and development for over 16 years. He was awarded the prestigious Faculty of the Year Award for the 2005 Academic Year at the School of Business and Entrepreneurship of NSU. He attended Habibia High School in Afghanistan, Fort Myers High School in the United States, Edison Community College, University of Central Florida, Nova University, and Nova Southeastern University for his terminal degree. His doctorate degree is in Management, and he has two post-doctorate specialties: Human Resource Management and International Management. Bahaudin is author and co-author of thirteen books and over 50 articles. During the past 25 years he has had the pleasure of working in the United States, Brazil, Bahamas, Afghanistan, St. Lucia, and Jamaica. He was born in Khoshie of Logar province, and raised in Kabul, Afghanistan. Bahaudin can be emailed at: mujtaba@nova.edu.

Dr. Michael Scharff is an Assistant Professor of Management and Chair of Graduate Studies at Limestone College, located in Gaffney, SC. Michael grew up in central New Jersey and went to college at The Citadel in Charleston, SC where he graduated with a degree in accounting. Upon graduation he was commissioned as a 2nd Lieutenant in the US Army. During his years in the military he was stationed at Fort Ben Harrison in Indianapolis, IN; Ansbach, Germany with the 1st Armor Division; Fayetteville, NC with the 82d Airborne Division and XVIII Airborne Corps; Atlanta, GA with Forces Command; and Fort Campbell, KY with the 160th Special Operations Aviation Regiment (Airborne). While in the military he was selected to go to fully funded graduate school and received an MBA from Syracuse University He completed his doctorate degree in management and organizational leadership in 2005 and also won the Dissertation of the Year award from the Doctoral School of Advanced Studies at the University of Phoenix. After leaving the military, he worked in various management roles in finance and corporate billing for MCI in Atlanta, GA. He left MCI in January 2006 to take his current position with Limestone College. He has had several articles published and has spoken at many national and international conferences on ethics and mentoring. Michael can be emailed at mscharff@limestone.edu

Contributor Biography:

Joann Adeogun is a full-time Doctoral Student at Nova Southeastern University with a specialization in Human Resource Management. Her background includes Consulting, Compliance, Accreditation, Regulatory Affairs, Institutional Effectiveness, Training and Instruction at several universities in the Atlanta, GA area. Joann is scheduled to complete her course work in April 2007 and Dissertation in December 2007. She received her graduate degree from Troy State University in Human Resource Management/ Specialization -Employment Law and her undergraduate degree from Shorter College in Business Management. She is PHR (Professional in Human Resource Management) Certified.

Charmaine Balfour is currently a doctoral student with concentration in finance at the Nova Southeastern University. Charmaine has over twelve years in the banking industry where she worked in accounting and finance. She is also a mortgage and tax specialist. Charmaine is multicultural as she has lived in both the United States and Jamaica. She currently resides in the Atlanta area of Georgia.

Dr. Thomas M. Box is a Professor of Management at Pittsburg State University. His Ph.D. is from Oklahoma State. From 1980 to 1984 he was Senior Vice President of Operations at Southwest Tube Manufacturing Co. From 1984 to 1990 Thomas was on the faculty of the University of Tulsa. He joined the PSU faculty in 1990. He has more than 75 journal and proceedings publications and five books. He is a member of the World Future Society, the Strategic Management Society and the Society for Advancement of Management. He can be reached at thobox@gmail.com.

Dr. Frank J. Cavico has been teaching Business Law and Ethics topics at Nova Southeastern University for nearly two decades. In 2000, he was awarded the Excellence in Teaching Award by the Huizenga School. In 2006, he was awarded the Faculty Member of the Year Award by the Huizenga School. His fine record is manifested by numerous research endeavors, principally law review articles in the broad sectors of business law and ethics as well as a business ethics textbook coauthored with Dr. Bahaudin G. Mujtaba, *Business Ethics: Transcending requirements through moral leadership*, which has been adopted for use by many national and international business schools. In 2007, he and Dr. Bahaudin G. Mujtaba coauthored the book, *Legal Challenges for the Global Manager and Entrepreneur*, published by Kendal Hunt. Professor Cavico holds a J.D. degree from St. Mary's University School of Law and a B.A. from Gettysburg College. He also possesses a Master of Laws degree from the University of San Diego School of Law and a Master's degree in Political Science from Drew University. Professor Cavico is licensed to practice law in the states of Florida and Texas.

Audrey Ellison has 25 years marketing and management experience working with organizations to develop and implement internal and external marketing strategies. She is also a business coach. Audrey teaches marketing and management courses at University of Phoenix, West Florida and Nova Southeastern University. She also teaches online and blended learning classes. She holds an MBA from Simmons College in Boston, Masters of Library Science and BS in History from Southern Connecticut State University. She is currently working on her Doctorate Degree in Marketing at Nova Southeastern University.

Natcha Limthanakom was born in Thailand and is currently completing the doctorate program at Nova Southeastern University's H. Wayne Huizenga School of Business and Entrepreneurship. Her research interests have included studies on cross-cultural value-orientation and clarification. Upon the completion of the doctoral program, she hopes to contribute to academic and practitioner-oriented studies and research on a global basis.

Eleanor Marschke is currently a doctoral student specializing in Human Resource Management. Eleanor is employed at Thomas & Betts Corporation where for the last twenty years she has been a top performer in the sales department of this Fortune 500 Company which manufactures electrical construction products. Her interest in *Spirituality in the Workplace* is a focus of here dissertation work. For further information on Eleanor please refer to her website at www.spiriteducator.com.

Robert J. Mullaney is a Licensed and Certified Occupational Therapist. After obtaining his Master's Degree in Business Administration with a specialization in Health Services Administration, he accepted a position at Miami Children's Hospital as a Satellite Facility Rehabilitation Director and left Baptist Health Systems of South Florida after 10 years. During his undergraduate studies at Florida International University, Robert worked as a Certified Personal Trainer and developed a wide variety of Corporate-Based Health and Wellness Programs for the Baptist Health Club. It was during this period that Robert took note of his entrepreneurial spirit and began to develop his own Strike Fitness Company, which he managed for 2 years before selling to investors. Robert is currently a Doctoral Student at Nova Southeastern University with a specialty focus on Management/ Management in Health Services.

Joel Rossmaier is an assistant professor of accounting and business at the University of the Ozarks in Clarksville, Arkansas. He received his B.S. in Business Administration from the University of Tennessee and his M.S. in Accounting from the University of Arkansas. He is currently pursuing his D.B.A. with Nova Southeastern University. A certified public accountant in Oklahoma, Mr. Rossmaier has over 20 years' experience in private industry as a public auditor, internal auditor, accounting manager and controller.

Dr. Freda Turner has assisted approximately 50 doctoral students in completing their dissertations. She is currently as a Dean, faculty and dissertation advisor to doctoral students. Three mentees that partnered with Dr. Tuner won Dissertation of the Year award for their scholarly contributions the literature. Dr. Tuner takes great pride in trying to make research scholarly, interesting, and fund for the doctoral learner. For further information, please contact her through email at: fturner@gcu.edu.

Dr. Ikwukananne I. Udechukwu received an MPA degree from Valdosta State University and a B.S. degree in Management from Park University. "Ike" just received a Doctorate in Business Administration (DBA) degree from Nova Southeastern University. He has served as a Classification and Compensation Analyst for both the Georgia Department of Corrections and the Georgia Department of Human Resources. He is now a Recruitment and Employment Specialist.

Dr. Albert A. Williams has been teaching at Nova Southeastern University in both graduate and undergraduate programs in finance, economics and business statistics. He also has lectured the same topics at the University of Phoenix and Broward Community College in South Florida. Before returning to academia, he was a commodity analyst at Restaurant Services Incorporated. In Belize, he was the chief executive officer of the Belize Marketing Board. In addition, he was an agricultural economist for the Government of Belize. He also was a project officer at the Development Finance Corporation in Belize.

Dr. Stefanie D. Wilson is the author of many recently published articles on multiple intelligence and leadership. Dr. Wilson worked at Motorola, Inc in a marketing management capacity for over 17 years. She has experience managing global product portfolios and introducing products such as two-way radios, and satellite communications equipment worldwide. She also managed marketing communication budgets totaling millions of dollars to support product launches that were global in scope. Dr. Wilson is an Assistant Professor of Management at the University of Hawaii West Oahu (UHWO). Dr. Wilson earned a Bachelor of Science in Business Management, Masters Degree in Business Administration with specializations in International Business and Marketing, and Doctor of Management in Organizational Leadership.

Index Table

Type A Personality, 91
Type B personality, 91

U

Udechukwu, 17, 188
United States, II, 1, 6, 17, 34, 36, 37, 38, 52, 54, 55, 56, 86, 88, 100, 101, 103, 149, 154, 169, 170, 186
Universal Responsibility, 43
University of Central Florida, 39
University of Florida's, 41
University of Georgia's Terry College of Business, 167
University of Phoenix, 51, 52, 57
Urgent, 80

V

Valdosta State University, 188
Value Driven Management, 183
Vantage Solutions LLC, 159

Varma, 16, 180

W

Wagoner, 42, 43
Walt Disney, 22
Washington, 37, 63, 70, 154, 158, 159, 181, 184
Washington D.C., 37
Weinstein, V
Western Academy of Management, 143
William Butler Yeats, 166, 195
William James, 23
Williams, V, 27, 132, 188
Wilson, S., V, 93, 175, 188
Winston Churchill, 21
Wolk, R., 163, 164

Z

Zebraski, 40
Zulm-Abaud, 34

"Education is not the filling of a pail, but the lighting of a fire."
(William Butler Yeats)

"The person who dares to teach must never cease to learn."
(Anonymous)

"The person who can make hard things easy is the educator."
(Ralph Waldo Emerson)

"Teachers can change lives with just the right mix of chalk and challenges."
(Joyce A. Myers)

"It is the supreme art of the teacher to awaken joy in creative expression and knowledge."
(Albert Einstein)

www.ingramcontent.com/pod-product-compliance
Lightning Source LLC
Chambersburg PA
CBHW022019090426
42739CB00006BA/202